Coleridge's Philosophy of Literature

Coleridge's Philosophy of Literature

The Development of a Concept of Poetry
1791–1819

J. A. Appleyard

HARVARD UNIVERSITY PRESS

Cambridge, Massachusetts

1965

Distributed in Great Britain by Oxford University Press, London

Publication of this book has been aided by a grant from the
Hyder Edward Rollins Fund

Library of Congress Catalog Card Number 65–22066

Printed in the United States of America

FOR MY MOTHER
AND IN MEMORY OF
MY FATHER

Preface

This study was begun as an attempt to see whether an examination of the actual development of Coleridge's thinking about the nature of literature would eliminate some of the obscurities involved in many descriptions of his mature ideas. Since, however, as Coleridge himself says, no one conceives a fact to be true who does not with equal confidence anticipate its necessity, the original hypothesis of this investigation has evolved into something of a firm assertion, namely that a chronological study of Coleridge's thought — especially as revealed in his lesser known works, his notebooks, and letters — is essential if one is to see his theory of literature in its true dimensions and to realize how incomplete our common notions of his philosophical and literary ideas are when they have been formed exclusively by study of the *Biographia Literaria.* That there should be a thesis rather than a hypothesis proves again an ineluctable law of epistemology — and a Coleridgean principle too — that one is the willing victim of one's own ideas and that insights once encouraged can shape a whole range of subsequent thinking, even evoke suitably convincing conclusions. The difficulty, Coleridge found, lay in beginning with the right idea and then adjusting it at every step to the exigent experience of whatever reality is under discussion. The reader must judge for himself how successfully this has been accomplished, in the light of the details that follow.

Two or three observations must be made on the method and scope of this study. The first concerns the subject matter. The term "philosophy of literature" conceals no occult or novel discipline. It seems useful mainly because of the scanty vocabulary that literary scholars employ to differentiate their interests. "Criticism," as it is commonly used, refers imprecisely both to speculation about the nature of literature and to the descriptive and evaluative analysis of particular works, genres, or periods — two very different, though not unrelated, activities. The theory of literature, insofar as it asks and answers questions about the phenomena of literature which are derived from more universal conceptual categories — questions of function, value, essence, and the like — is best considered as a philosophical inquiry. The term "philosophy of literature" is therefore only a convenient omnibus term for the body of speculation which, explicit or only implied, underlies every attempt to make, or to talk about, the concrete image or analogon of experience that we call literature.*

Further, the study of literary theory, if it is a philosophical inquiry, must also be a historical inquiry. R. G. Collingwood's reluctant meditations on the Albert Memorial are instructive on this point. He tells in his *Autobiography* how each day during the first World War, as he walked to his government work through Kensington Gardens, he confronted Scott's monument. Its ugliness obsessed him. He was unable to understand how anyone could ever have considered it beautiful. But then he began to ask himself what the relation was between Scott's purpose and his accomplishment. Perhaps his aim had not been to make a thing which *we* would think beautiful, but something quite different — and in this purpose he may possibly have succeeded. The answer that finally occurred to Collingwood may seem obvious, but it implies an epistemological correlative of some significance for the method of historical investigation: "A body of knowledge consists not of 'propositions', 'statements', 'judgments', or whatever name logicians use in order to designate assertive acts of thought . . . but of these together with the questions they are meant to answer." To broaden this principle somewhat, we might say that, as discourse is possible only within a framework of assumptions, meanings, and values common to both

---

* It will be obvious that only imaginative literature is under discussion throughout this study. Here too language fails us, for there is no term by which we can signify a work whose structure is imaginative as distinguished from rhetorical or expository, whether it be in verse or prose. Coleridge tried to establish the distinction between "poesy," which would express the common element of the fine arts or *muta poesis* in general, and "poetry," or the species which is not *muta* but expressed in language. The terminology does not seem to have caught on. See "On Poesy or Art," *Biographia Literaria*, ed. with his aesthetical essays by J. Shawcross, 2 vols. (Oxford, 1907; repr. 1958), II, 255. It is this "poetry" or imaginative literature in general that is the subject of this study.

speaker and audience, so in the same way the understanding of past discourse or event or artifact is possible only by creating, through an effort of the historical imagination, a framework which includes both the past and our contemporary selves, which captures the "circum-stantial immediacy" of historical events. Without this historical imagi-nation we are prone to univocal interpretations of ideas, statements, and events, assuming that they have an essential content or significance which remains absolute through the flux of time. Coleridge has suf-fered more than most literary theorists from this kind of analysis, and if we would avoid the fault we must keep in mind that the study of history is the study of questions as well as of answers.

And if the meaning of answers depends on the nature of the ques-tions to which they respond, it is also true that questions arise because answers are wanting. The history of thought thus becomes a dialectic of problem and solution. Coleridge's intellectual development repeats this paradigm. He continually attempted to give an intelligible structure to his own pre-philosophic experience, but partial solutions fell away one after another under the criticism of his inquiring mind. His search moved constantly in the direction of unity, though the path led back and forth in dialectical question and answer. To the student this movement becomes intelligible only if he re-creates the problems and their solutions in order, as Coleridge experienced them. J. H. Muirhead notes that "The philosophical development of a mind like Coleridge's, sensitive, growing to the last, is necessarily a tangled tale." Exactly. It is *a tale*, and therefore best told historically, locating Coleridge's thought not only in a time and place but extending it, so to speak, lineally, to show what he called, in speaking of the works of a poet studied chronologically, the "progress, maturity, and even the decay of genius."

What is wanting in the sizable bibliography of literature on Cole-ridge is a full-scale study of the development of his philosophy which will consider him on his own terms and not as a representative of something else, whether it be German idealism, English Platonism, pantheistic mysticism, semantic analysis, or depth psychology. The idea or organizing insight ought to be internal to his thought, so as to see what that thought is and not merely what it is like or unlike.

For this task a salutary respect for the particular and a methodical caution in generalizing are indispensable equipment. The investigation undertaken here can amount, at most, to a part of such a study, a test of whether or not the methodology proposed is as fruitful as it seems. It is limited by its subject matter to only one part of Coleridge's thought, the development of his philosophy of literature, and then only up to 1819, the date of Coleridge's last explicit statements about literary theory and apparently the end of his overt interest in the matter. It includes almost nothing about the vast subject of Coleridge's poetry and what we might learn from it about his philosophy of literature. It is limited, finally, by the inevitable subjectivity which is the condition of all attempts to discern the shape of events and ideas, and from which the only appeal is to the ultimate criterion of utility: does it provide at this point in Coleridge studies a useful insight into the content of his literary theory?

One final reservation must be made. It involves the question of the sources of Coleridge's thought. Writers from Thomas De Quincey and Sara Coleridge to René Wellek have exercised their skill in essays and books addressed to the problem of the "borrowings." The result of this scholarship has been to increase our knowledge of Coleridge's relationships to writers of his own and earlier ages, and our admiration for his learning and catholicity, but little has been added to our understanding of the value and meaning of Coleridge's thought in itself. Lately a different attitude toward sources has prevailed in Coleridge studies. The use to which the borrowings were put now seems of greater significance than the question of where the elements came from, or whether, indeed, they were borrowed at all. Coleridge regularly cannibalized the works and ideas of others, and employed the results quite opportunistically, to suit a momentary need, to prop an argument for a time, to suggest a new direction for his own thought. Rarely was he much concerned with the precise and actual meaning an idea had for another writer; almost always it was its interaction with his own thinking that mattered most to him. Relatively little attention, therefore, will be given here to sources. They will be used only where corroborative and illustrative. In this way it is hoped to avoid lingering over relatively unprofitable matter — which in any case is beyond the competence of all but the most learned Coleridgeans — in order to get to the proper subject of this study, the development of Coleridge's philosophy of literature as a structure in itself.

There are one or two details of procedure to be noted. I have followed Coleridge's irregular spelling and sometimes hasty grammar wherever the sense of a passage was not seriously impaired by doing so. However in several instances I have silently normalized the text of Griggs's edition of the *Letters*, whose editorial apparatus preserves Coleridge's peculiarities accurately but in far greater detail than is necessary for this study.

Finally, I wish to acknowledge several substantial obligations, in particular to former teachers: to P. Albert Duhamel and Edward L. Hirsh, of Boston College, for the first lessons which have since become fast and tested principles; to John D. Boyd, S.J., now of Fordham University, who several years ago first set me the task of finding out what the *Biographia* was about; and to Herschel C. Baker, of Harvard University, in whose seminar on Hazlitt and Coleridge the ideas underlying this study were tentatively put forward and helpfully criticized. I am especially indebted to Walter Jackson Bate, of Harvard University, whose own writings on the Coleridge period are models of judgment and scholarship, for his generous encouragement and for his advice on the manuscript of this work in its several stages. The defects which remain must be credited entirely to my own inability to profit by his intelligent criticisms. I am also grateful for the kindness and assistance shown me by the staffs of several libraries: the Harvard College Library, the Boston College Library, the Boston Athenaeum, the British Museum, the Royal Library at The Hague, and the library of the Canisianum at Maastricht, The Netherlands. Miss Kathleen Coburn very kindly answered a request for information which only her wide knowledge of the notebook manuscripts could provide. Henry Ansgar Kelly, S.J., handled many burdensome details of the manuscript preparation at a time when the inconvenience to his own work was not slight. And I consider myself fortunate in having had the services of two superior typists, Mrs. J. A. Robinson and Mv. O. de

Ley-Vogt. I am grateful for the permission given by Mr. A. H. B. Coleridge, of Whitford, Axminster, Devonshire, to quote from unpublished notebook manuscripts of Coleridge's in the British Museum; to the Clarendon Press, Oxford, for permission to quote from *The Collected Letters of Samuel Taylor Coleridge*, edited by Earl Leslie Griggs, 4 vols. (Oxford, 1956–1959); and to Pantheon Books, Inc., New York, for permission to quote from *The Notebooks of Samuel Taylor Coleridge*, edited by Kathleen Coburn, 2 vols. (New York, 1957–1961). Lastly, I must acknowledge the valuable contributions of the many friends who listened, read, made suggestions, and rendered assistance of a hundred kinds that I could not have done without.

J.A.A.

Maastricht
August 1965

Contents

The office of philosophical *disquisition* consists in just *distinction*; while it is the priviledge of the philosopher to preserve himself constantly aware, that distinction is not division. In order to obtain adequate notions of any truth, we must intellectually separate its distinguishable parts; and this is the technical *process* of philosophy. But having so done, we must then restore them in our conceptions to the unity, in which they actually co-exist; and this is the *result* of philosophy.

Biographia Literaria, chap. xiv

But you cannot *make* anything true which results from, or is connected with, real externals; you can only *find* it out.

Table Talk, April 14, 1835

AP	*Anima Poetae*
BL	*Biographia Literaria*, ed. Shawcross
CL	*Collected Letters*, ed. Griggs
C Works	*Complete Works*, ed. Shedd
EOT	*Essays on His Own Times*
Friend	*The Friend of 1818*
Friend (1809)	*The Friend of 1809–1810*
MC	*Coleridge's Miscellaneous Criticism*, ed. Raysor
N	*Notebooks*, ed. Coburn. The number following refers to the entry.
PW	*Complete Poetical Works*, ed. E. H. Coleridge
ShC	*Shakespearean Criticism*, ed. Raysor
SM	*Statesman's Manual*

CHAPTER I

Background, 1791–1800:

Coleridge as Democrat and Physico-Theologian

My speculative Principles were wild as Dreams — they were
'Dreams linked to purposes of Reason'; but they were perfectly
harmless — a compound of Philosophy and Christianity.

Letter of October 1, 1803

❧❧❧❧❧❧❧❧❧❧❧❧❧❧❧❧❧❧❧❧❧❧❧❧❧❧

Coleridge was by habit of mind a philosopher and yet he came somewhat slowly to the actual study of philosophy. The discursive formulation of principle to explain experience is a characteristic that is apparent
in his earliest writings, but the philosophical enthusiasms of his youth
were often indulged uncritically, and it was not until 1800 or so — after
his student days, his best poetry, his travels in Germany, and several unsuccessful literary and commercial enterprises were behind him — that
mental anxiety, combined with the involuntary idleness of sickness,
provoked him to a thorough study of the varied theories that were
juxtaposed somewhat uneasily in his intellectual system. It would seem
reasonable, therefore, for this study to begin at the point where his mature philosophy begins, with the review and criticism of his earlier
thought that are embodied in the four letters to Josiah Wedgwood in
February 1801. This would involve, however, the severe handicap of
passing over the first twenty-eight years of Coleridge's life, and therefore of ignoring the influential contributions to his later thought which
came not only from the philosophies he espoused in his youth, from his
passionate commitment to social justice and political causes, and from

his early religious enthusiasm, but also from his poetry, almost all of which was written in these years, and from the effect that the personalities of several friends, notably William and Dorothy Wordsworth, had on his character and intellectual development. Furthermore, to begin anywhere but in Coleridge's earliest years would be to neglect his first efforts to integrate his philosophical and theological principles, an attempt whose failure was doubtless responsible for the more exact philosophizing of the period 1800–1808, and so for the direction of much of his later thought.

This chapter and the following one, then, will attempt to indicate Coleridge's intellectual development up to the summer of 1800, and so provide the background for an understanding of the self-criticism of the Wedgwood letters and the philosophical developments that followed soon after. Within the limits of a few pages a detailed study of Coleridge's early thought is impossible, not only because of the astonishing variety of his mental activity and the sources which stimulated it, but also because scholars are far from agreed on the interpretation of much of his thought, and there are large areas of which no satisfactory studies exist. For instance, the idealistic elements of Coleridge's early thought are perhaps most in need of investigation, and there is no fully adequate treatment of Coleridge's poetry. For these reasons, and because these first chapters are primarily propaedeutic in relation to what follows, no apology seems necessary for offering a comprehensive rather than a detailed view of Coleridge's early philosophy. The emphasis here will be on the functional nature of his intellectual synthesis, the motive for its development and the reason for its relative inadequacy as a tool for his work, stressing certain things which it will be useful to have in mind when we begin to look in greater detail at Coleridge's philosophy of literature: the habits of mind which constitute in a general way Coleridge's conceptual framework, the elements of his thought in the decade 1791–1800 that can be isolated in reference to the associationist school of psychology, the characteristics that seem to come from the opposite tradition of transcendentalism and idealism, and finally the aspects of his philosophical outlook at this time which directly anticipate later developments in his literary philosophy.

MY PARTICULAR MIND

In the autobiographical letters he wrote for his friend Tom Poole in 1797 Coleridge separated the events of the first three years of his life from those that followed, and rather solemnly remarked that he made this division because the earlier years seemed to have contributed nothing to the formation of his "particular mind." [1] As post-Freudians we take this sort of remark in stride, but even in an age of precocity Coleridge's philosophic cast of mind seems to have been formed unusually early, according to his own letters. His autobiographical remarks are therefore of great interest insofar as they reveal those characteristics of intellectual temperament that are antecedent to philosophical influences and are the categories and forms in which those influences take shape. Four or five of these habits of mind are distinctive enough to be mentioned here as guides to Coleridge's later thought.

In the first place there is the fact of the primacy of his own inner experience as a source and criterion of his ideas. Coleridge himself attributed this disposition to his lonely and imaginative childhood. "I took no pleasure in boyish sports — but read incessantly." His books were of the sort that would stimulate the fantasy of an eager youth — the annals of Belisarius' campaigns, the adventures of Robinson Crusoe and his literary descendant Philip Quarll, the Arabian Nights' entertainments. When his father found and burned these tales, Coleridge resorted to his own imagination. "So I became a *dreamer* . . . and I was fretful, and inordinately passionate, and as I could not play at any thing, and was slothful, I was despised and hated by the boys; and because I could read and spell, and had, I may truly say, a memory and understanding forced into almost an unnatural ripeness, I was flattered and wondered at by all the old women . . . and before I was eight years old, I was a *character*." [2] The result, if we may believe Coleridge's retrospective impressions, was that the world of ideas and imaginative creations became more real to him than the workaday world of rationally con-

---

[1] *Collected Letters of Samuel Taylor Coleridge*, ed. Earl Leslie Griggs, 4 vols. (Oxford, 1956–1959), I, 312. The autobiographical letters are nos. 174, 179, 208, 210, and 234. This collection is hereafter cited as *CL*.

[2] *CL*, I, 347, 347–348.

ceived objects. He accepted his father's explanation of the solar system, he says, "without the least mixture of wonder or incredulity. For from my earlier reading of Faery Tales, and Genii etc etc — my mind had been habituated *to the Vast* — and I never regarded *my senses* in any way as the criteria of my belief. I regulated all my creeds by my conceptions not by my *sight* — even at that age." [3] This dependence on introspection was a lifelong habit of Coleridge's. He was fascinated by accounts of mental states, and no topic receives more attention than the topography of his own mind and heart.[4] There are dozens of instances of this self-analysis in his early letters and the focus of his introspection is on his emotional states as often as it is on intellectual processes. The remark he made to Thelwall in 1796 — "My philosophical opinions are blended with, or deduced from, my feelings" — was especially significant for the later development of his thought.[5]

Much as he is concerned with his own experience as the source of the data of his intellectual life, Coleridge cannot exactly be described as a romantic subjectivist. The objectivity of his experience is therefore another characteristic that must be mentioned. At first glance this may seem to run counter to some of the observations already made, even to deny the sense of Coleridge's own words quoted above. It is true that he spoke with contempt of knowledge gained from purely sensory evidence. After the passage already cited — "I never regarded *my senses* in any way as the criteria of my belief" — Coleridge went on to criticize the current theories (which he had himself supported, as we shall see) of how transcendental ideas can be formed by sensible impressions: "Those who have been led to the same truths [that is, awareness of the Vast] step by step thro' the constant testimony of their senses, seem to

---

[3] *CL*, I, 354.
[4] "Metaphysics, and Poetry, and 'Facts of mind' — (i.e. Accounts of all the strange phantasms that ever possessed your philosophy-dreamers from Tauth, the Egyptian to Taylor, the English Pagan) are all my darling Studies." *CL*, I, 260. Miss Coburn finds this habit of mind significant: "That the fulcrum of Coleridge's thought is his awareness of the psychological factors in any kind of human experience, and that it derives its power from his own subtle and complex personal realizations, is, at the very least, a part of the truth about Coleridge." *Inquiring Spirit: A New Presentation of Coleridge from His Published and Unpublished Prose Writings*, ed. Kathleen Coburn (London, 1951), pp. 19–20.
[5] *CL*, I, 279. For some examples of introspective analysis see *CL*, I, 78, 125–127, 259–260, 349, 398, 454–455, 628–629.

me to want a sense which I possess — They contemplate nothing but *parts* — and all *parts* are necessarily little — and the Universe to them is but a mass of *little things*." [6] Though Coleridge was in little danger of becoming a positivist, the opposite extreme of radical subjectivism was equally repugnant to him. His earliest philosophical theories were, after all, derived from association psychology and its sensate explanation of knowledge, and even after he rejected this position the clarification of the relationship of external nature to the mind and imagination was one of the central problems of his philosophy.

The notion of objectivity involved here possibly turns on the meanings of the word "empirical." Coleridge would have rejected its positivist implication of the limits of knowledge, but there was no reason why his own experiences, mental and spiritual as well as physical, could not be termed "empirical" and therefore "objective." There is no question here of a solipsistic self-reliance; that can be shown by instancing the enormous variety of data that Coleridge assembled in his notebooks as material for his reflections, and the earnest and extensive searching of others' theories that accompanied his own speculations. But all particulars are only *parts* of a larger whole and when contemplated by themselves lead to nothing further. Regarded as evidences of order, of mind, sensory and spiritual data alike furnish objectivity to the philosopher. The key to this objective order is not discursive analysis (which he would later call *understanding*), but rather an intuition or a kind of instinctive apprehension of truth — what he once referred to as a "philosophic tact for what is truly important in facts," and which is recognized as "right in the abstract, by a living feeling, by an intuition of the uncorrupted Heart." He says of some lines suggestive of the doctrine of pre-existence that they allude to "a *Feeling* which if you never have had yourself, I cannot explain to you." [7] This gap be-

[6] *CL*, I, 354.

[7] *BL*, I, 148; *CL*, II, 1000, and I, 260. The lines are from the "Sonnet composed on a journey homeward; the author having received intelligence of the birth of a son, Sept. 20, 1796," in *The Complete Poetical Works of Samuel Taylor Coleridge*, ed. Ernest Hartley Coleridge, 2 vols. (Oxford, 1912), I, 153–154. This collection is hereafter cited as *PW*. In his pioneering attempt to survey Coleridge's mind, Norman Wilde made a remark relevant to this discussion: "His thought moves along the *via media* between sensationalism and intellectualism, rejecting the brute facts of the one and refusing to rest content with the lifeless abstractions of the other, insisting always on the primacy of the spiritual

tween an insight capable of grasping a "vast" truth or an ineffable feeling and, on the other hand, the sense knowledge of the "rationally educated" which contemplates only parts or little things is basic to Coleridge's thought. Through all the changes in his subsequent philosophy, he regularly opposes this insight, or some version of it, to various inadequate expressions of what knowledge is. In one form or another it is the criterion of all his concepts and the guarantee of the "objectivity" of his ideas.[8]

This dependence upon a personal intuition as a standard of judgment suggests, as a corollary to these observations, the metaphysical character of Coleridge's philosophy. From the moment he first began to criticize the associationist epistemology, it was apparent that the starting point of philosophy for him was an insight into being-as-experienced, and the goal was the total apprehension of being. "The term, Philosophy, defines itself as an affectionate seeking after the truth; but Truth is the correlative of Being." [9] And, though the instrument of this analysis was necessarily reasoning or the discursive faculty, the subject matter of philosophy included more than rationally verifiable conclusions. The ultimate apprehension of being therefore depended on sources which included discursive reasoning but included also whatever other kinds of knowledge could be winnowed from experi-

---

vision." "The Development of Coleridge's Thought," *Philosophical Review*, 28 (1919): 160.

[8] In spite of Coleridge's own words, it is misleading to locate the distinction, as some critics do, between mind and heart, as though it were intellect and feeling that were being separated. From the time he first understood the need for a distinction, and thus the inadequacy of association psychology on this point, Coleridge saw the problem in terms of the disparity between our rational conceptions of things and their concrete individualities. See the notebook entry 334: "All our notions husked in the phantasms of Place and Time, that still escape the finest sieve and most searching Winnow of our Reason and Abstraction." *The Notebooks of Samuel Taylor Coleridge*, ed. Kathleen Coburn, 2 vols. Bollingen Series L (New York, 1957–1961); this edition is hereafter cited as *N*. Nor did Coleridge ever condemn sense knowledge as such, but rather the superficial notions of those who live by their gross senses and inferior mental faculties, the kind of knowledge Bacon's "idols" gave. His own physical sensitivity was extraordinary, as the detailed entries in his notebooks and the exact figures of his poetry show. "His quivering alertness to every stimulus of sense was . . . the ground of his strengths and of his weaknesses." Humphrey House, *Coleridge: The Clark Lectures 1951–1952* (London, 1953), p. 14. Miss Coburn notes his extraordinary ability to identify himself with natural phenomena, at the time of experiencing them or in memory. *N* 335, note.

[9] *BL*, I, 94.

ence. Since the nature and extent of these possible kinds of knowledge cannot be defined a priori, Coleridge's epistemology is an open-ended system, beginning with discursive reason but moving outward to include whatever kinds of intuition and insight experience reveals. Thus the discovery of the defect of discursive reasoning as a source of complete and satisfactory knowledge — which was the chief cause of his disenchantment with associationism — was the most important event of his early philosophical development, insofar as it led to his interest in intuitive forms of knowledge and to the whole structure of his later thought. At the same time, his reliance upon a metaphysically realistic viewpoint saved him from the inherent defeatism of the critical philosophy. We shall have to come back to this point after examining some of the data that lie ahead.

Another distinctive element of Coleridge's thought was the result of his strong personal need for a religious view of life. This may have been a consequence of his pious upbringing at the hands of his father, vicar of Ottery St. Mary, "a first-rate Christian," who "in learning, good-heartedness, absentness of mind, and excessive ignorance of the world . . . was a perfect *Parson Adams*."[10] The younger Coleridge was himself destined for the ministry, and in later life considered the possibility of taking a Unitarian pulpit as a means of support. The religious spirit that resulted from this early training was intensely personal, and it is this aspect of Coleridge that needs emphasis, rather than the more familiar transcendental philosophy-religion that we know from the poems. The need for an individual faith is behind most of the crises of his early years. Though he "sported infidel" for a time at Christ's Hospital in a show of schoolboy independence, the atheism never seems to have touched his heart.[11] His letters to his brother George, even allowing for a desire to satisfy that stern judge of conduct, show the same qualities of anxious questioning, cautious skepticism, and eager belief that are evident in later letters on religious subjects to Southey, Thelwall, Poole, and Josiah Wedgwood.

It may be that his failures commercially and artistically, or more

[10] *CL*, I, 310.
[11] James Gillman, *The Life of Samuel Taylor Coleridge* (London, 1838), I (the only part published), 23–24.

likely his continual ill-health, threw him back on religion for consolation. He says wryly to Poole at one point, "O me, my dear fellow! the notion of a Soul is a comfortable one to a poor fellow, who is beginning to be ashamed of his Body." [12] But a better explanation is simply that a religious view of life was a consequence of the moralism which is so strong a feature of his character. This shows up in the passionate criticism of self (and of ideas and institutions) which is the motive of much of his best poetry from "Religious Musings" to the "Dejection" ode, and in his ardent social idealism and lifelong concern for improving the political order. Raysor notes: "It was not due a misconception of his temperament that he thought of entering the Unitarian ministry, that he wrote sermons for incapable clergymen. When he asked Lamb if he had ever heard him preach, Lamb was almost obvious in replying that he had never heard him doing anything else." [13] His text might well have been taken from his own life; among other characteristics of Coleridge, House lists: "An inability to cope with what presented itself as the plain immediate duty . . . coupled with a very exact knowledge of what the immediate duty was." [14] This seems to be confirmed by the fact that the passages in which Coleridge indulged in self-pity and justified his sloth are confined almost entirely to his letters, where he could usually count on sympathetic auditors. In his own notebooks Coleridge never deceived himself about his capacities or his motives.

Coleridge's religious needs intensified as he grew older. His last years were devoted almost exclusively to the explication and defense of his synthesis of philosophy and orthodox Christianity and its application to moral and social life. In fact, throughout the development of his thought there is little distinction between theology and philosophy. Since he had rejected the purely rational criticism of experience, it was natural that the alternative reliance on intuition, with its idealistic and mystical implications, should be strongly religious. His epistemology was one of the sources of the spiritual vision that integrated all of his thought from his early struggles with associationism, and the

[12] *CL*, II, 661.
[13] *Coleridge's Shakespearean Criticism*, ed. Thomas Middleton Raysor, 2 vols. (London, 1930), I, l. Hereafter cited as *ShC*.
[14] House, *Coleridge*, p. 37.

major poems, to the theological speculations of his last years. D. G. James contrasts the "willing suspension of disbelief," which Coleridge requires for poetic faith, with the "unbroken habit of belief" which he earnestly sought through his life, and finds in the consideration an insight into the nature of Coleridge's romanticism: "The Romantic poet of *Kubla Khan*, the *Mariner*, and *Christabel*, and the theologian and Christian philosopher of *Aids of Reflection* are not two, and disparate, people. Those who see the Christian writer as one who has escaped from the Romantic poet fail to discern the true nature both of Romanticism and of Christianity." [15] Both are total world views. One is based on the empathic and unitive identification in the self of the qualities of the external universe of things and persons. The other is based on the imitation by the individual person in himself of that perfect commitment to God, as the only certainty, that Christ exemplified and made possible. The subjective motive of the unitive realization of the "other" is nearly the same in both, and Coleridge's transition from his early romantic sympathy with the "one life" in things to his later Christian vision of the divine nature as the ground and guarantee of the unity of the created universe represents in one sense only a consistent maturing of his most fundamental convictions.

Finally, something must be said about the functional purpose of Coleridge's philosophy, and the qualitative correlative of this, the dialectical pattern by which his thinking proceeds. The fact that for Coleridge philosophy is a necessary way of life, an imperative unraveling of the problems presented by experience, must be quite clear from what has already been said about his habits of mind. The struggle to conceptualize a personal intuition and to unify the concepts in a satisfactory framework requires a motivation stronger than intellectual curiosity as it is commonly conceived. Religious uncertainty, creative incapacity, physical suffering — these were the very existential sources of Coleridge's philosophy. In his mature thought there is a very clear idea of function and the value of an ends-and-means philosophy; in his youth the notion was more implicit in his thinking, but is still quite characteristic of him.

[15] *The Romantic Comedy* (London, 1948), p. 169.

If philosophy is conceived of as a search for meaning in experience, and method as an orderly process toward ever fuller formulations, then the pattern of progress will inevitably be dialectical as the original insight is amplified or refined by comparison or contrast with new experience. In one of Coleridge's fanciful etymologies, he associated the word "mind" with the German *mähen*, to reap, and this suggested to him the "vibratory yet progressive motion" of the scythe as characteristic of the mind's progress.[16] His philology is unsound, but the idea is striking, especially when we consider that some of Coleridge's most typical utterances are distinctions — understanding and reason, fancy and imagination, primary and secondary imagination, thought and attention, imitation and copy, fabrication and generation, genius and talent, poetry and science, subject and object, law and idea. Coleridge's mind seems to have worked, in his youth, by dividing subjects into opposing parts and rejecting the unsatisfactory half. Later he came to see that the opposition was one of polar tendencies within a complex whole and he espoused a theory of "reconciliation of opposites." This evolved, as his thought progressed, into the more sophisticated "trichotomous" logic in order to express the integrative aspect of true dialectic synthesis. It was no accident that Coleridge had such a brilliant reputation as a conversationalist — though the frequent testimony to this is sometimes puzzling to the student who knows only his middling prose — for the progressive clarification of back-and-forth discussion was the natural process of his mind. Of course, the mind which sees truth now on one side of a question, now on the other, is liable to the charge of vacillation and inconsistency, especially when the direction of the dialectical process is not clear. Coleridge sometimes exasperated his friends. Hazlitt in his reminiscence of their first meeting recalls that on their way to Shrewsbury Coleridge shifted constantly from one side of the footpath to the other as he walked. Years later he thought this indicative of a characteristic instability. "He seemed unable to keep on in a strait line." [17]

It seems possible now to say that the confused eclecticism with which

[16] N 378 and note; see also *CL*, II, 696–697.

[17] "My First Acquaintance with Poets," *The Complete Works of William Hazlitt*, ed. P. P. Howe, 21 vols. (London and Toronto, 1930–1934), XVII, 113.

Coleridge is often charged can best be explained, in part at least, as the instinctive inclination to see all sides of a problem, and to move, by opposing true but partial solutions, toward more inclusive and complicated explanations. Unity is of course the motive and hoped-for result of dialectical procedure. Coleridge's single aim in his speculations was the integration of insights and observations into a total philosophical outlook. "I feel too intensely the omnipresence of all in each, platonically speaking — or psychologically my brain-fibres, or the spiritual Light which abides in the brain marrow, as visible Light appears to do in sundry rotten mackerel and other *smashy* matters, is of too general an affinity with all things/ and tho' it perceives the *difference* of things, yet is eternally pursuing the likenesses, or rather that which is common." [18] This achievement of unity on the conscious level by means of a dialectical operation of imperfect principles is echoed on the unconscious level by the indeliberate and intuitive unity achieved through the agency of the associative capacity. Coleridge calls this "the streamy Nature of Association, which Thinking = Reason, curbs and rudders." [19] The associative stream of sense particulars, memories, images, and feelings moves within the channel set for it by discursive ratiocination, but it has a force and effect of its own. Lowes, whose work is a detailed study of the sources and operation of the associative capacity in Coleridge, calls it "the prime instrument in the hands of genius" and says that its implications lie at the very roots of all art.[20]

These characteristics of Coleridge's mental set are obviously not to be considered purely as innate forms or categories. They developed as Coleridge's mind grew and his experience widened, along lines determined by his most native capacities and influences. They are "given" in the sense that inquiry into their origin and priority with respect to each other would be difficult if not impossible, yet they are manifestly regulative in Coleridge's intellectual processes and to understand them is of great help in discerning the subsequent course of his philosophy.

One substantive consequence of this analysis of Coleridge's mental

---

[18] N 2372.
[19] N 1770.
[20] John Livingston Lowes, *The Road to Xanadu: A Study in the Ways of the Imagination* (Boston and New York, 1927), pp. 71–73.

habits is the conclusion that his early years were marked by strong
tensions between disparate tendencies in his thought. Philosophy was a
problem-solving activity precisely because Coleridge had intellectual
problems, and they stemmed for the most part from discordant positions strongly held. Possibly the topography of Coleridge's mind outlined in the previous pages has prematurely suggested a unity of viewpoint which in fact was the result of a lifetime of speculation. In his
youth the reconciliation of so many opposite views was a desirable rather
than an actual accomplishment, and even his guiding intuitions could
only have been inchoate, based as they were on so little experience.
The keenly religious temper was uneasily accompanied by an intellectual skepticism. "Fond of the dazzle of Wit, fond of subtlety of Argument, I could not read without some degree of pleasure the levities of
Voltaire, or the reasonings of Helvetius — but . . . my Heart forced me
. . . to *love* the Jesus, whom my Reason (or perhaps my *reasonings*)
would not permit me to *worship*." [21] The scientific and empirical mind
that was fascinated by his brother's medical studies and later by Davy's
chemical researches was the same one that had at an early age become
"habituated *to the Vast*" and to stories of fairies and genii, and which
did not regard the senses in any way as the criteria of belief.[22] The
demand for rationally convincing explanations of problems was rather
inconsistent with the emotionalism that emerges in some of the poetry,
and with the condemnations of the "Laodicean self-confidence of human Reason" and "vain Philosophy's aye-babbling spring." [23] None of
these antipathies was insoluble, and we shall see the resolution of many
of them in Coleridge's subsequent thought. Indeed, it might well be
true that his philosophy would have been poorer without the motive
impulse of these warring enthusiasms felt early in life. Nevertheless,
the oppositions, though they were partly the necessary stages in the
dialectical advance of his mind, were acutely and painfully present to
him in the years when he had left school behind and his mature intellectual life was just beginning.

[21] *CL*, I, 78.
[22] *CL*, I, 354.
[23] *CL*, I, 267. "The Eolian Harp," *PW*, I, 102.

POLITICS AND DISSENT

The decade which concerns us is the 1790's. At its beginning Coleridge was not yet a student at Cambridge; at its end he had been soldier, journalist, preacher, political tractarian, poet, and traveler, and was about to retire to the country and become a philosopher. If we look for a starting point from which to investigate the elements of Coleridge's intellectual outlook during these first crowded years of his adult life, we cannot do better than to begin with the man to whom he attributed the inspiration for so much of his thought at this time, David Hartley, the "great master of *Christian* Philosophy." [24] Coleridge first read Hartley's *Observations on Man* while he was an undergraduate at Cambridge, in the fall of 1794, and subsequently testified to the influence he felt by naming his eldest son Hartley in 1796. Because of the repeated acknowledgments in his letters of his youthful interest in Hartley, and because of the prominence he gives to the refutation of association psychology in the *Biographia*, it is customary to consider that the Hartleyan system of Christian rationalistic psychology was the substance of Coleridge's philosophy during this period.[25] With certain qualifications this seems true, especially of the middle years of the decade. However, the fact that he could praise the master of Christian Philosophy in glowing terms long after he had rejected the mechanism of the origin of ideas, and had altered in his own mind the association of ideas into something radically different, suggests that Coleridge was never equally enthusiastic about all parts of Hartley's system. In what sense then is

[24] *CL*, I, 236.

[25] Whether Coleridge derived his ideas of associationism mainly from Hartley, or from remoter sources in Locke and Hobbes, or even from contemporary associationists such as Priestley, is a question that cannot be settled here. There is in Coleridge's own acknowledgment of Hartley's influence on him, and in the Hartleyan concepts and terminology employed in his letters and poetry during these years, ample justification for supposing a significant relationship. In addition, there are no references to Hobbes before 1801, when Coleridge was reviewing his whole attachment to associationism and studying the question of its legitimate genealogy. His first mention of Locke is in company with Hartley as the subjects of his "intense study," but he says later, in 1801, that "he had never really *read*, but only *looked thro'* " Locke's *Essay*. *CL*, I, 126; II, 679. Compared with these remarks the Hartley citations are abundant and specific on the question of indebtedness. They are discussed below.

it accurate to speak of his acceptance of Hartley? And what elements of the association philosophy exerted a more than temporary influence on his thought? Two observations must be made.

In the first place, if we consider what Coleridge wrote in the years 1791–1800, we find that, with the exception of the poetry of 1797–1798, and the journals and letters of the year in Germany, 1798–1799, his published works were almost entirely devoted to politics and social theory. This was to be expected, if we recall that the event which most strongly affected the minds of Englishmen in the last decade of the century was the revolution in France. If it was not exactly the source of the liberal theories in theology, philosophy, and social thought that were current in the 1790's, the revolution was certainly the catalyst of most of this intellectual activity, the concrete fact which had to be accounted for in every theory, and the touchstone by which men and opinions were judged. Politics thus formed the natural interest of the educated youth of the period.

Coleridge, as much as anyone, was shaped by the spirit of the times.[26] He was conventionally democratic, egalitarian, and optimistic. When he arrived at Cambridge in October 1791 he already had to his credit an ode on the destruction of the Bastille, full of worn epithets and personifications, unreservedly saluting the defeat of Tyranny and the birth of glad Liberty for France and all nations.[27] Sympathy with events across the channel and criticism of the Pitt government were strong among the undergraduates. A friend, C. V. Le Grice, has described the political evenings in Coleridge's rooms at Jesus, "when Aeschylus, and Plato, and Thucydides were pushed aside," and the latest pamphlet of Burke's heatedly discussed. "There was no need of having the book

---

[26] For an excellent brief description of the age and Coleridge's relation to it, see "The Young Man in His Time," the second chapter of Carl R. Woodring's *Politics in the Poetry of Coleridge* (Madison, Wis., 1961). This book complements with detailed information another useful analysis of Coleridge's political and social thought, John Colmer's *Coleridge: Critic of Society* (Oxford, 1959). Much of the material in this section is taken from these two studies. The first three chapters of Herschel Baker's *William Hazlitt* (Cambridge, Mass., 1962) survey the religious and political controversies that both Coleridge and Hazlitt were heir to. The comparison that can be made between their two reactions to the common spirit of the times is instructive. For Hazlitt's view of Coleridge's "decline" into orthodoxy, see Baker, pp. 61–65, 113–114, 354–364.

[27] *PW*, I, 10–11.

before us. Coleridge had read it in the morning; and in the evening he would repeat whole pages verbatim." [28] As an undergraduate Coleridge's most notable accomplishment was winning a prize for a Greek Sapphic ode; his subject was the iniquity of the slave trade. And in the same summer in which he and Southey conceived the scheme of a communistic society on the banks of the Susquehanna they wrote the verse tragedy *The Fall of Robespierre*, which is colored with regret at the corruption of the republican hero but also with confidence in democracy's future after his fall.

Immediately after leaving the university for the final time, in December-January of 1794–1795, Coleridge published in the *Morning Post* eleven "Sonnets on Eminent Characters." Nine were forthrightly political. Burke is addressed by Freedom as "Great Son of Genius!" but chided for the error of giving consolation to "Oppression's hireling crew" by his attack on the revolution. Priestly is praised as the promoter of Justice, for having freed Religion "from the papal spell," and as a scientist for whom "Meek NATURE slowly lifts her matron veil." The sonnet to Godwin describes the author's debt, when he "roam'd the bleak Heath of Distress," to the writer of *Political Justice*, whose vision of the future beatitude of mankind identified social justice with happiness. Pitt is labeled a traitor who "kiss'd his country with Iscariot mouth." Even the ostensibly unpolitical sonnet to Bowles attributes to him the author's awakening to "Fancy, Love, and Sympathy," as well as to the sense of brotherhood.[29]

In the series of addresses given in Bristol in 1795 Coleridge involved himself directly with matters of current controversy.[30] The true friends of freedom in England, he said, are those who believe that vice originates not in the heart but in the understanding and surrounding circumstances, and who therefore place their faith in the future happiness of man when illumination and education will have removed the sources of ignorance. He urged negotiation with France and an end to the

---

[28] *Gentlemen's Magazine*, December 1834, quoted in Joseph Cottle, *Reminiscences of Samuel Taylor Coleridge and Robert Southey* (London, 1847), p. 304.

[29] *PW*, I, 80–84.

[30] Printed in *Essays on His Own Times: Forming a Second Series of The Friend*, ed. Sara Coleridge, 3 vols. (London, 1850), vol. I. Hereafter cited as *EOT*.

censorship and denial of liberty under the Pitt government, with its consequent atmosphere of panic and suspicion.

The first half of 1796 was devoted to the ill-fated *Watchman*, Coleridge's contribution to the political education of England's citizens. The prospectus stated quite directly: "In an enslaved state the rulers form and supply the opinions of the people. A People are free in proportion as they form their own opinions. In the strictest sense of the word Knowledge is Power." [31] The themes of the original contributions to this journal are similar to those of the Bristol addresses and to the ideology of the political sonnets. Popular education and personal reform must precede parliamentary changes if they are to be effective. The high ideals of the revolution must not be compromised by the militarism of France's leaders. The repression by the government of citizens' rights to free speech and fair trial is excessive and intolerable. Religious dissent from the Establishment — he has the Methodists in mind — fosters the love of freedom because it involves the examination of ultimate principles; further he praises Methodism for its genuine concern for the poor and because it urges sobriety and domestic habits which dispose the people to liberty.

The spirit of social consciousness also pervades much of the poetry of the later 1790's. "Reflections on Having Left a Place of Retirement" (1795) culminates in the resolution "to fight the bloodless fight/ Of Science, Freedom, and the Truth in Christ." "The Destiny of Nations" (1796), a redaction of lines once contributed to Southey's *Joan of Arc*, is a mélange of republican sentiments, prophecy, religious enthusiasm, and historical allegory, in pseudo-Miltonic diction and devices. The "Ode on the Departing Year" (1796) mournfully reviews the events of the previous months, finds some joy in the death of the "Northern Conqueress," Catherine of Russia, but ends in gloomy prophecy of the downfall of Albion because she has abused the light and freedom she might have offered to others. "Fire, Famine, and Slaughter" (1798) is an anti-Pitt allegory, and the theme of England's abuse of her God-given freedom, morality, and justice is central to "Fears in Solitude" (1798). "France: An Ode" (1798) is something of a summary of Cole-

---

[31] Colmer, *Coleridge: Critic of Society*, pp. 32–33.

ridge's politics and a turning point. He reviews the causes that first prompted him to support the revolution. The invasion of Switzerland, however, has shown him how far French militarism has perverted its original ideals; now his hopes for the ultimate triumph of freedom rest not on governments but on individual moral reformation according to the principles of religion and social philosophy.

When he resumed political journalism for the *Morning Post* in 1799, his attitude toward many of the principles he had hitherto embraced was ambivalent. France was disillusioning his democratic enthusiasm. His German sojourn had perhaps whetted a homesickness and an incipient patriotism. The philosophical underpinnings of his politics and social theory were being examined somewhat critically. It was but a short step to the first great turning point of his intellectual development.

The second observation that must be made as a preliminary to an assessment of Coleridge's commitment to Hartley's system concerns Coleridge's religion. If the main subjects of his published writings during the 1790's are politics and social theory, it is also true that one of the primary interests of Coleridge in his letters during the period is the exploration of the necessity and extent of religious faith for the conduct of both personal and public life. It will become clear, too, that for him there was no separation of the two spheres in which religious belief might operate; the bases of his political philosophy are identical with those of his personal faith.

Coleridge's devout upbringing and his native transcendentalism have already been noticed. Along with these characteristics went a youthful skepticism and rationalism. The result was that he was never in his early years an uncritical believer. Whether he was ever an "infidel" may be doubted; the only clear reference to such a possibility is in a letter to Thelwall, where it may be accounted an exaggeration for the sake of making a point with his atheistic correspondent.[32]

As he grew into manhood belief responded to need. Thus, in the relatively untroubled years of his schooling, religious faith was a matter of assent to a reasonable natural theology, with enough home truths

[32] "I have studied the subject [of religion] deeply and widely — I cannot say, without prejudice: for when I commenced the Examination, I was an Infidel." *CL*, I, 205.

thrown in to warm a heart of rather limited capacity. "My Faith . . . was made up of the Evangelists and the Deistic Philosophy — a kind of *religious Twilight*." [33] When he got to Cambridge he felt the need of a stronger faith. Possibly this was one of the consequences of his interest in the poetry of the Rev. William Bowles; at any rate Coleridge ascribes to him an increased awareness of "the feelings of the heart." [34] More likely the strengthening of his religion was the result of his coming under the influence of William Frend, who showed him that a political radical could also be a pious believer. Frend's combination of social philosophy and Unitarian theology must have satisfied Coleridge's liberal instincts as well as his basic theism. Thomas Poole wrote of Coleridge a month after he had first met him in July 1794: "In religion he is a Unitarian, if not a Deist; in Politicks a Democrat, to the utmost extent of the word." [35] To be a Unitarian meant to be a Socinian, that is, a believer in the adoptive divinity of Christ. By the standards of the day, the position was considered a more reasonable one than the Trinitarianism of the Established Church which, furthermore, was associated in the public mind with the abuses and inadequacies of the government and the prevailing social order. At Cambridge dissent was fashionable as well as reasonable. Frend's position became a rallying point for liberal undergraduates when the university attempted to deprive him of his tutorship by a trial, ostensibly on the charge of unorthodox religious opinions, but patently for his political writings, which urged negotiation with France rather than war, and support of the cause of freedom. Coleridge publicly stamped himself a Jacobin and narrowly missed expulsion from the university because of his part in a demonstration in the courtroom.[36] Actually he thought his own position more benevolent than fanatic: "And I am [called] a Dýmocrat because I will not join in the maledictions of the Despotist — because I will *bless all* men and *curse* no one!" [37]

The reaction between Coleridge's religion and his politics seems

[33] *CL*, I, 78.

[34] *BL*, I, 10.

[35] E. K. Chambers, *Samuel Taylor Coleridge: A Biographical Study* (Oxford, 1938), p. 29, quoting Mrs. H. Sandford, *Thomas Poole and His Friends* (n.p., 1888), I, 95.

[36] Arthur Gray, *Jesus College* (London, 1902), pp. 179–180.

[37] *CL*, I, 126–127.

to have been reciprocal; if his faith was elaborated to include the doc-
trinal basis of universal brotherhood, his political theory also grew to
include a notion of personal responsibility in social matters that was
ultimately religious. He wrote at this time (November 6, 1794) to his
brother George, in some distress at the charges that he was a democrat
and an infidel, which he attributed to "youthful disputatiousness mistaken for the result of fixed Principles." In taking up the question
"what is the best conceivable mode of meliorating Society," Coleridge
answers by saying, in effect, that only the moral reform of individuals
will enable reforms on the level of government or society to succeed.
"Did Jesus teach the *Abolition* of it [slavery]? No! He taught those
principles, of which the necessary *effect* was — to abolish all Slavery. He
prepared the *mind* for the reception before he poured the Blessing —.
You ask me, what the friend of universal Equality *should* do — I answer
— 'Talk not of Politics — *Preach the Gospel*!' " [38] It may be suspected
that religion was so prominent in the discussion because the correspondent on this occasion was his clerical brother George. In fact, however,
this point was one of Coleridge's persistent principles in discussing
the renovation of society, and one of the main topics on which he differed from Godwin whose system was otherwise so attractive to him at
this time. For Godwin, a philosophical anarchist, the answer to society's
ills was the clarification of principles and the spread of illumination;
"melioration" would inevitably follow. Coleridge, however, advocated
the path of individual reform.

That general illumination should precede revolution, is a truth as obvious, as that the vessel should be cleaned before we fill it with a pure liquor.
But the mode of diffusing it is not discoverable with equal facility . . . He
would appear to me to have adopted the best as well as the most benevolent
mode of diffusing truth, who uniting the zeal of the methodist with the
views of the philosopher, should be *personally* among the poor, and teach
them their *duties* in order that he may render them susceptible of their
rights.[39]

The concept of personal responsibility becomes a fundamental principle

[38] *CL*, I, 126.
[39] *EOT*, I, 21–22.

of Coleridge's social philosophy and an indication of the direction of his subsequent religious thought.

The reference to Methodism in this last passage is interesting. Colmer thinks that *The Watchman* essays show Coleridge's increasing dissatisfaction with Unitarianism, at least with the reasonable worldliness that it allowed and its lack of real sympathy for the suffering. He suggests that this is the cause of the irritable tone of the article "On Fasts," the satiric references to a minimal religion being necessary for a devotee of "Modern Patriotism," and the indifference of prosperous Britons to the war-born distress of their indigent countrymen in the essay "We See Things with Different Eyes." [40] Methodism, on the other hand, offered enthusiastic personal commitment and a genuine social consciousness.

This was exactly the direction Coleridge's religious views were to take in the latter half of the decade. In the earlier years, however, his outlook was more rooted in the elements of religion and of applied religion that could be derived from analyses of man's nature and duties, and in a select belief in the more reasonable parts of revelation. This seems to have been his basic attitude toward Unitarianism. When he was later in doubt about taking the pulpit offered him at Shrewsbury, one of the causes of his anxiety was that the ministry made "one's livelihood hang upon the profession of *particular opinions*," which reason might "at length dissever." His confusion on this point was moderated by the reflection that: "The *necessary* creed in our sect is but short — it will be necessary for me, in order to my continuance as an Unitarian Minister, to believe that Jesus Christ was the Messiah — in all other points I may play off my intellect *ad libitum*." [41] When he described in the *Biographia* the sermons he gave while on a tour seeking subscribers for *The Watchman* in 1796, he noted that they were

[40] Colmer, *Coleridge: Critic of Society*, p. 40.

[41] *CL*, I, 365, 366. For another summary of the modest content of Christian doctrine see the letter to Thelwall, December 17, 1796: "Now the Religion, which Christ taught, is simply 1 that there is an Omnipresent Father of infinite power, wisdom, and Goodness, in whom we all of us move, and have our being, and 2. That when we appear to men to die, we do not utterly perish; but after this Life shall continue to enjoy or suffer the consequences and natural effects of the Habits, we have formed here, whether good or evil. — This is the Christian *Religion* and all of the Christian *Religion*." *CL*, I, 280.

"preciously peppered with Politics," and that he spoke in a blue coat and white waistcoat, lest he seem to be of the orthodox church, "that not a rag of the woman of Babylon might be seen on me. For I was at that time and long after, though a Trinitarian (i.e. ad norman Platonis) in philosophy, yet a zealous Unitarian in Religion; more accurately, I was a *psilanthropist*, one of those who believe our Lord to have been the real son of Joseph, and who lay the main stress on the resurrection rather than on the crucifixion." [42] Emphasis on the resurrection followed the belief in adoptive sonship, and was thought more consistent with an optimistic vision of man's future.[43]

[42] *CL*, I, 176; *BL*, I, 114–115.

[43] To what extent these positions represent the influence of Joseph Priestley cannot be determined here. Priestley, the central figure in the formation of English Unitarianism, was in the same tradition of rational Christianity as Nathaniel Lardner, who influenced him strongly, and Hartley, whose *Observations* he revised. All these names occur in Coleridge's pantheon about this time. Priestley's doctrine was one of scientific materialism combined with a Christian faith of a Socinian kind. Philosophical necessity was a corollary of the materialism, but a benevolent God has ordained a mechanism toward universal salvation rather than the awful judgment of Calvinism. The hope for immortality was based upon the expectation of the resurrection of the whole man. See the chapter "Joseph Priestley and the Socinian Moonlight," in Basil Willey's *The Eighteenth Century Background: Studies on the Idea of Nature in the Thought of the Period* (London, 1940).

A recent study by Herbert Piper, "The Pantheistic Sources of Coleridge's Early Poetry," *Journal of the History of Ideas*, 20 (1959): 47–59, has suggested that there is evidence that Coleridge adopted along with Priestley's Unitarian theology his materialistic pantheism as well. The world view of "The Destiny of Nations" and "Religious Musings," it is asserted, rests on two ideas common in France (among Diderot, de Maupertuis, d'Holbach, and others) and of which Priestley and Erasmus Darwin were the chief English spokesmen: that nature was a living force acting through the whole natural world, and that this nature had an intelligent purpose, expressed in evolutionary terms or in a provident technology. Both ideas are contained in the lines from "Destiny of Nations" which salute God the Father as:

> Nature's vast ever-acting Energy!
> In will, in deed, Impulse of All to All!   (*PW*, I, 147).

In a later note to this passage Coleridge attributed the possibly "dangerous" interpretation of these lines to his early membership among the "sons of Joseph," a punning allusion to Priestley and to Socinian Unitarianism. Whether Coleridge's tentative materialism and faint pantheism of this period are as striking as Piper asserts may be doubted. That the influences, such as they were, came from Priestley is quite possible, in view of Coleridge's esteem for the scientist-theologian and his general cast of mind at the time. The parallels that Piper has assembled are persuasive on Coleridge's reading of Priestley and Darwin, but his argument for extensive influence rests mainly on the text of "The Destiny of Nations," and it is questionable how much the muddled doctrines of that work ever meant to Coleridge, or how extensively the same positions appear in "Religious Musings." What Piper's analysis makes clear is that Coleridge was reading Priestley and that science and theology in Priestley offered complementary theories for a rational world view.

HARTLEY AND ASSOCIATIONISM

It must be clear by now that Coleridge's religious and political views during the first half of the 1790's have certain common and fundamental themes; indeed they are so closely related that it is not too much to say that for Coleridge politics and social philosophy are the exteriorization of the principles of religion. It was the point of view of Frend and Priestley and of the Dissenters who formed the body of reformist opinion generally. In the light of these similarities in both of Coleridge's primary interests during this period, what conclusions can be made in regard to his commitment to Hartley? An answer to this question must be postponed a moment longer, until we can examine the outlines of Hartley's philosophy and distinguished its principal emphases.

The *Observations on Man*, Hartley's two-volume *summa*, was first published in 1749.[44] It is in two parts. The first, "Containing observations on the frame of the Human Body and Mind, and on their Mutual Connexions and Influences," develops the theory of vibrations, the association of sensations, and the parallel association of ideas and of pleasures and pains, concluding with general remarks on the mechanism of the human mind. The second part, "Observations on the Duty and expectations of Mankind," treats of natural and revealed religion from a rational and apologetic point of view; it subsumes under these topics much of the psychology of the first part, now put to the purposes of religion.

Hartley begins in the first part by establishing the doctrine of vibrations as the key to the sensory process. He records his indebtedness to Newton's *Principia* and *Optics* for the idea that all phenomena are resolvable into motions. His own problem is to explain how these physical motions are transformed into sensations, which are internal feelings of the mind. Correlative to these are ideas, or "other internal feelings," which "appear to spring up in the mind of themselves," or

[44] *Observations on Man, His Frame, His Duty, and His Expectations*, 2 vols. (London, 1749). Apparently Coleridge used the octavo edition of 1791, of which the first two volumes reprint the 1749 text without alteration, and the third volume contains notes and commentary by H. A. Pistorius on the second part of the original treatise. See the note by Coleridge to line 43 of "Religious Musings," *PW*, I, 110. References here are to the 1791 octavo edition. There was a folio edition the same year.

"are suggested by words," or "arise in other ways." "The ideas which resemble sensations, are called *ideas of sensation*: all the rest may therefore be called *intellectual ideas*," and these latter are compounded out of the ideas of sensation.[45] Sensations, then, are the elements of this knowledge theory, and their origin is what he wishes to explain. In Hartley's language, the process begins when external objects are impressed on the sensory nerves, and vibrations occur in the aether residing in the pores of these nerves. These vibrations in the aether agitate the small particles of the medullary substance of the sensory nerves with synchronous vibrations, which are then propagated along the course of these nerves up to the brain, where they are propagated freely, in diminishing strength, over the whole medullary substance of the brain, though preserving the line of direction of the nerve which conveyed them, thus allowing for differentiation.[46] Since ideas correspond to sensations, or are compounded from them, it is also true that the white medullary substance of the brain is the immediate instrument by which ideas are presented to the mind; in other words, what ever changes are made in this substance, corresponding changes are made in our ideas, and vice versa.[47]

In a scholion Hartley tries to answer the objection that no causal relationship has been proved between vibrations and mental sensations, by suggesting an analogy from mathematics and physics. Just as the quantity of matter in bodies is always found to be proportional to their gravity and so we may either make the quantity of matter the exponent of the gravity, or the gravity the exponent of the quantity of matter, so, "if that species of motion which we term vibrations, can be shown by probable arguments, to attend upon all sensations, ideas, and motions, and to be proportional to them, then we are at liberty either to make vibrations the exponent of sensations, ideas, and motions, or these the exponent of vibrations, as best suits the inquiry." Hartley's answer to the question would be perfectly valid, were he considering only the

[45] Hartley, I, 2. The first four pages proper of volumes I and II of the 1791 octavo edition are numbered i–iv, though the small Roman numbers had already been used for preliminary material. I have substituted Arabic numbers in referring to these pages.
[46] Hartley, I, 21–24.
[47] Hartley, I, 8.

expression or manipulation of relationships between vibrations and sensations; however, he had set out to provide a mechanism which would explain the actual causal influences, and he is forced to conclude that it is impossible to say how vibrations are connected with sensations. Though he offers the notion of an "infinitesimal elementary body to be intermediate between the soul and gross body," which will provide the causal relationship, he does not elaborate on this additional entity. His final remark is that ideas and sensations may have some other source than vibrations, and so, though his proposals about the mechanism are true "in a very useful practical sense, yet they are not so in an ultimate and precise one." [48]

The doctrine of the association of ideas is developed independently of Hartley's notions of vibrations, and he attributes the concept to John Gay, who had written on the association of pleasures and pains, and to Locke, who had discussed habit in terms of association.[49] Simply stated, the theory proposes that sensations, by being often repeated, leave certain vestiges or images of themselves. These are the simple ideas of sensation, and they are the most vivid where the corresponding sensations are most vigorously impressed or most frequently renewed.[50] Furthermore, "Any Sensations A, B, C, etc. by being associated with one another a sufficient Number of Times, get such a Power over the corresponding Ideas a, b, c, etc. that any one of the Sensations A, when impressed alone, shall be able to excite in the mind b, c, etc. the Ideas of the Rest." [51] The moral life is subject to the same principles of association, for affections or passions (pleasures and pains) are only complex aggregates of simple ideas, and are greater or less according as each person unites more or fewer, more vivid or more languid, miniature vibrations. Since the simple parts of these affections and passions can be discovered by analysis, "we may learn how to cherish and improve good ones, and check and root out such as are mischievous and immoral." [52] And, since sensible (and therefore in-

[48] Hartley, I, 33, 34.
[49] Hartley, I, iii, 5.
[50] Hartley, I, 56.
[51] Hartley, I, 65.
[52] Hartley, I, 81; also I, 368.

tellectual) pleasures are far more numerous than sensible (and intellectual) pains, and by association are drawn into unified states in which the pains are gradually overcome, the whole of life tends by a benevolent disposition of God toward "pure ultimate spiritual happiness." [53] This calculus of association, operating in the direction of ever more spiritualized ideas and pleasures (Hartley enumerates those of imagination, ambition, self-interest, sympathy, and finally of theopathy or the pleasures and pains involved in the contemplation of God), culminates in a moral sense which has its own authority, as the result of all the rest, and leads us to the love of virtue and the hatred of vice, and finally "to the pure love of God, as our highest and ultimate perfection, our end, centre, and only resting-place, to which yet we can never attain." [54]

Hartley concludes his first volume with a disquisition on the mechanism of the human mind, and the consequent necessity of thought and action involved. "Each action results from the previous circumstances of body and mind, in the same manner, and with the same certainty, as other effects do from their mechanical causes; so that a person cannot do indifferently either of the actions A, and its contrary a, while the previous circumstances are the same; but is under an absolute necessity of doing one of them, and that only." [55] This is how he understands the mechanism of the mind. Though he denies free will in the philosophical sense (if either A or a could equally follow is the same as "affirming that one or both of them might start up into being without any cause"), he admits it in the practical order ("if free will be defined as the power of doing what a person desires or wills to do," then it is consistent with the doctrine of mechanism since a person's desires and affections are developed by the association of ideas).[56] This

[53] Hartley, I, 83–84. Coleridge noted on the end papers of his copy of Hartley — interestingly enough, it is one of the very few annotations in the book — some implications of these ideas for a thoroughly spiritualized poetry: "P. 81 — Ideas may become as vivid and distinct, and the feelings accompanying them as vivid, as original impressions — and this may finally make a man independent of his senses. — one use of poetry." The note is on the end paper facing page 512 of volume I of the copy of Hartley's *Observations*, 1791 octavo, in the British Museum.

[54] Hartley, I, 497.

[55] Hartley, I, 500.

[56] Hartley, I, 503, 501.

mechanism, Hartley says, has among its happy consequences the disso-
lution of the problem of God's prescience as opposed to man's free will,
the tendency to abate resentment against men since what they do to
us they do by God's appointment, a support of the doctrine of universal
restoration, and a motive for us to labor more earnestly because of the
certainty of our mechanically determined course.[57]

The second part of Hartley's treatise, "Observations on the Duty
and expectations of Mankind," is divided into four sections. In the first
is developed a theology based mainly on the conclusions of reason
without the assistance of revelation. It covers such topics as the existence and attributes of God; the necessity of a natural religion, whether
it be considered as the duties which unaided reason dictates, or as the
promptings of the moral sense, or merely as rational self-interest, all of
which come to the same thing; and also the impossibility of the human
will being free in the philosophical sense, due to the infinite power and
knowledge of God. The second section is a lengthy apologetic for the
truth of the Christian religion, covering the authenticity, historicity, and
reasonableness of the scriptures, the truth of miracles, the force of
prophecies, the moral evidence of Christ's character and the fact of the
Church's flourishing condition, and finally many reflections on the philosophical content of Christian revelation — its superior excellence,
political wisdom, and so forth. The third and principal section, "Of the
Rule of Life," consists of an elaborate review of the various kinds of
pleasures and pains enumerated in the first book (those of sensation,
imagination, ambition, self-interest, sympathy, theopathy, and the
moral sense), now criticized from the viewpoint of their regulation by
the religious virtues of piety, benevolence, and the moral sense, with
a great many practical rules and applications. The fourth division
treats of the expectations, founded both in reason and in revelation, of
the untimate future happiness of all mankind.

Criticism of Hartley's *Observations* on the ground of a supposed
dichotomy between the theoretical bases of the two parts of the work
seems rather misguided. Several critics have argued that the science

was confined to the first part and the religion to the second,[58] but this interpretation fails to take into account the purpose of Hartley's first book, which can really be understood only in relation to the second. His argument proceeds from the mechanism of the origin of ideas, to the theory of the association of ideas and feelings in our intellectual and moral activity (in Book I), and finally to the essentially rational analysis of the proper conduct of our lives (Book II).

The argument is quasi-scientific and superficially empirical; it seems to proceed from the details of experience to abstract principles of behavior. However, it is really Hartley's end in view that directs his choice of details. The final state of man is "theopathy" or "perfect self-anihilation, and the pure love of God." In discussing the "rule of life" by which this state is to be achieved, Hartley bases it on a threefold analysis — of "the frame of our natures," "the dictates of natural religion, and the precepts of the scriptures taken together." The last two elements derive from revelation, both natural and direct. The first element is our own empirical knowledge of our nature. All three are necessary if we are to understand the rules by which we are to achieve happiness. Christian revelation is a "far clearer light" and "a more definite rule" but, given "the frame of our natures," the empirical psychology of the first book must be equally well understood.[59] The unity of Hartley's system lies in this teleology of moral and religious purpose and in the rational method of analysis.[60]

Granted the assumption that a benevolent deity has prearranged the operation of our natures toward ultimate bliss, it follows in Hartley's mind that we must discover the conditions of this process so as best to cooperate with it. Morality thus demands a mechanism, which he elects

---

[58] J. H. Muirhead, *Coleridge as Philosopher* (London, 1930; repr., 1954), p. 42. Coleridge himself encouraged this view in *BL*, I, 84.

[59] Hartley, *Observations*, II, iii.

[60] "He is attempting . . . to understand this creature, known *a priori* to be fallen, whose mind operates mechanically by association of simple sensations (and perhaps has material particles vibrating in its medullary substance), in order better to ascertain how its natural *behavior* can be regulated according to the rules of *conduct* revealed by God." Robert Marsh, "The Second Part of Hartley's System," *Journal of the History of Ideas*, 20 (1959): 268.

psychology to provide, acting on the hints of Gay and Locke. The association of ideas requires only the premise that ideas are unitary things whose complexity results from their being related according to empirically discoverable laws of association. Going further back, he provides a mechanism for the origin of ideas themselves by making a threefold assumption: of the existence of vibratory motions, of an intermediate aether, and of the possibility of transmuting corporeal motions in the brain into sensations and ideas in the mind. In Hartley's terms the two parts of his work are quite consistent, and the psychological mechanism of mind in the first part leads quite logically to the possession of beatitude. It is when one's conception of some detail in the system changes (as in realizing, as Coleridge came to do, that association was a mechanical and lifeless process, and that the moral life demanded personal freedom) that the two parts are bound to be seen as contradictory. On its own grounds the Hartleyan doctrine is quite unified.[61]

The apparatus of association psychology which Hartley takes such pains to describe does not seem to be the source of the structural themes of Coleridge's religious philosophy. Much closer resemblances to Coleridge's thought can be found in the moral and religious principles which are implicitly assumed in Hartley's work from the beginning and which show up primarily in the second part as the organizing ideas of the whole treatise. These might be summarized as: the theistic conception that underlies the work, the idea of the perfectibility of man, the mechanism of necessity by which this process toward happiness is accomplished, and the confidence in rational analysis which pervades

---

[61] For a slightly different explanation of the same conclusion, see Hoxie N. Fairchild, "Hartley, Pistorius, and Coleridge," *PMLA*, 62 (1947): 1010–1021. "There is indeed a chasm between Hartley's natural religion and his Christianity, but the gap would probably not be apparent to him or to the eighteenth-century readers who thought of Christianity as a 'republication' of natural religion and a practical means of implementing its teachings. Granting his dubious premises, there is a continuous relationship between his associative system and his natural religion; and his pseudo-mystical pantheism, though he does not quite recognize the fact, belongs to his natural religion rather than to his Christianity" (pp. 1017–1018). Fairchild observes that Coleridge later asserted (in *BL*, I, 84) the independence of the second part of Hartley's work from the first. "When the poet wrote *Religious Musings*, however, it was precisely the *dependence* of Hartley's religion upon Hartley's psychology that appealed to him" (p. 1018).

the study. These are the themes of Coleridge's theology and his politics in the early 1790's. They define what was the precise attraction and the most enduring, though sometimes negative, influence of Hartley's "Christian Philosophy."

The first and last elements — theism and rationalism — were fairly elementary dispositions of Coleridge's mind during these years. The combination places him in the long tradition of English thinkers who combined supernatural faith with scientific analysis of the state of man — Bacon, Newton and Locke, the Cambridge Platonists of the seventeenth century, Shaftesbury, Paley, Butler, Priestley, and of course Hartley. The other two doctrines — perfectibility and necessity — define a somewhat narrower segment of this illustrious line, and must be examined more closely. There is the strongest reason for thinking that they characterized Coleridge's outlook at this time. Whenever he felt the need of a terse summary of his position these were the two doctrines he mentioned. To Thelwall he writes in 1796: "A Necessitarian, I cannot possibly disesteem a man for his religious or anti-religious Opinions — and as an *Optimist*, I feel diminished concern. — I have studied the subject deeply and widely — I cannot say, without prejudice: for when I commenced the Examination, I was an Infidel." Almost two years before, he had written to Southey: "I would ardently, that you were a Necessitarian — and (believing in an all-loving Omnipotence) an Optimist." About the same time he praised Lamb for his equanimity in the face of his sister's illness, "as beseemed him who like me is a Unitarian Christian and an Advocate for the Automatism of Man." [62] Religious optimism and philosophical necessity may seem strange bedfellows but for Coleridge and many of his contemporaries in the last years of the eighteenth century they formed a convincing point of view.

The optimistic view of man's nature was the offspring of deistic rationalism and "scientific" psychology. When the classical Christian concept of man, with its reservations about his ability to persevere unassisted in the path of goodness, narrowed into the Calvinistic vision of man's total iniquity and helplessness apart from grace, the obvious

[62] *CL*, I, 205, 145, 147.

counterbalance appeared in the idea of his natural goodness. This was the invention of a different theology, one that was self-confidently grounded in the light of reason and the truths of Nature which, in the face of endless controversies over revelation, were thought to be clearer and more certain guides.[63] In its extreme form the theory of the innate goodness of man was open to the obvious criticism of experience; but when considered in relation to the Lockean psychology, which taught that the content of the mind was composed entirely of external impressions, the notion of natural perfection became one of natural perfectibility, which could be achieved by controlling the circumstances that formed the mind, and in this version innate goodness became almost scientifically credible.

The doctrine of perfectibility or optimism, to call it by its most general name, is not capable of simple definition. It took many forms, some of which may be considered as they occur in Coleridge. There is first of all the rather primary aspect of it which asserts a eudaemonistic teleology. In Coleridge's first reference to Hartley this is the point that interests him: "And after a diligent, I *may* say, an intense study of Locke, Hartley and others who have written most wisely on the Nature of Man — I appear to myself to see the point of *possible* perfection at which the World may perhaps be destined to arrive —." He is confident in the outcome of this benevolent system — "as an *Optimist*, I feel diminished concern [about subjective guilt]." [64] The notion that the white paper of the mind was inscribed only with impressions received from without was developed by Godwin and others into the assertion that all vice originated in man's surroundings and that the cure of the ills of society could be encompassed by removing the factors that inhibit the progress of man: government, which prevents the natural development of social justice; and ignorance of principles, which hinders intellectual and moral development. This revolution in Godwin was to be nonviolent, carried on largely by means of education. In the first of the "Conciones ad Populum," delivered in Bristol, Febru-

---

[63] See the first chapter of Willey's *The Eighteenth Century Background*, especially pp. 1–14.

[64] *CL*, I, 126, November 6, 1794; I, 205.

ary 1795, Coleridge described a member of the "small but glorious band" of true patriots:

Convinced that vice originates not in the man, but in the surrounding circumstances; not in the heart, but in the understanding; he is hopeless concerning no one — to correct a vice or generate a virtuous conduct he pollutes not his hands with the scourge of coercion, but by endeavouring to alter the circumstances would remove, or by strengthening the intellect, disarms, the temptation. The unhappy children of vice and folly, whose tempers are adverse to their own happiness as well as to the happiness of others, will at times awaken a natural pang; but he looks forward with gladdened heart to that glorious period when justice shall have established the universal fraternity of love.[65]

The confidence in education as a means of eradicating bondage to surroundings was, it will be remembered, one of the motives behind the publication of *The Watchman*.[66] And the assumption that men would be good but for the inhibitions that government placed on their development (this was the period of Pitt's strenuous censorship and the suspension of habeas corpus) was obviously fortified by the events in France in the early 1790's.

The most interesting evidence of Coleridge's commitment to a philosophy of social optimism was the pantisocratic vision. Conceived by Coleridge and Southey on their first meeting, during a respite from a walking tour in the summer of 1796, the plan called for the emigration of several couples to the Delaware regions of America where an agricultural and communistic society would be set up on the banks of the Susquehanna. It was more than just a plan for agrarian retirement, as is evident from the vigor with which Coleridge wished to arrange circumstances so that no taint of received opinions or cant orthodoxy might enter the ideal community. He objects to children accompanying them on the grounds that the prejudices and error, the fear and selfishness, they have learned from their schoolfellows will be subver-

---

[65] *EOT*, I, 17.

[66] "In the present perilous state of our Constitution the Friends of Freedom, of Reason, and of Human Nature, must feel it their duty by every mean in their power to supply or circulate political information." Prospectus for *The Watchman*, quoted in Lawrence Hanson, *The Life of S. T. Coleridge: The Early Years* (London, 1938), pp. 91–92.

sive of a permanent system. He queries Southey as to whether the women are not thinking of the novelty of the scheme, are sufficiently concerned with essentials, and are strong enough not to spoil the plan. He is worried lest Christianity, or "that mongrel whelp that goes under it's name," be introduced.[67] Besides insisting on this purity of doctrine, Coleridge wants the pantisocratic community to be free of concern for money (one of the rocks on which the scheme foundered, when Southey's prospects improved), and to be completely egalitarian (Southey made the mistake of suggesting the introduction of a servant class, and thereby provoked one of Coleridge's most democratic outbursts).[68] The fundamental theory behind the utopian venture was the Godwinian and Priestleyan principle that freedom from artificial restraints was the key to the formation of the perfect natural society. Coleridge did not subscribe to the doctrine of innate goodness, and his differences with Godwin over the emphasis to be placed on personal religious reform have already been noticed, but he was so far a perfectibilist as to hold that the removal of temptation was the only requirement for man's goodness. "Wherever Men *can* be vicious, some *will* be. The leading Idea of Pantisocracy is to make men *necessarily* virtuous by removing all Motives to Evil — all possible Temptations." [69]

The necessity of the moral process toward universal happiness is a concomitant of the doctrine of perfectibility in Hartley, Priestley, Godwin, and, for a time, Coleridge. We have seen that Hartley's system, if looked at as a psychology, centers on the apparently empirical analysis of the origin of sensation or ideas in the mind. In order to effect a transition, however, from material sensations to immaterial ideas, his system must assume precisely what it should, according to its ostensible method, discover by evidential means, namely the immateriality of ideas. Furthermore, in order to discover a unity among ideas, it must assume the existence of that very unity. And, in order to show that better ideas cancel out less perfect ones, it must assume the progressive organization of ideas. In other words, it is a mistake to think of Hartley's psychology as empirically derived, with the necessity of the process

[67] *CL*, I, 119, 123.
[68] *CL*, I, 114–115, 121–123.
[69] *CL*, I, 114.

as a scientific conclusion. Hartley's psychology is basically a structure of contemporary physiological data, intended to provide a "scientific" explanation of several principles drawn from moral and religious philosophy, and resting on a set of assumptions about the physiological data which have validity only in terms of the philosophical truths that they were invented to explain. Hartley's necessity is the "reluctant consequence" (his own diffident words) only of his own determinism, which is assumed with his very definition of the content of the mind as equivalent to the sensory impressions, and with the reduction of the will to a state of mind. "The *will* is that state of mind, which is immediately previous to, and causes, those express acts of memory, fancy, and bodily motion, which are termed voluntary." [70]

Apparently Coleridge adopted this philosophical necessity during the years in question. As early as 1794 he announced: "I am a compleat Necessitarian — and understand the subject as well almost as Hartley himself — but I go farther than Hartley and believe the corporeality of *thought* — namely, that it is motion —." [71] The reduction of Hartley's psycho-physical parallelism to a purely materialistic explanation of knowledge had been one of the principal accomplishments of Priestley in his redaction of Hartley's *Observations*,[72] and this was the time when Coleridge was coming under the influence of Priestley and Unitarianism generally. The materialism must have been uncongenial to most of Coleridge's instincts. He mentions it only this once. On another occasion, in disputing the source of morality with Thelwall, and averring that adultery would be wrong in any ethical system, he says: "*Guilt* is out of the Question — I am a Necessarian, and of course deny the possibility of it." He can even be enthusiastic about the melioristic aspects of determinism: "What we *must* do, let us love to do. It is a noble Chemistry, that turns Necessity into Pleasure!" [73]

However frequent and specific his remarks were at this time, it seems that Coleridge always had reservations about extreme philosophical

[70] Hartley, *Observations*, I, 3.
[71] *CL*, I, 137.
[72] *Hartley's Theory of the Human Mind, on the Principle of the Association of Ideas; with Essays Relating to the Subject of It* (London, 1775).
[73] *CL*, I, 213; *N* 31.

necessity, and it is doubtful that the concept played a large part in his philosophy, except by stimulating him to an opposite line of thought. Like atheism, it went too much against the grain. As early as March 1795 Coleridge wrote to George Dyer, "Almost all the physical Evil in the World depends on the existence of moral Evil" — "unexpected sentiments," says Miss Coburn, "from a complete Necessarian," though it is true that in the context Coleridge is discussing how man corrupts nature and perhaps he did not see the contradiction in his principles.[74] A year later, however, there is an interesting entry in a notebook, showing a distinct uneasiness about philosophical necessity and a feeling that some parts of the theory need explanation: "Doctrine of necessity rendered not dangerous by the Imagination which contemplates immediate, not remote effects — hence vice always hateful and altho equally monotonous as Virtue." [75] His explanation, similar to Hartley's comments on "practical" freedom, seems to be that necessity is a fact, but that the imagination, by leading us to think in terms of our causal influence on things and our voluntary activities, makes us unaware of its effect and so moderates any tendency toward fatalism.

This kind of hesitation is apparent in many of Coleridge's comments on the subject of necessity. In the dispute with Godwin, discussed above, over the possible improvement of society, Coleridge's insistence on personal moral renovation shows a distrust of the determinist process toward happiness; this is a classical, conservative element in Coleridge's social philosophy, which may reflect his own ample experience of the intrusion of self between intention and fulfillment. Another instance of this breakdown of the perfectibilist scheme is the passage quoted above from the first of the "Conciones." Coleridge is saying that the true patriot changes society not by coercion but by improving the circumstances or strengthening the intellects of those less fortunate. Almost lost in the benevolent onrush of the passage are those for whom these means do not work: "The unhappy children of vice and folly, whose tempers are adverse to their own happiness as well as to the happiness of others, will at times awaken a natural pang

---

[74] *CL*, I, 154; *N* 161, note.
[75] *N* 156.

[in the observer]." This is experience speaking, not perfectibilism, and the defect of the necessitarian vision is not lessened by disguising the free will as "tempers."

A few years later, when Coleridge was moved by the early death of the Irish patriot Robert Emmet to reminisce about the philosophy of his youth, he chose to emphasize precisely the elements of religion and social theory that we have stressed here:

> My speculative Principles were wild as Dreams — they were 'Dreams linked to purposes of Reason'; but they were perfectly harmless — a compound of Philosophy and Christianity. They were Christian, for they demanded the direct reformation and voluntary act of each Individual prior to any change in his outward circumstances, and my whole Plan of Revolution was confined to an experiment with a dozen families in the wilds of America: they were philosophical, because I contemplated a possible consequent amelioration of the Human Race in it's present state and in this world; yet christian still, because I regarded this earthly amelioration as important chiefly for it's effect on the future State of the Race of man so ameliorated.[76]

The necessitarian aspects of perfectibility were by then considerably muted.

What part did Hartley's specific psychology play in Coleridge's philosophy? If we consider first the mechanism of the origin of ideas in Hartley's work, it is safe to say that it had very little influence on Coleridge. There are one or two passages in his letters and writings which might seem to indicate the opposite. The much-quoted passage from "Religious Musings" describing Hartley as

> he of mortal kind
> Wisest, he first who marked the ideal tribes
> Up the fine fibres through the sentient brain,[77]

is thought to indicate the philosopher's chief distinction in Coleridge's eyes. But there are not many such texts. Even his single dramatic assertion of "the corporeality of *thought* — namely that it is motion" is followed by a parody of the Hartleyan vocabulary which suggests that

---

[76] *CL*, II, 999–1000, October 1, 1803.
[77] *PW*, I, 123.

he is somewhat amused by the extremity of his own position.[78] If even
Hartley had his doubts about the apparatus of vibratiuncles ("the doctrine of association may be laid down as a certain foundation . . .
whatever becomes of that of vibrations"[79]), it is not surprising that
Coleridge, in spite of (more likely as a result of) his curiosity about
empirical psychological data, was unhappy with a completely mechanical explanation of the mind's operation.

Hartley's explanation of the origin of ideas was based upon a simple
mechanism so inflexible as to be all but useless in the analysis of any
kind of knowledge above the level of simple apprehension. Not so his
speculations on the association of ideas. He rightly distinguished between the value of the two doctrines. The notion of vibrations was
the offspring of a crudely materialistic pseudo-empiricism. The theory
of the association of ideas has a respectable history from the time of
Aristotle. Hartley, following Locke's hint that complex ideas are made
up of simple ones, made it not only a kind of operation of the mind,
but the mind's sole activity, and attributed to it all progress in moral
as well as intellectual activities. In other words, he built upon the un-
controversial premise that ideas recall other ideas by reason of similarity,
contrast, contiguity in space or time, or causal influx a structure which
defined the whole operation of the mind in terms of this association.
And he added another premise, somewhat concealed, that this association worked in the direction of progressive perfection, ideas of good
overcoming ideas of evil, or ideas of truth overcoming those of error.
It is important to maintain the distinction between the two kinds of
associationism, the traditional — ultimately Aristotelian — view and
the Hartleyan, in discussing Coleridge's use of association psychology.
There is no difficulty gathering texts to show in a superficial way that
Coleridge accepted the associationist doctrine in his early years. To
Mary Evans he writes, explaining how completely she has become the

[78] It is a note written to a younger friend who had been thrashed by James Boyer, the
Christ's Hospital master: "I condole with you on the unpleasant motions, to which a
certain Uncouth Automaton has been mechanized; and am anxious to know the motives,
that impinged on its optic or auditory nerves, so as to be communicated in such rude
vibrations through the medullary substance of It's Brain, thence rolling their stormy
Surges into the capillaments of it's Tongue, and the muscles of it's arm." CL, I, 137.

[79] Hartley, Observations, I, 72.

object of his reveries: "My associations were irrevocably formed, and your Image was blessed with every idea." To Thelwall, on the comparative sublimity of classical and Christian myths: "The difference in our tastes it would not be difficult to account for from the different feelings which we have associated with these ideas." In criticizing a poem of Southey's to him: "You, I doubt not, have associated feelings dear to you with the ideas . . . and therefore do right in retaining them." Again: "As to Harmony, it is all *association* — Milton is *harmonious* to me, and I absolutely nauseate Darwin's Poem." [80] But this aspect of Hartley's system never interested him as much as its ethical and religious principles. Even the studies of the influences of associationism on Coleridge's poetry rarely center on the specific psychology that distinguished Hartley's theories, but rather on the notions of optimism, the perfectibilist process, necessity, or the moral problems these ideas raise.

The real cause of the attention paid to association psychology in the study of Coleridge is not to be found in his political and religious thought during the decade of the 1790's, but in the later years when he turned to psychology and epistemology. It was then that he realized retrospectively the errors of the Hartleyan system and of its foundations in Locke and Hobbes. There is more about associationism in the *Biographia Literaria* than anywhere else in Coleridge's writings, because he was at that time concerned not to refute a philosophy which he had never followed in its extreme for more than a year or two but to reject the whole drift of contemporary thought in the direction pointed out by Locke and Hobbes, of which Hartley was only a prominent popularizer and a convenient adversary.[81] Another reason why Hartley is studied in search of Coleridge is because so much of Coleridge's later psychology seems to have its roots in associationism. Here again the distinction between traditional association theory and

---

[80] *CL*, I, 130, 281, 290, 216. *The Botanic Garden* of Erasmus Darwin was published in two parts, 1789 and 1791.

[81] Priestley, who had carried Hartley's thought to extremes, was spared refutation. Was this because he was Unitarianism's saint? Perhaps Woodring is right in suggesting that Hartley is the noncontroversial surrogate for Priestley in much of Coleridge's early praise and later damnation of associationism. *Politics in the Poetry of Coleridge*, pp. 98–99.

the contributions of English theorists such as Hartley must be kept in mind. By 1800 — indeed long before — Coleridge had rejected all of the characteristically Hartleyan elements of associationism. The general theory of the association of ideas, but not the exclusive explanation of the mental life by such a theory, formed a part, and really only a small part, of the structure Coleridge later elaborated. Yet he had to develop this system by using the philosophical language and framework that were generally available at the end of the eighteenth century — the Hartleyan one. The task of working out his own forms of expression was one that could only be accomplished gradually, and if some of his ideas seem grounded in purely associationist doctrine it is not to be concluded that the one and the other are the same. No one can create a philosophy and a language for it overnight. That is why emphases are more important than verbal echoes in deciding Coleridge's meaning. Except for a brief period, Hartleyan associationism — the specific psychology of it — was not a significant element in Coleridge's thought.

RELIGIOUS MUSINGS

If the "Christian Philosophy" of Coleridge's early years, roughly 1793–1796, includes the various doctrines of political and religious philosophy noted above, one way of seeing them organized as a unified outlook and animating a creative work of some dimension is to look briefly at "Religious Musings." The first version of the poem was written on Christmas Eve of 1794, and it was revised over and over until March 1796 [82] (and indeed after that for subsequent editions); thus it spans almost exactly the period under study here. It was not an idle exercise. Coleridge thought of it as a turning point in his poetical career, and later used as a motto for the poem several lines from Mark Akenside which begin:

> What tho' first,
> In years unseason'd, I attun'd the lay
> To idle Passion and unreal Woe?
> Yet serious Truth her empire o'er my song
> Hath now asserted.

[82] CL, I, 187.

And he said shortly afterwards, "I rest for all my poetical credit on the *Religious Musings*." [83]

In introducing the poem Coleridge gives the following outline as an "argument": "Introduction. Person of Christ. His prayer on the Cross. The process of his Doctrines on the mind of the Individual. Character of the Elect. Superstition. Digression to the present War. Origin and Uses of Government and Property. The present State of Society. The French Revolution. Millenium. Universal Redemption. Conclusion." [84] The religious interpretation of contemporary political events is the subject of the poem, and the essential element of the interpretation is the optimistic reliance upon the eventual triumph of social justice and religious beatitude by means of a moral process that is essentially Hartleyan. The identification of social justice with heavenly glory is perhaps a marriage of Godwin and Hartley. It is evident from the start of the poem that the subject is at least as political as it is religious. The distinctive reflection of the narrator in meditating on Christ's passion is that God, "The Great Invisible," shines forth "chiefly in the oppressed Good Man's face" who, regardless of himself, "Mourns for th' oppressor." [85] Christ's prayer is one of mercy for humankind. This mercy has its effect on individuals and on society — these are the major divisions of the poem.

For the individual, the effect of Christ's love is shown in the process by which the soul of the "thought-benighted Sceptic" passes from the state of Terror, where he is "spell-bound with earthy lusts" and unable to feel the "Dim recollections" of its "nobler nature," to Hope, "From Hope and stronger Faith to perfect Love," and ends finally in the beholding of God:

> Till by exclusive consciousness of God
> All self-annihilated it shall make
> God its Identity: God all in all! [86]

Coleridge notes: "See this *demonstrated* by Hartley," and cites two passages in the *Observations*. The first occurs when Hartley is discuss-

[83] *PW*, I, 108, note; *CL*, I, 197, April 1, 1796.
[84] *PW*, I, 108, note.
[85] *PW*, I, 109. Reference is to the 1796 version.
[86] *PW*, I, 110–111.

ing the six stages of moral growth, beginning in imagination, passing through ambition, self-interest, and sympathy, and culminating in theopathy and a developed moral sense. It reads: "Since God is the Source of all Good, and consequently must at last appear to be so, *i.e.* be associated with all our pleasures, it seems to follow . . . that the idea of God . . . must, at last, take place of, and absorb all other ideas, and HE himself become, according to the language of the scriptures, *all in all*."[87] The second passage Coleridge refers to is an elaborate algebraic analysis using W as Love of the World, F as Fear of God, and L as Love of God, to show that W equals F^2 divided by L, so that, if W is a constant, F^2 equals L, and therefore an increase in the fear of God, the point where Coleridge's process begins in the lines cited, will lead to the final love of God.[88] The elect individual, like the true patriot in Coleridge's other writings, is the one who corresponds to this teleological movement and considers "all visible things/ As steps, that upward to their Father's throne/ Lead gradual." God, for his part, cooperates by "Alike from all educing perfect good." [89] The triumph of good over evil is accomplished by a Hartleyan resolution of both powers, good being the stronger: "Our evil Passions, under the influence of Religion, become innocent, and may be made to animate our virtue." [90] The result is a sense of membership in "one wondrous whole," which "fraternises man" and "constitutes/ Our charities and bearings." The implication is clearly that democracy is the form of government most suited to the children of God. The only obstacle to the individual's happiness is superstition, or ignorance of God as Supreme Reality, which only Faith can overcome.[91]

----

[87] Hartley, *Observations*, I, 114. Miss Dorothy Waples, in her study of Coleridge's drawings from associationism, "David Hartley in *The Ancient Mariner*," *Journal of English and Germanic Philology*, 35 (1936): 342, interprets these lines from "Religious Musings" as a version of the Hartleyan process. Fairchild, in *PMLA* 62 (1947): 1010–1021, discusses the background and implications of this footnote of Coleridge's. "After 1797, the note to line 44 of *Religious Musings* was carefully omitted and thenceforward Coleridge never disclosed the fact that he had once prized Hartley as a non-enthusiastic demonstrator of the beatific vision" (p. 1021).

[88] Hartley, *Observations*, II, 329–330.

[89] *PW*, I, 111.

[90] *PW*, I, 112, note.

[91] *PW*, I, 114–115.

The social equivalent of this paradigm occurs in the second part of the poem, which begins with the Hartleyan and Godwinian notion that out of evil will come good in "the great process of divine Benevolence." [92] The horrors of the present war with France are such evils; the war party advances under the Christian banner and they seek "Thee to defend, meek Galilean" by means of treachery, the suffering of widows and orphans, foul alliances (with Russia, Austria, and "each petty German princeling" — all "Soul-hardened barterers of human blood"). But God has so disposed things that these evils are "the immediate source/ Of mightier good" and that "by brief wrong" there will result "Truth lovely"; the state of future happiness has a power that is "Magnetic o'er the fixed untrembling heart." [93] Coleridge repeats in slightly different form the process of benevolence that society goes through, this time in a more precise version of Hartley's terms. In primitive times the "vacant Shepherd" wandered with his flock, pitching his tent "where'er the green grass waved." Soon, however, his imagination suggests the desirability of having his own property. The spirit of self-interest and ambition thus leads man into sensual indulgence and the evils of a materialistic society. But at the same time these make him take thought about his condition and his intellectual and spiritual necessities. "From Avarice thus, from Luxury and War/ Sprang heavenly Science; and from Science Freedom." This spirit of freedom represents the highest conception of the philosophers of the past, who looked forward to "the fated day" when eloquent men would rouse "the unnumbered tribes/ That toil and groan and bleed, hungry and blind" and shape their confusion "to such perfect forms" as they had dreamed of in their most ecstatic moments, the beauty of which made them muse on "Why there was misery in a world so fair." [94]

This gap between vision and fact is illustrated by the present state of society, which Coleridge pictures in Godwinian terms as resulting from the oppressions of the powerful. The wretch "made wild by want" roams for prey but it is nevertheless with an "unnatural hand" that he

[92] *PW*, I, 116, note.
[93] *PW*, I, 115–117.
[94] *PW*, I, 116–118.

commits "deeds of blood." The dissipated working man is a "victim of seduction." The aged woman depending on official charity dies so slowly that it cannot be called murder. The antidote to all this unjust suffering, and the instauration of the millenium, is to be accomplished by the French Revolution, whose divine mandate is indicated by Coleridge's comparison of it with the destruction following the breaking of the fifth seal in the Apocalypse.[95] What follows will be social justice warmed by Love, the millenium in heaven and on earth, and the resurrection of those who "from earliest time/ With conscious zeal had urged Love's wondrous plan,/ Coadjutors of God." They are: Newton, Hartley, and Priestley.[96] The poem ends in a vision of universal salvation and an invocation of the "Contemplant Spirits" who supervise the organization of creative energy, suggesting the pantheistic materialism spoken of above. Coleridge will one day join their mystic choir. Until then he will busy himself in "ministries of heart-stirring song," and in meditation on that Love which warms and animates all things.[97]

In outlining here the social and religious philosophy which underlies "Religious Musings," much has been unavoidably omitted that a complete discussion of the poem would call for. Though doctrine is a substantial part of the poem, enough to justify Coleridge's self-criticism, in a contemporary letter, that his poetry "sweats beneath a heavy burthen of Ideas," [98] the work is not versified rhetoric. An intense personal vision animates "Religious Musings" and the details are conveyed with occasional grace and with some sense of his later poetic power. The work is noteworthy, however, not so much for its art as for its philosophy. It offers an admirable emblem of Coleridge's mind in the middle of the 1790's, before the experience either of poetic creation or of failure and illness caused second thoughts about the simple principles of his "Christian Philosophy."

[95] PW, I, 119–121.
[96] PW, I, 122–123.
[97] PW, I, 124–125.
[98] CL, I, 137.

CHAPTER II

Background, 1791–1800:

Transcendentalism, Enthusiasm, and Literary Theory

Hartley was ousted by Berkeley, Berkeley by Spinoza, and
Spinoza by Plato; when I last saw him Jacob Behmen had
some chance of coming in.

Southey, letter of July 11, 1808

One aspect of "Religious Musings" was deliberately slighted in the
preceding discussion because it deserves consideration in detail. This is
the presence in the poem of a philosophical point of view which, even
if it can be derived from the Locke-Hartley-Priestley tradition, as some
critics claim,[1] appears here in a mature form that is unrecognizable in
the works of those predecessors, and in any case points toward the future development in Coleridge's thought of ideas inimical to the unified
system of the associationists which he embraced at the start of his literary and philosophical career. This is the powerful strain of idealism
and transcendentalism in the poem.

The central theme of the poem has two aspects: the perfectibilist
process in the individual and in society, and the exalted concept of love
in which that process begins and ends. The perfection of this state is a
mutuality of divine and human love. The love of Christ on the cross
initiates the stages by which men rise to the contemplation of God all
in all. The process itself is "Love's wondrous plan."[2] And man, by

[1] For example, Fairchild in *PMLA*, 62 (1947): 1010–1021. Also Richard Haven,
"Coleridge, Hartley, and the Mystics," *Journal of the History of Ideas*, 20 (1959): 477–
494.

[2] *PW*, I, 110, 122.

feeding and saturating his soul with the truth that God's "most holy name is Love" passes out of his "small particular orbit" and attains a vision of the unity of all things:

> From himself he flies,
> Stands in the sun, and with no partial gaze
> Views all creation; and he loves it all,
> And blesses it, and calls it very good!
> This is indeed to dwell with the Most High! [3]

This unity of man and creation in God is another facet of the transcendental strain in the conception of the poem:

> 'Tis the sublime of man,
> Our noontide Majesty, to know ourselves
> Parts and proportions of one wondrous whole!
> This fraternises man, this constitutes
> Our charities and bearings. But 'tis God
> Diffused through all, that doth make all one whole. [4]

Sometimes this unity seems to be achieved by the traditionally religious love of God and by charity toward fellow man. At other times it is accompanied by an imaginative sympathy so great that all things are drawn into the subjective person: the savage who thinks "his own low self the whole" is contrasted with the enlightened man who

> by sacred sympathy might make
> The whole one Self! Self, that no alien knows!
> Self, far diffused as Fancy's wings can travel! [5]

This subjective identification seems to have a Berkeleyan element, though there is also Coleridge's schoolboy passion for Plotinus on which to draw. He does, however, identify Berkeley in a note as the inspiration of another passage on the uncertainty of knowledge:

> Life is a vision shadowy of Truth;
> And vice, and anguish, and the wormy grave,
> Shapes of a dream!

[3] *PW*, I, 113.
[4] *PW*, I, 113–114.
[5] *PW*, I, 114–115.

Even the panpsychist version of the unity of being has a place here; Coleridge asks parenthetically about the spirits that organize the "grosser and material mass" of things: "Holies of God!/(And what if Monads of the infinite mind?)." [6]

In analyzing this conception of the transcendental unity of creation through sympathetic love, we must distinguish carefully between the Hartleyan elements involved here and the contributions of more authentic sources. It is quite possible that Coleridge saw in the momentum of associationist theory toward a unity of perception the possibility of extending this unity into the cosmos or the world of nature, but it does not seem likely that this inspiration could have come purely from within the associationist psychology. Though Hartley's system operates in the direction of a constantly more unified moral and intellectual organization, it is essentially a psychology rather than a metaphysic, and does not concern itself with the bonds between things, but rather with the conditions of their perception. Likewise, on the moral side, though Hartley's system begins in a benevolent disposition on the part of God and culminates in the perfect happiness of divine contemplation, the process is mechanical and only apparently voluntary, and emotion, since it is merely a less organized kind of idea, plays little part except in so far as it affects the regulation of our desires. On the other hand, the unity of being in Coleridge's poem is objective in nature, as well as in the divine mind, and is realized in man by means of a personal vision contingent upon his own contemplation of the loveliness of God and its reflection in things. In the same way, the love that Coleridge is speaking of is a dynamic and voluntary exchange between man and God, or at least an active sympathy with mind and order in existence; Hartley's intellectualized and largely unselfconscious response to the benevolent impulse in creatures is something quite different.

The presence of these unmechanistic and nonrational elements in "Religious Musings" is indicative of the direction Coleridge's thought took in the latter years of the decade 1791–1800. New ideas and elaborations of implications that were already present grew up and, in rela-

[6] *PW*, I, 124.

tion to older viewpoints, created dissonances which persisted until the weight of dissatisfaction with partial truths caused him to revaluate his whole outlook. Some of these dissonances must be looked at more closely.

ONE MIGHTY ALPHABET

First place among the non-Hartleyan ideas must be given to the conception of the unity of man with the natural world and with God. The basic doctrine of eighteenth-century associationism was, of course, the Lockean assumption that the content of the mind was wholly composed out of sense impressions, with the moral and psychological corollary that character is formed by circumstance. This is the starting point for the development of a distinctively Romantic idea, one which is central to Coleridge's thought through his whole life, the notion of the formation of the mind by sympathetic identification with nature. "It is melancholy to think," he wrote in 1795, "that the best of us are liable to be shaped and coloured by surrounding Objects." So far, this is the standard associationist doctrine. But Coleridge adds:

— and a demonstrative proof, that Man was not made to live in Great Cities! Almost all the physical Evil in the World depends on the existence of moral Evil — and the long-continued contemplation of the latter does not tend to meliorate the human heart. The pleasures, which we receive from rural beauties, are of little Consequence compared with the Moral Effect of these pleasures — beholding constantly the Best possible we at last become ourselves the best possible.[7]

There is some confusion of ideas in this passage. Physical evil comes from moral evil which is subsequently identified with "the felon-crowded Dungeon of a great City!"[8] But in the country moral effects come from the contemplation of rural beauties. Presumably Coleridge's train of thought is something like this: in the city the absence of na-

[7] CL, I, 154.
[8] CL, I, 155.

tural beauty leads men to moral evil, of which the result is sin and squalor (physical evil). What is interesting is the concealed assumption that rural beauty is naturally good. That all experience is a source of moral formation is a Hartleyan doctrine, and morally good experience results in morally good formation. But that natural beauty is on the same level with rational analysis, good example, instruction, and other sources of moral improvement was a notion that was no part of Hartley's philosophy; it could have come to Coleridge through poets like James Thomson and William Lisle Bowles, if any source is necessary. It was certainly strengthened and elaborated by the influence of Wordsworth.[9]

The explanation which Coleridge gives of this phenomenon ("In the country, all around us smile Good and Beauty — and the Images of this divine καλοκἀγαθόν are miniatured on the mind of the beholder, as a Landscape on a Convex Mirror") is still on the level of perception.[10] The action of the mind receiving images of the "beautiful-good" is described in strictly Lockean terms. However, an anticipation of the direction that the development of this idea will take is found in a notebook entry for about 1796: "Love transforms the souls into a conformity with the object loved." Miss Coburn suggests that the source is Burnet's *Telluris theoria sacra* (1689), and that the "object loved" is not physical nature, but rather "Omnipotency, Omnisciency, and Infinite Goodness" which enlarge the soul as it contemplates them.[11] The transition from divine attributes to natural beauty was not long in coming. In March 1798 Coleridge writes to his brother George that he is devoting his energy to the consideration of "fundamental and general causes": "in poetry, to elevate the imagination and set the affections in right tune by the beauty of the inanimate impregnated, as with a living soul, by the presence of Life — . . . I love fields and

---

[9] Coleridge quotes *The Castle of Indolence* in the passage under discussion. *CL*, I, 154–155. Willey attributes this attitude toward nature partly to Coleridge's distrust in mechanism and partly to the deflection into imaginative channels of the political impetus of pantisocracy. *Eighteenth Century Studies*, p. 256. But expressions of Coleridge's attitude antedate his disillusionment with both mechanism and pantisocracy.

[10] *CL*, I, 154.

[11] *N* 189, and note.

woods and mountains with almost a visionary fondness." And he
quotes from Wordsworth the lines beginning:

> Not useless do I deem
> These shadowy Sympathies with things that hold
> An inarticulate Language: for the Man
> Once taught to love such objects, as excite
> No morbid passions, no disquietude,
> No vengeance and no hatred, needs must feel
> The Joy of that pure principle of Love.[12]

The theoretical justification for this empathetic identification of mind
with Nature seems to have been the theistic immaterialism of Berkeley.
Without going too far into the question of exact influence, it is possible to assert a relationship because of several clear statements of indebtedness and some passages where a doctrine similar to Berkeley's
is undoubtedly at work. In the spring of 1796 Coleridge borrowed an
edition of Berkeley from the Bristol Library,[13] and about this time there
is a notebook entry which lists a variety of future literary projects,
among them six hymns to the Sun, the Moon, and the Elements, end-
ing with "a sublime enumeration of all the charms or Tremendities
of Nature — then a bold avowal of Berkeley's System!!!!!" [14] In November 1796 he writes to Poole, apropos of Southey's sonnet on Rousseau, "I do not particularly admire Rousseau — Bishop Taylor, Old
Baxter, David Hartley and the Bishop of Cloyne are *my men*." [15] The
next month he writes to Thelwall, discussing the psycho-physical relationship of soul to body: "Now this opinion I do not hold — not that
I am a Materialist; but because I am a Berklian." [16] And the following summer he appends to some lines from "This Lime-Tree Bower
My Prison" the note to Southey: "You remember, I am a Berklian."
The lines in question are these (from the version in the letter to
Southey):

[12] *CL*, I, 397.

[13] George Whalley, "The Bristol Library Borrowings of Southey and Coleridge, 1793–
8," *The Library, Transactions of the Bibliographic Society*, fifth series, 4 (September
1949): 122.

[14] *N* 174 (16). The hymns are a remote source of the inspiration of *The Ancient
Mariner*. See Lowes, *The Road to Xanadu*, pp. 74–79 *et passim*.

[15] *CL*, I, 245.

[16] *CL*, I, 278.

So my friend
Struck with joy's deepest calm, and gazing round
On the wide view, may gaze till all doth seem
Less gross than bodily, a living Thing
That acts upon the mind, and with such hues
As cloathe the Almighty Spirit, when he makes
Spirits perceive His presence! [17]

The lines are a poetic rendering of the Berkeleyan doctrine that nature is the language of God, that the existence of sensible beings consists in their being perceived by a mind, that these things of nature are ideas directly communicated to us by God to reveal his creative and conserving presence, and that the apprehension of these ideas is the function of pure intellect, spirit responding to spirit. The same idea, along with the rejection of urban life, is involved in the familiar lines to his child Hartley from "Frost At Midnight":

For I was reared
In the great city, pent 'mid cloisters dim,
And saw nought lovely but the sky and stars
But *thou*, my babe! shalt wander like a breeze
By lakes and sandy shores, beneath the crags
Of ancient mountain, and beneath the clouds,
Which image in their bulk both lakes and shores
And mountain crags: so shalt thou see and hear
The lovely shapes and sounds intelligible
Of that eternal language, which thy God
Utters, who from eternity doth teach
Himself in all, and all things in himself,
Great universal Teacher! he shall mould
Thy spirit, and by giving make it ask.[18]

The language figure is also found in "The Destiny of Nations":

For all that meets the bodily sense I deem
Symbolical, one mighty alphabet
For infant minds.[19]

The source is clearly Berkeley, who employs the idea to combat what he considers the overly minute analysis of the formal or operational

[17] *CL*, I, 335.
[18] *PW*, I, 242.
[19] *PW*, I, 132. See also Wordsworth's lines quoted above.

aspects of philosophy, such as the mechanism of sense perception, to the neglect of more substantial considerations.[20]

Berkeley's interpretation of sense phenomena as the language of God, however, is basically idealistic and immaterialistic. Sensible signs are, like true language, arbitrary and have "no resemblance or necessary connexion with the things they stand for and suggest." [21] They are merely the medium by which ideas are directly communicated to us by God. Coleridge's lines from "Religious Musings" convey this idea:

> Life is a vision shadowy of Truth;
> And vice, and anguish, and the wormy grave,
> Shapes of a dream! The veiling clouds retire,
> And lo! the Throne of the redeeming God
> Forth flashing unimaginable day
> Wraps in one blaze earth, heaven, and deepest hell.[22]

In a footnote he says the text is intelligible to those who, like himself, "believe and feel the sublime system of Berkeley." It would not seem, however, that this part of Berkeley's thought ever gained a strong hold over one so conscious of sense stimuli and so willing to learn from them. The theory of symbol which Coleridge eventually evolved was based on a more realistic metaphysics and a concept of analogy which insisted on the participation of symbol and referent in a common nature as the foundation of the symbolic knowledge.

It is therefore quite likely that Coleridge used Berkeley as he used most of the sources that are claimed for his thought; he took from

---

[20] "As in reading other books, a wise man will choose to fix his thoughts on the sense and apply it to use, rather than lay them out in grammatical remarks on the language; so in perusing the volume of Nature, it seems beneath the dignity of the mind to affect an exactness in reducing each particular phenomenon to general rules, or shewing how it follows from them. We should propose to ourselves nobler views, such as to recreate and exalt the mind, with a prospect of the beauty, order, extent, and variety of natural things: hence, by proper inferences, to enlarge our notions of the grandeur, wisdom, and beneficence of the Creator: and lastly, to make the several parts of the Creation, so far as in us lies, subservient to the ends they were designed for, God's glory, and the sustentation and comfort of ourselves and fellow-creatures." *The Principles of Human Knowledge*, pt. I, § 109, in *The Works of George Berkeley, Bishop of Cloyne*, ed. A. A. Luce and T. E. Jessop, 9 vols. (London, 1948–1957), II, 89.

[21] Alciphron or the Minute Philosopher, Dialogue IV, no. 7, in *Works*, III, 149.

[22] *PW*, I, 124.

him what best suited his own purposes at the time. The influence does not seem to have been a consistent or steady one. Sometimes the idea of nature as the language of God becomes more explicitly pantheistic. In "The Eolian Harp" Coleridge asks:

> Or what if all of animated nature
> Be but organic Harps diversely fram'd,
> That tremble into thought, as o'er them sweeps
> Plastic and vast, one intellectual breeze,
> At once the Soul of each, and God of All? [23]

This was written in 1795, only a short time before the passage already mentioned from "The Destiny of Nations" (1796), where God is

> All-conscious Presence of the Universe!
> Nature's vast ever-acting Energy!
> In will, in deed, Impulse of All to All! [24]

and almost contemporaneously with "Religious Musings" where the Contemplant Spirits are

> Holies of God!
> (And what if Monads of the infinite mind?) [25]

— both of which passages have been cited as evidence of the influence of Priestley's and Darwin's materialistic pantheism on Coleridge.[26] Priestley's materialism and Berkeley's immaterialism are quite contradictory, though not in the precise area of Coleridge's interest, namely the understanding of God through nature. It is certainly doubtful, however, that Coleridge ever embraced a pantheism in the exact sense. Doubtless these borrowings and expressions of indebtedness merely illustrate his eclectic spirit trying to work out an explanation for a viewpoint to which he was sympathetic by nature.

Spinoza should be mentioned as another possible influence on the concept of man's identification with the natural world. Coleridge certainly knew Spinoza but — aside from the anecdote about the gov-

---

[23] *PW*, I, 102.
[24] *PW*, I, 146–147.
[25] *PW*, I, 124.
[26] Piper, in *Journal of the History of Ideas*, 20 (1959): 49.

ernment agent's report that he and Wordsworth were overheard discussing "one Spy Nozy" in 1797 — there is no evidence that he was reading him before the fall of 1799 ("sunk in Spinoza . . . as undisturbed as a Toad in a Rock"), and some doubt that this was very extensive (he writes to Davy in June 1800: "As soon as I settle, I shall read Spinoza and Leibnitz.").[27] The reading was part of his quest for a theory of unity. A notebook entry for November 1799 envisions a beginning for a poem on Spinoza: "I would make a pilgrimage to the burning sands of Arabia, or etc. etc. to find the Man who could explain to me there can be *oneness*, there being infinite Perceptions — yet there must be a *one*ness, not an intense Union but an Absolute Unity, for etc." [28] The main influence of Spinoza seems to have come later. Southey in 1808 described Coleridge's intellectual development: "Hartley was ousted by Berkeley, Berkeley by Spinoza, and Spinoza by Plato; when I last saw him Jacob Behmen had some chance of coming in. The truth is that he plays with systems, and any nonsense will serve him for a text from which he can deduce something new and surprising." [29]

The possibility that Coleridge was attracted to a doctrine because of its poetic utility as a means of expressing a feeling or insight cannot be ignored. In a letter to Thelwall, December 1796, he explains why he employed the notion of the pre-existence of the soul in a sonnet on his first son's birth: "Now that the thinking part of Man, i.e. the Soul, existed previously to it's appearance in it's present body, may be very wild philosophy; but it is very intelligible poetry [because poets all employ the notion of a soul inhabiting a body] . . . So I, who do not believe in this descending, and incarcerated Soul, yet said, if my Baby had died before I had seen him, I should have *struggled* to believe it." [30] Probably it is this imaginative usefulness that is the reason for employing the pantheism of the above lines, while the Berkeleyan notion of nature as the language of God (though in the nonidealistic sense)

[27] *BL*, I, 126–127; *CL*, I, 534, 590.

[28] *N* 556.

[29] Letter to William Taylor, July 11, 1808, *Memoir of the Life and Writings of William Taylor of Norwich*, ed. J. W. Robberds, 2 vols. (London, 1843), I, 215, quoted by Hanson, *The Life of S. T. Coleridge*, p. 295.

[30] *CL*, I, 278. See *PW*, I, 153–154.

represents a deeper and more permanent addition to his philosophy.

This monistic spiritualism in the interpretation of nature has been attributed also to the influence of the seventeenth-century German mystic Jacob Boehme (Behmen in Coleridge, the form used in the so-called Law translation). Newton Stallknecht has suggested that Boehme trancendentalized Hartley in Coleridge's philosophy, and that Coleridge absorbed from him the idea that all natural substances are "signatures" or outer manifestations of the divine power.[31] He finds support for this viewpoint in the analogous use of the musical instrument's relation to the artist, to express the soul's relation to God, in both "The Eolian Harp" and in Boehme's *Signature of All Things*.[32] Boehme also describes the inner core of reality as "self-hood," and Stallknecht finds this similar to Coleridge's remark, after discussing various theories of life, Beddoes', Darwin's, Plato's, and others: " — on the whole, I have rather made up my mind that I am a mere *apparition* — a naked Spirit! — And that Life is I myself I!"[33] Unfortunately, Coleridge adds the words: "which is a mighty clear account of it," suggesting less than total agreement. Stallknecht's opinion has in its favor Coleridge's own words in the *Biographia*, where he speaks in defense of Boehme's positive contributions to philosophy and mentions his own debt of gratitude to him, "formed at a much earlier period" than that to Schelling.[34] How early and how extensive were the influences is not stated.

Another scholar, Richard Haven, in a monograph on Coleridge's mysticism, undertakes to show that the influence of the mystical and idealist traditions represented by Boehme, Plotinus, Proclus, and Cudworth has been greatly exaggerated, and that the early transcendentalism of Coleridge can be accounted for by a reassessment of Hartley.[35] By concentrating on the elements of personal union with God, Haven is able to show that all the requisites for this state are in Hartley's system. His argument is sound as far as it goes, and it serves to cor-

[31] Newton P. Stallknecht, *Strange Seas of Thought* (Durham, N.C., 1945), pp. 43, 105.

[32] Stallknecht, pp. 106–107.

[33] *CL*, I, 295; Stallknecht, p. 106.

[34] *BL*, I, 95, 103.

[35] In *Journal of the History of Ideas*, 20 (1959): 477–479.

rect the view of Hartley as advancing a psychology which has a merely materialistic end in view. Furthermore, he sees that, if only personal mystical insight is discussed, Coleridge needs no other source than his own experience.[36] And he is accurate in stating that there is little evidence for asserting extensive study by Coleridge of these writers prior to 1800. There is only one citation of Boehme before 1801–1802, in a notebook entry of 1795–1796, where his name is mentioned without comment in a list of projected works, the same cited above in connection with Berkeley.[37] However, the doctrine most in need of explanation in Coleridge's thought at this time, and which it is assumed he got from Boehme and the Platonists, is the spiritual interpretation of nature and the consequent unity of being, which Haven does not discuss.

Putting both arguments together, it seems possible to say that Boehme's influence on Coleridge came at a later date, or possibly that, as with the details of association psychology, it came to have a greater significance to him in retrospect than it did at first — thus the testimony in the *Biographia* to Boehme's influence.[38] The most likely source of the monistic immaterialism is still Berkeley, and the mystical and pantheistic aspects of it must be cautiously avoided.[39]

[36] Haven, p. 487.

[37] N 174 (4); Haven, pp. 489–491.

[38] It should also be kept in mind that in the *Biographia*, in the passage in question, Coleridge is attempting to show that he had these ideas before he read Schelling. Possibly this purpose led him to Boehme as a convenient source in his reading, and accounts for his somewhat contradictory remarks: "I never brought away from his [Boehme's] Works any thing I did not bring to them." *CL*, III, 278. "All Schelling had said he [Coleridge] had thought out for himself, or found in Jacob Boehme." Crabb Robinson's Diary, May 29, 1812, quoted by Shawcross, *BL*, I, 243.

[39] Both commentators, incidentally, find that *The Ancient Mariner* illustrates their interpretations. Stallknecht finds in it an illustration of the Boehme-influenced philosophy of the last books of *The Prelude*, in which is expressed the poet's faith in imagination as the faculty of aesthetic enjoyment and creation by which he may "love whate'er he sees." Stallknecht, *Strange Seas of Thought*, p. 148. The Mariner by his crime (reason's conquest of feeling) inhabits "a universe of death," the world apprehended solely by the lower faculty of reason (in Boehme's terms understanding is higher), subject to determinism and without freedom. In blessing the water snakes is pictured the awakening of aesthetic love which rescues the Mariner from his spiritual isolation. He must still regain his love and understanding of *man*, which the last stanzas describe. The lines "He prayeth best . . ." thus refer to a union of natural things and to a communion of charity among human creatures. Stallknecht, pp. 149–156. In Haven's interpretation, the transcendent

This attitude toward nature results in a conception of the unity of all being that is very marked in Coleridge's thinking during these years. To Thelwall he writes in October 1797:

I can *at times* feel strongly the beauties, you describe, in themselves, and for themselves — but more frequently *all things* appear little — all the knowledge, that can be acquired, child's play — the universe itself — what but an immense heap of *little* things? — I can contemplate nothing but parts, and parts are all *little* — ! — My mind feels as if it ached to behold and know something great — something *one and indivisible* — and it is only in the faith of this that rocks or waterfalls, mountains or caverns give me the sense of sublimity or majesty! — But in this faith *all things* counterfeit infinity!

He then quotes a version of the lines from "This Lime-Tree Bower":

'Struck with the deepest calm of Joy' I stand
        Silent, with swimming sense; and gazing round
        On the wide Landscape gaze till all doth seem
        Less gross than bodily, a living Thing
        Which acts upon the mind . . . ![40]

This was written only a few days before the fourth of his autobiographical letters to Poole (October 16, 1797), in which he argues that the reading of romances and tales of giants and genii gave him a love of the Great and the Whole. "Those who have been led to the same truths step by step thro' the constant testimony of their senses, seem to me to want a sense which I possess — They contemplate nothing but *parts* — and all *parts* are necessarily little — and the Universe to them is but a mass of *little things* . . . [They] uniformly put the negation of a power for the possession of a power — and called the want of imagina-

---

experience which is the highest truth in Coleridge's version of Hartley's system is not a turning from a world of physical reality to one of supernatural reality. "Rather he [Coleridge] presents the familiar world of sense as turning *into* the unfamiliar world of spirit. The 'self-annihilated' contemplate as paradise the same 'reality' which is to the self-centered an 'anarchy of spirits.' The Ancient Mariner is not redeemed by a vision of angels but by a vision of watersnakes which exist both in the world of his torment and in the world of his salvation. The relationship between the two worlds is the relationship between two states of mind." Haven, in *Journal of the History of Ideas*, 20 (1959): 486.

[40] *CL*, I, 349–350.

tion Judgment, and the never being moved to Rapture Philosophy!
—." [41] This sense of an insight into the unity of things and an imaginative identification with them is the controlling experience behind Coleridge's aesthetic. The absence of it, due to illness, anxiety, or whatever
cause, is the occasion of his deepest depressions. The familiar instances
of this state of mind occur during the years 1802–1803, and the well
known text of the ode "Dejection" furnishes examples. Even in the
earlier years, however, there are similar trials. He writes from Germany: "I have, at times, experienced such an extinction of *Light*
in my mind, I have been so forsaken by all the *forms* and *colourings*
of Existence, as if the *organs* of Life had been dried up: as if only simple
BEING remained, blind and stagnant!" [42]

EMOTION AND PERSONAL RELIGION

This psychological dependence on a conviction of the unity of self
with the world of perception leads us to another non-Hartleyan theme
in Coleridge's outlook in the later years of the decade, the importance
of emotion and feeling. In his younger days he was something of a
Stoic, relying upon the instruction of Reason and the exercise of the
intellect. By his own admission it was his contact with the poetry of
Bowles, in 1789 and later, that showed him that feeling was at least as
strong a motive to virtue as logical argument.[43] In 1796 he could still
rebel at being called an enthusiast, and about that time he records without comment in his notebook a phrase which tells heavily against
emotionalism in religion: "The prayers of enthusiast a pious drunken-

---

[41] *CL*, I, 354–355.

[42] *CL*, I, 470. Though the figure is a commonplace, it may be worth noting that the
use of color as a metaphor for the spiritual meaning behind sense knowledge occurs elsewhere when Coleridge is talking about God in nature. Cf. The "hues" which "cloathe
the Almighty Spirit" in "This Lime-Tree Bower," quoted above. Color was the common
example in philosophical discussions of a secondary quality, which in Newtonian terms
existed solely in the mind. Berkeley held that both secondary qualities and primary ones
(for him, extension, figure, motion, and solidity) existed in the mind, and were the
means of God's communication with us.

[43] *BL*, I, 7, 10, 15–16. Lucyle Werkmeister, in "Coleridge, Bowles, and 'Feelings of
the Heart,' " *Anglia*, 78 (1960): 57–58, attributes the youthful Stoicism to Coleridge's
Plotinian researches.

ness, a spiritual concupiscence, presumptuous self-idolatry —." [44] He grew increasingly aware, however, of the effect of his own feelings on his mental states; at first he cautiously allowed that emotion was a concomitant of thought: "I feel strongly, and I think strongly; but I seldom feel without thinking, or think without feeling . . . My philosophical opinions are blended with, or deduced from, my feelings." He was ready to admire both "the *head* and the fancy of Akenside, and the *heart* and fancy of Bowles." [45] When he began to feel the loss of sympathy with things mentioned above, he explained it in terms of feelings of dejection without the counterbalancing moderation of thought, and, in the lines from Germany already quoted in part, placed his hopes for mental stability in love, without which intellect withers: "I languish after Home for hours together, in vacancy; my *feelings* almost wholly unqualified by *Thoughts*. I have, at times, experienced such an extinction of *Light* in my mind, I have been so forsaken by all the *forms* and *colourings* of Existence . . . I am deeply convinced that if I were to remain a few years among objects for whom I had no affection, I should wholly lose the powers of Intellect — Love is the vital air of my Genius, and I have not seen one human Being in Germany, whom I can conceive it *possible* for me to *love* — no, not one." [46]

By 1800 Coleridge had completely reversed his former suspicions of feeling: "Life were so flat a thing without Enthusiasm — that if for a moment it leave me, I have a sort of stomach-sensation attached to all my Thoughts, like those which succeed to the pleasurable operation of a dose of Opium." [47] Not only did emotion become for Coleridge a necessary concomitant to intellectual insight, but it functioned as the primary substrate in the associative process. A hint of this occurs in a discussion of the difficulties of writing description. "I could half suspect that what are deemed fine descriptions, produce their effects almost purely by a charm of words, with which and with whose combinations, we associate *feelings* indeed, but no distinct *Images*." [48] The no-

---

[44] *CL*, I, 200; *N* 190.
[45] *CL*, I, 279.
[46] *CL*, I, 470–471.
[47] *CL*, I, 558.
[48] *CL*, I, 511. The gift of describing objects seems here to be related proportionately

tion is fully developed only after the re-examination of philosophy that occurred in 1800–1801; apropos of his criticism of Locke in the letters to Wedgwood, he says: "My opinion is this — that deep Thinking is attainable only by a man of deep Feeling, and that all Truth is a species of Revelation." [49] We shall go somewhat beyond the temporal limits of this present discussion to cite the mature expression of the rejection of the association mechanism and the substitution for it of a ground of feeling:

> I hold, that association depends in a much greater degree on the recurrence of resembling states of Feeling, than on Trains of Ideas . . . Believe me, Southey! a metaphysical Solution, that does not instantly *tell* for something in the Heart, is grievously to be suspected as apocryphal. I almost think, that Ideas *never* recall Ideas, as far as they are Ideas — any more than Leaves in a forest create each other's motion — The Breeze it is that runs thro' them/ it is the Soul, the State of Feeling — . If I had said, no *one* Idea ever recalls another, I am confident that I could support the assertion. [50]

This is a long way from the Stoic distrust of enthusiasm that colored Coleridge's early philosophizing.

Finally, to ravel up some threads of Coleridge's thought previously distinguished, we may simply say that this transcendental element had its effect on his religious life and, as this became more personal, the earlier confidence in the perfectibility of man waned somewhat. If he did not exactly become a Methodist, Coleridge's faith during the latter half of the decade was a more intensely personal and less intellectual one. In September 1796 he wrote to John Colson of his faith in Christ, "It is my wealth in poverty, my Joy in sorrow, my peace amid tumult." He smiles with pity at the infidel who imagines he would barter it "for a few subtleties from the school of the cold-blooded Soph-

---

to the poet's empathic identification with them. See W. J. Bate's discussion of the impulse which the doctrine of sympathy gave to verisimilitude of representation in late eighteenth-century theory: *From Classic to Romantic: Premises of Taste in Eighteenth Century England* (Cambridge, Mass., 1946), pp. 142–147. This seems to be related also to Shakespeare's "meditation" of events and characters. See below, Chap. IV.

[49] *CL*, II, 709.

[50] *CL*, II, 961. August 7, 1803.

ist!" [51] A few weeks later: "I am daily more and more a religionist." [52] No reader of the letters of these years can doubt the sincerity of Coleridge's concern for the state of his soul. Once more his faith is developing in compliance to his need. The wreck of his academic career, the disappointment of the expectations of family and friends, failure as journalist and editor, combined with the first evidences of chronic poor health, all these exacerbated his "constitutional despondency" and caused him to seek the consolations of religion. "My philosophical refinements, and metaphysical Theories lay by me in the hour of anguish, as toys by the bedside of a Child deadly-sick. May God continue his visitations to my soul, bowing it down, till the pride and Laodicean self-confidence of human Reason be utterly done away with; and I cry with deeper and yet deeper feelings, O my soul! thou art wretched, and miserable, and poor and blind, and naked!" [53] Where before he could talk in Stoic terms about the theoretical and experimental conviction of the necessity of faith as a source of regularity in virtue, now he censures this attitude as a fault. "I have been too neglectful of practical religion — I mean, actual and stated prayer, and a regular perusal of scripture as a morning and evening duty! . . . tho' Christianity is my *Passion*, it is too much my *intellectual* Passion." [54] Thought and Feeling were two poles between which his religious life made irregular progress at this time. In his own terse summary: "Socinianism moonlight — Methodism a Stove! O for some Sun to unite heat and Light!" [55]

Related to this emergence of a personal religion, adding strong feeling to the intellectual deistic position of earlier years, is a growing skepticism in regard to the inevitability of the perfectibilitarian process. The basic direction of this development was indicated in Coleridge's controversies with Godwin over the melioration of social evils. Personal imputability was not a strong point in associationist religious theory, nor in Unitarian theology. In Hartley it is treated ambiguously:

[51] *CL*, I, 235.
[52] *CL*, I, 253.
[53] *CL*, I, 267. See also *BL*, I, 132.
[54] *CL*, I, 407.
[55] *N* 1233.

in the first part of his work philosophical necessity eliminates the possibility of personal guilt, while in the second there is the notion of responsibility for our choice of the circumstances which further or retard the moral process. This was one of the points Coleridge was to attack. He had earlier dismissed the possibility of guilt as inconsistent with his necessitarianism, but after psychological and physical anxieties matured his outlook, he became more aware of the existential limitations of human nature and expressed this view in traditional religious terms: "I believe most steadfastly in original Sin; that from our mothers' wombs our understandings are darkened; and even where our understandings are in the Light, that our organization is depraved, and our volitions imperfect; and we sometimes see the good without *wishing* to attain it, and oftener *wish* it without the energy that wills and performs — And for this inherent depravity, I believe, that the *Spirit* of the Gospel is the sole cure." [56] This passage cautiously anticipates elements of Coleridge's later religious philosophy: the emphasis on volition and the consequent denial of any kind of associationist determinism, the notion of grace, and the development of a redemptive rather than merely benevolent theology. The absolute trust in rational analysis previously manifest is now moderated, not only by an increasing reliance on the lessons of feeling and sentiment but also by this gradual rejection of one of the principal conclusions of rational religion, the inevitably optimistic process of being.

On reviewing the direction of Coleridge's thought in the decade 1791–1800, it seems possible to characterize its distinctive note as the growing consciousness of the person. Coleridge's native inclination to self-analysis drew his intellectualist religious speculations and his social theories into closer integration, resulting in a unity which was based on a personal assimilation of what had heretofore been rather abstract principles. The motive force behind association psychology had been the need for achieving a unity of mental activity, but the result was an intellectualized organization of capacities rather than a subjectively realizable integration of the whole person. Likewise, Unitarian theology was a Christianity filtered through the rational cloth of deism, saved

[56] *CL*, I, 396.

from utter frigidity by a benevolent and optimistic teleology which emphasized the fatherhood of God and the brotherhood of men, but which said little about the possibilities of a personal response to God through love and prayer. The abstract and objective aspects of the Hartleyan system gave way in Coleridge's thought to an apprehension of things and events more grounded in the subjective response, just as rational theology was gradually complemented by a voluntarism that placed more emphasis on private responsibility and personal effort. The distrust of "organization" as an explanation of the mind, and of "Socinian moonlight" as a theology for the whole Christian man, developed apace. The confused and partly contradictory positions that Coleridge held during these years reveal a novice in the intellectual life, but they also reveal an honesty of judgment that is not content with simple answers, but willing to struggle through many partial truths in order to find the unity that will satisfy his complex experience.

THE BEGINNING OF A LITERARY PHILOSOPHY

We have said that the roots of Coleridge's literary theory are to be found in his general philosophy, and we have to some extent outlined the early growth of that philosophy. In the period 1790–1800 there is little explicit analysis of literature in his writing other than some criticism of specific poems which is largely nontheoretical. His philosophical interests, tentative and uncritical as they were, were centered mainly on social and religious problems, and on a simple psychology of mind in general. These speculations do not seem to have led him to theorize about the literature that he was very much interested in creating, until Wordsworth's accomplishments canalized some of his own instinctive capacities and undeveloped insights. When Coleridge did begin to analyze literature philosophically, he employed forms and distinctions taken from association psychology, perhaps to a greater extent than he realized. This was mainly after 1800, indeed considerably after. But the elements of the association philosophy that were later to develop into characteristic parts of Coleridge's literary theory are visible in a very imperfect way even in the years when Coleridge was devoting very little effort to a philosophy of literature. An outline of some of the evidence for their presence in Coleridge's early thought suggests that his mature philosophy is closely related to the tradition of English psychology and that it developed along lines which that system might have been expected to take, with or without the addition of European idealism.

The thrust of associationist psychology, we have said, was in the direction of unity. It was developed as an explanation of the unity of the mind in the face of the empirical supposition of the atomistic and wholly sensate nature of perception.[57] Its success lay in the fact that it seemed to preserve the particularity of individual perceptions and yet to assert the integrating process of the mind as it develops gradually more complex ideas out of simple ones. This double emphasis, on both unity and the particulars unified, resulted on the aesthetic level in the principle of uniformity amidst variety. Much of the positive criticism of the associationist theorists took the form of discussing the "beauties" or individually pleasing elements in a work of art, and how they contributed to the unity of the whole. This kind of language is very common in Coleridge's early discussions of Bowles's and Southey's poetry.[58]

The conception of the unity which controls this variety was changed radically by associationist theory from what it had been in the neoclassical criticism of the earlier part of the century.[59] According to this psychology, the stronger and more frequently repeated impressions gradually overcame the weaker ones and came to control the associative process; likewise, in the ambiguous voluntaristic-necessitarian theory of

[57] For the purposes of literary theory, the regularity and unity of the association process produced for some critics the "objectivity" which the introduction of taste and sensibility had destroyed, since association is a "natural" process. On the other hand, association principles were also invoked to explain the irregularity and subjectivity of the mind's operation, especially by those who followed the Locke-Addison-Burke tradition, who saw association as a defect of the mind's working. See the articles by Martin Kallich, "The Association of Ideas and Critical Theory: Hobbes, Locke, and Addison," *English Literary History*, 12 (1945): 290–315; "The Associationist Criticism of Francis Hutcheson and David Hume," *Studies in Philology*, 43 (1946): 644–667; "The Association of Ideas and Akenside's *Pleasures of Imagination*," *Modern Language Notes*, 62 (1947): 166–173.

[58] For example: *CL*, I, 94, 104, 565.

[59] This point is developed by Ralph Cohen, "Association of Ideas and Poetic Unity," *Philological Quarterly*, 36 (1957): 465–474.

will which the associationists proposed, it was possible for a person to direct this associative process by concentrating on better thoughts and feelings so as to have them prevail. The unity of the mind thus became one of viewpoint, originating in and controlled by a subjective process. In aesthetics this meant that the unity of the work of art, which had heretofore been based on its correspondence to the requirements of the genres which expressed the "kinds" of literature which the general principles of human nature allowed, now found itself defined by the "dominant idea" which animated the work. Unity was therefore a matter of tone, of the attitude of writer to audience or to subject matter.

Coleridge shows both aspects, and the confusion of the two. His own criticism is often based on genre distinctions, at least in his early years, as when he queries whether his "Ode on the Departing Year" possesses "that Impetuosity of Transition, and that Precipitation of Fancy and Feeling, which are the *essential* excellencies of the sublimer Ode." [60] The notion of the dominant idea is also common in his analysis of poems; the best illustration is his remark to Southey: "Before you write a Poem, you should say to yourself — What do I intend to be the *Character* of this Poem — Which *Feature* is to be predominant in it? — So you may make it a Unique." [61] Again he criticizes Southey's *Joan of Arc*; though the language is natural, perspicuous, and dignified, and there is manly pathos, sonnetlike description, unrivaled character, and dramatic dialogue, still its author does not possess that "opulence of Imagination, lofty-paced Harmony, or that toil of thinking, which is necessary in order to plan *a Whole*." [62] Further, to Thelwall he answers the charge of obscurity in a sonnet by questioning whether it was the "obscurity residing in the uncommonness of the thought," or "that which proceeds from thoughts unconnected and language not adapted to the expression of them?" The test of this is the test of the integrity of the poem: "When you *do* find out the meaning of my poetry, can you (in general, I mean) alter the language so as to make it more perspicuous — the thought remaining the same?" [63]

[60] *CL*, I, 289.
[61] *CL*, I, 139.
[62] *CL*, I, 293–294.
[63] *CL*, I, 277.

This assertion of the unique meaning to which all the parts of the poem contribute recalls the lesson which Coleridge claimed to have learned very early in his school days, from James Boyer, the formidable master of Christ's Hospital: "I learnt from him, that Poetry, even that of the loftiest and, seemingly, that of the wildest odes, had a logic of its own, as severe as that of science; and more difficult, because more subtle, more complex, and dependent on more, and more fugitive causes. In the truly great poets, he would say, there is a reason assignable, not only for every word, but for the position of every word." [64] In neoclassical poetic theory the reason for the place of every word depended equally on the end in view, but this was established by very precise rules for each "kind" of poetry, which only genius might transgress and then only rarely and under the inspiration of the higher law of decorum. In associationist and romantic theory the rightness of words and ideas became dependent on an increasingly subjective quality of thought. The unity which resulted from this source encouraged theories of intuitive perception such as are implied in some of Coleridge's later descriptions of the imagination and, partly, in his notion of reason. An interesting by-product of these theories of poetic unity is the notion of an ends-and-means view of poetic composition and therefore of poetic criticism. This concept, which much later became a central part of Coleridge's philosophical method, emerges distinctly only in the lectures on Shakespeare.

It should also be observed that Coleridge's enthusiasm for the many-sided doctrines of associationism contained the seeds of the future distinction between reason and understanding as different sources of knowledge. To a personality inclined to credit insight and the feelings of the heart more than logical processes, there must have appeared an ever widening gap between the mechanism by which sense data are thought to be organized and the unity-of-being perceived in the study of the language of God. Coleridge's various qualifications of the associative doctrine — that it was too abstract, did not tell in the heart, and disallowed the personal element — show him tending toward a distinction which would allow him to retain the idea of association itself

[64] *BL*, I, 4.

but add to it the superior insight which he discovered as a result of extending to their logical conclusions, with the motive of Berkeley's view, the associative aspirations toward unity.

It seems that the same source must be credited as the ultimate origin of the distinction between fancy and imagination. Critics have argued over whether this distinction is correlative in any sense with that between reason and understanding. Even prescinding from the claim that the one distinction was used in dealing with creative activity alone and the other in dealing with the whole knowledge process, it is true that in their maturest development they express quite different divisions of the mind's operations. Still, the imagination-fancy distinction was first described in 1802, and more vividly in 1804 (though its full expression had to wait for some years), which was considerably prior to the explication of the reason-understanding distinction, suggesting that both took their origin in the dissatisfaction with a mechanical, even materialistic, explanation of the mind's organization.[65]

The notion of imagination as a modifying and coadunating faculty, analogous to the creative capacity of God, could only have arisen after (and because) the associative explanation of the mind's operation (that is, by an aggregative power, or fancy) was rejected as inadequate to experience. Though this criticism of the mechanism of association is hinted at throughout the latter half of the decade, it is not made explicit until the philosophical studies of 1800–1801. Before that the notions of imagination in Coleridge's writings are quite traditional: either as the power of visualizing absent things, or as invention, or as the total power of associative response (in the Humean sense), but most often as the faculty which reproduces in various combinations images from the storehouse of memory and which is therefore liable to be the enemy of reason. "Whence arise our Miseries? Whence arise our Vices? From *imaginary* wants . . . Providence . . . forbids him [man] to be contented. It has given us the restless faculty of *Imagination*." [66] Or he criticizes Godwin for having "neither the strength of intellect that dis-

---

[65] The imagination-fancy distinction is clearly stated in a letter of September 10, 1802, and again on January 15, 1804. *CL*, II, 865–866, 1034. The definitions will be considered below.

[66] "On the Slave Trade," *The Watchman*, no. 4, March 25, 1796, *EOT*, I, 137–138.

covers truth, or the powers of imagination that decorate falsehood." [67] Where imagination has a positive function, as in ornamenting and embodying the truth, this is regarded as suited primarily to children as a means of instruction while they are yet unfit for rational milk. In eighteenth-century philosophizing this viewpoint was often bolstered by an argument based on the supposed predominance of the arts in primitive epochs, before the more civilized scientific and philosophical ages. Hartley takes this position in his *Observations*, when discussing the imagination. It is suitable for the infancy of knowledge. "And agreeably to this it may be observed, that music, painting, and poetry, were much admired in ancient times." [68] Coleridge versifies this doctrine in "Religious Musings," where, in discussing the progress of civilization, he passes from the primitive sheep-herding age to the stage where Imagination took hold and "all the inventive arts . . . nursed the soul/ To forms of beauty, and by sensual wants/ Unsensualized the mind," which thereby "Learnt to forget the grossness of the end" and became "pleasured with its own activity." [69] It is still quite a distance from these doctrines of the imagination to the notion of it as the distinctive power of Milton and Shakespeare and the closest approach we can have to the experience of divine creation.[70]

Coleridge attributed his insight into the nature of imagination to his acquaintance with Wordsworth. Certainly their friendship is responsible for determining in great part the direction Coleridge's literary theories take after 1797. Coleridge positively venerated the older poet. "Wordsworth is a very great man — the only man, to whom *at all times* and in *all modes of excellence* I feel myself inferior." "I have now known him

[67] *CL*, I, 215.

[68] Hartley, *Observations*, I, 431.

[69] *PW*, I, 117.

[70] Possibly Coleridge's use of taste as a critical touchstone anticipates some of the functions which imagination later performs. For Coleridge at this time the term seems to have what Bate calls its general romantic sense, the "assumption that an immediate, comprehensive, and unified conception of the particular is achieved through an instinctive employment of experience." *From Classic to Romantic*, p. 122. One of Coleridge's persistent metaphors suggests this immediate instinctive response: to Thelwall he says, your "criticism had convinced me that your nerves are exquisite *electrometers* of Taste." *CL*, I, 307. He compliments in the same way Dorothy Wordsworth and Thomas Wedgwood, *CL*, I, 331; II, 877.

a year and some months, and my admiration, I might say, my awe of his intellectual powers has increased even to this hour." "He is a great, a true Poet — I am only a kind of a Metaphysician." [71] In answering the charge of prostration with regard to Wordsworth, he asks if it is impossible that the greatest poet since Milton should be living in their time, and he compares his acquaintance with Wordsworth with what it would be like to have known Milton when he was thirty.[72] "If I die, and the Booksellers will give you anything for my Life, be sure to say — 'Wordsworth descended on him, like the Γνῶθι σεαυτόν from Heaven; by shewing to him what true Poetry was, he made him know, that he himself was no Poet.' " [73]

Though Wordsworth's personal life was far from stable when he came to live at Alfoxton in the summer of 1797, he seems to have provided the example of a self-possession and a sureness both in his philosophical principles and in his poetic craft that Coleridge, harassed by the self-doubt brought on by failure and ill-health, badly lacked. Wordsworth was everything that Coleridge then aspired to be. Two obligations are specifically mentioned in the *Biographia*, relating to the writing of poetry. The first was the realization which Coleridge experienced listening to Wordsworth's poetry, that it was possible to describe nature with a fresh simplicity and exactness that surpassed anything he had thought possible. The second was the theory of imagination, about which he was led to speculate as the source of the union of deep feeling with profound thought and the idealizing of common objects that Wordsworth accomplished in his poems.[74]

Together Coleridge and Wordsworth set out to discuss the principles and theories which might result in a new kind of poetry which would embody these elements. The result was the *Lyrical Ballads* of 1798, the preface to the second edition of which, written by Wordsworth, is taken to express their theoretical position in 1800, though both Coleridge and Wordsworth soon came to disclaim many of its features. The notions of poetic diction, which are thought to be Wordsworth's revolu-

[71] *CL*, I, 334, 410, 658.
[72] *CL*, I, 584.
[73] *CL*, II, 714.
[74] *BL*, I, 58–60.

tionary contribution, may be passed over here, as they were the principal focus of Coleridge's later objections. There are two assumptions in the preface, however, which fit in, whoever their immediate author, with Coleridge's later thought, and which are consequences, though in different ways, of associationist beginnings. The first of these is the idea that it is a "feeling" which gives rise to a poem and which controls its unity. "Another circumstance must be mentioned which distinguishes these Poems from the popular Poetry of the day; it is this, that the feeling therein developed gives importance to the action and situation, and not the action and situation to the feeling." [75] Since "the Poet is chiefly distinguished from other men by a greater promptness to think and feel without immediate external excitement, and a greater power in expressing such thoughts and feelings as are produced in him in that manner," [76] the degree of feeling becomes an essential element in the production of poetry. Though this use is romantic, it is not inconsistent with the "dominant idea" theory of the associationist critics, especially when feeling becomes the bond of ideas, as it does in Coleridge's developed associationism. Wordsworth calls this controlling attitude the "purpose" that guides each poem.[77]

A second theme of Wordsworth's preface that anticipates a central idea in Coleridge's literary philosophy is the superiority of poetic knowledge and its characteristically human pertinence. This was a logical consequence of the emancipation of imagination. Poetry, says Wordsworth, has as its object truth, general and operative, "carried alive into the heart by passion." It is "the image of man and nature." It is, he says, misquoting Aristotle, "the most philosophic of all writing." [78] Unlike the biographer or historian, the poet needs only one source of

---

[75] *The Poetical Works of William Wordsworth*, ed. E. de Selincourt and Helen Darbishire, 2nd ed., 5 vols. (Oxford: vols. I–III, 1952–1954; vols. IV and V from the first edition, 1947 and 1949), II, 388–389.

[76] *Poetical Works of William Wordsworth*, II, 397.

[77] *Poetical Works of William Wordsworth*, II, 388. In this insistence on a conscious final cause, as in other elements of poetic theory common to Wordsworth and Coleridge, we can see how far both were from the extremes of romantic inspirationism, from the view that the creation of a poem is, in the words of Meyer Abrams, "a spontaneous process independent of intention, precept, or even consciousness." *The Mirror and the Lamp: Romantic Theory and the Critical Tradition* (New York, 1953), p. 187.

[78] *Poetical Works of William Wordsworth*, II, 394.

appeal to his audience — what constitutes them as men. Unlike the
scientist, his knowledge is not a laboriously acquired understanding of
"particular parts of nature," but is "a necessary part of our existence, our
natural and unalienable inheritance"; thus, poetry is "the first and last
of all knowledge — it is as immortal as the heart of man." [79]

Aristotle's doctrine of the differentiation of ways of knowing according to their formal objects seems to have become, by virtue of the dubious separation of imaginative insight from logical and discursive
analysis, a division into inferior and superior modes of knowledge. But
for the mechanistic tendency of associationist psychology, the unity of
the human mind might have been preserved in the midst of its differ-
entiating operations. As things turned out, the future of literary theory
and of literature itself was profoundly altered by the rise of romantic
subjectivism and all the other subjectivisms ultimately based on the
doctrine of imagination. Coleridge later came to see the confusions
latent in the unlimited authority of this individual imagination, though
his attempts to qualify the scope of its operation were largely unsuccessful and have even been labeled a retreat into the older orthodoxy. The
inability to relate to his complete satisfaction the demands of both
imagination and reason was the cross of his mature years, and accounted
in part for his endless philosophizing and his ultimate silence on the
whole problem of the imagination.

[79] *Poetical Works of William Wordsworth*, II, 396.

CHAPTER III

Shaping a Philosophy, 1800–1808

To him who is compelled to pace to and fro within the high
walls and in the narrow courtyard of a prison, all objects may
appear clear and distinct. It is the traveller journeying onward,
full of heart and hope, with an ever-varying horizon, on the
boundless plain, who is liable to mistake clouds for mountains,
and the *mirage* of drouth for an expanse of refreshing waters.

The Friend

In May 1799 Coleridge wrote from Göttingen, his principal resi-
dence during the year he spent in Germany, saying that he would have
bought by the end of his stay about thirty pounds worth of books,
"chiefly metaphysics/ and with a view to the one work, to which I
hope to dedicate in silence the prime of my life." [1] He returned to
England two months later, but "bread-and-cheese" occupations during
the following year kept him from the life of study and reflection he
desired. For several months during the winter of 1799–1800 he lived in
London, attempting to combine political journalism for the *Morning
Post* with literary enterprises that would relieve his finances — probably the often mentioned biography of Lessing and certainly the translation of Schiller's *Wallenstein*, two parts of which appeared the following summer. In July 1800, whether because of the failure of the
Schiller translation commercially, or from distaste for the frantic demands of political writing and parliamentary reporting, or possibly
because of his lifelong antipathy to the city, Coleridge retired with his
family to Keswick, in Cumberland. Most likely a complex of reasons
prompted the move, and prominent among them may have been the

[1] *CL*, I, 519.

realization that the necessities of earning a living as a London journalist and literary day laborer would never allow him to achieve "the
one work" that he had written about from Germany.

Once before he had retired to the country after commercial failure.
When *The Watchman* ceased publication in May 1796 Coleridge occupied himself for a time in "shilling-scavenger employments" and then
settled at Stowey in Somersetshire, near the house of his good friend
Tom Poole, where he devoted his energy "to poetry and to the study
of ethics and psychology" or, in another account, "to the foundations
of religion and morals."[2] Doubtless he was interested in all these topics,
though it was poetry that distinguished the Stowey period, and he
later said of his speculative immaturity at this time: "A more thorough
revolution in my philosophic principles, and a deeper insight into my
own heart, were yet wanting."[3]

This deeper insight Coleridge achieved during a prolonged illness
at Keswick in the winter of 1800–1801. As a boy he had suffered attacks
of rheumatic fever, and the letters of his early years are full of notes
about his indispositions. The removal to Keswick, however, was coincident with a complete breakdown in Coleridge's health, possibly because of the climate of the Lake District with its excessive rainfall.[4]
For a year he suffered almost constantly from fever, dysentery, swell-
ing of the joints, and stomach disorders, and never through the remainder of his life was he free of any of these afflictions for very long.
It was probably in these circumstances that he became a constant user
of opium as a pain killer.[5]

A certain amount of controversy attends the interpretation of Coleridge's turning to "metaphysics." The view that his interest in speculation was a result of the failure of his poetic talent, or, at least, that
philosophizing killed his creative ability, receives some support from
Coleridge's own words. In July 1800, even before his illness, he signed

[2] *BL*, I, 121, 132.

[3] *BL*, I, 137.

[4] Chambers, *Coleridge*, p. 137.

[5] Chambers, p. 138. Miss Elisabeth Schneider says that we do not know when he
became addicted, but that the habit was permanently fixed by 1801. *Coleridge, Opium
and Kubla Khan* (Chicago, 1953), p. 62.

two letters as "Gentleman-poet and Philosopher in a mist."[6] A few months later (February 1801) he wrote to Poole, "I hope, Philosophy and Poetry will not neutralize each other, and leave me an inert mass."[7] And in the following month he told Godwin — in a brilliant series of metaphors which paradoxically invokes the imaginative gift he is denying — that he had been "chasing down metaphysical Game . . . The Poet is dead in me — my imagination (or rather the Somewhat that had been imaginative) lies, like a Cold Snuff on the circular Rim of a Brass Candle-stick, without even a stink of Tallow to remind you that it was once cloathed and mitred with Flame. That is past by! — I was once a Volume of Gold Leaf, rising and riding on every breath of Fancy — but I have beaten myself back into weight and density, and now I sink in quicksilver."[8] Even three years later he could describe himself as "ci devant Poet in rus and now Metaphysician."[9]

The obvious contemporaneity, however, of Coleridge's philosophical speculations and the decline or stagnation of his poetic powers does not argue a causal connection. A much more plausible explanation is that both were the result of his prolonged and enervating illnesses. Or, rather, that whatever energy he was able to keep in reserve from his bouts with sickness was expended on philosophy, since it served best the immediate purpose of providing a rationale and a source of comfort in his suffering. "I shall look back on my long and painful Illness only as a Storehouse of wild Dreams for Poems, or intellectual Facts for metaphysical Speculation," he wrote to Poole in 1801.[10] Again, in the letter to Godwin quoted above, March 1801, he noted that he had been chasing down metaphysical game precisely because by doing so he "compelled into hours of Delight many a sleepless, painful hour of Darkness."[11] In the often quoted disparagement of his own verse at this time — "instead of a Covey of poetic Partridges with whirring wings of music, or wild Ducks *shaping* their rapid flight in forms

[6] *CL*, I, 612, 614.
[7] *CL*, II, 668–669.
[8] *CL*, II, 714.
[9] *CL*, II, 1085.
[10] *CL*, II, 668.
[11] *CL*, II, 713–714.

always regular (a still better image of Verse) up came a metaphysical Bustard, urging it's slow, heavy, laborious, earth-skimming Flight, over dreary and level Wastes" — he says quite clearly that "Sickness and some other and worse afflictions, first forced me into *downright metaphysics*." [12] That he did not despair of his creative ability is clear from the parenthetical remark immediately following this: "for I believe that by nature I have more of the Poet in me." And indeed his poetic gift was not completely inoperant during these years of speculation. The ode "Dejection" (first draft, April 1802) deals directly with this critical experience of "intellectual *exsiccation*," but it betrays no great loss of creative capacity. It is, in fact, as A. O. Lovejoy says, a paradox "in that it not merely — like many other poems — makes melancholy enjoyable, but achieves beauty by the description of the loss of the feeling for beauty." [13] The cause of this loss, however, is not intense speculation but rather the poet's inability to summon the joy which in the pure of heart animates a vision of the world about them. This failure of the "genial spirits" is explicitly attributed to physical and mental suffering ("But now afflictions bow me down to earth"), and metaphysical reflection on his ills, far from causing the difficulty, is rather a surrogate for the higher insight:

> And haply by abstruse research to steal
> From my own nature all the natural man —
> This was my sole resource, my only plan.[14]

Not philosophy then, but a variety of griefs robbed Coleridge of the motive and perhaps the ability to do more than communicate his malaise.

THE ONE WORK

As anodyne, however, speculation was remarkably effective. Bustards or not, Coleridge started a number of philosophical projects during the years 1800–1804, and it was then that we hear for the first time the

[12] *CL*, II, 814.
[13] *CL*, II, 713; A. O. Lovejoy "Coleridge and Kant's Two Worlds," *Essays in the History of Ideas* (Baltimore, 1948), p. 263.
[14] *PW*, I, 366, 367.

details of "the one work," the system to which he was, in one way or another, to dedicate much of the remainder of his life.

It was natural to Coleridge's mind, apparently, to be continuously planning great works. Most of these were no more than "literary air-castles," to use Chambers' expressive phrase, and the lists of projected works that occur regularly in the notebooks are mainly indicative of transient enthusiasms and momentary inspirations.[15] There is more to be said, however, of Coleridge's plans for a philosophical synthesis. The various schemes from 1800 on for a work which would sum up his speculations show that he was beginning to find solutions for some of the antithetic views that he had held a few years earlier. Moreover the changes and developments in the proposed metaphysical works give us some idea of the coherent growth of Coleridge's philosophy. A chronological view of Coleridge's speculative schemes and the contexts of their origin and maturing goes a long way toward overturning the notion that his philosophy was a hodgepodge of unassimilated borrowings. The number of references to his synthesizing opera of one kind or another justifies the conclusion that Coleridge was striving for a unity of thought; the purpose of this chapter will be to trace among his fragmentary and completed works the early growth of this conceptual structure.

His occupations during the years 1800–1814 alternated between bouts of illness, dejection, and philosophizing, and periods of industrious activity. After the sickness and speculation of 1800–1804, he was a diplomatic secretary in Malta and then a traveler in Italy from 1804 until the summer of 1806. Another period of idleness and diverse occupations was followed by the writing and publication of *The Friend* in 1809–1810. The next four years were mainly active; philosophical reflection, at least insofar as the notebooks and letters record, yielded to the business of lecturing, and we find that much of the earlier speculation emerged in the criticism of Shakespeare and in the aesthetic and specifically poetic theory that he outlined before his audiences.

Through all these years the idea of a great work was never far from

---

[15] See, for instance, *N* 161 (1796), *N* 174 (1795–1796), *N* 1646 (1803).

Coleridge's thoughts, however much its theme was redefined as the grounds of his conclusions shifted over the years from 1800 on. We first hear of it, aside from the earlier reference to the thirty pounds worth of books, as an "Essay on Poetry . . . it's Title would be an Essay on the Elements of Poetry/ it would in reality be a *disguised* System of Morals and Politics — ."[16] Later in the same year he mentions that he is seriously occupied with "a metaphysical Investigation of the Laws, by which our Feelings form affinities with each other, with Ideas, and with words."[17] In the following February he is afraid that illness will prevent him from devoting his energy "to the affinities of the Feelings with Words and Ideas under the title of 'Concerning Poetry and the nature of the Pleasures derived from it.' . . . the Work would supersede all the Books of Metaphysics hitherto written/ and all the Books of Morals too."[18] In December of this year Coleridge is "reading in the old Libraries for my curious metaphysical Work," and two months later he notes that "in a very short time the first sheet of my metaphysical work will go to the Press."[19] The "History of the opinions concerning Space and Time for Mackintosh," which he mentions in a letter of 1802, does not seem to be connected with the larger work; Southey says that it is a preface to a work of Thomas Wedgwood's of which James Mackintosh is to be midwife. Both preface and work, as Southey suspected, proved to be abortions.[20] A year later Coleridge writes that his book "is not, strictly speaking, metaphysical, but historical. It perhaps will merit the title of a History of Metaphysics in England from Lord Bacon to Mr. Hume, inclusive."[21]

Abruptly, in June 1803, these inchoate plans took on an elaborate design. The work "which I consider as introductory to a *System*" is not "the labour of one year or of two/ but the result of many years' meditations, and of very various Reading." "I entitle it Organum verè

---

[16] *CL*, I, 632. October 9, 1800.
[17] *CL*, I, 656. December 17, 1800.
[18] *CL*, II, 671. February 3, 1801.
[19] *CL*, II, 776, 787. December 14, 1801, February 19, 1802.
[20] Southey to William Taylor, February 6, 1802, quoted by Griggs, *CL*, II, 787, note.
[21] *CL*, II, 927. February 17, 1803.

Organum, or an *Instrument* of practical Reasoning in the business of real Life." To it he will prefix a history of logic from Aristotle through Raymond Lully, Peter Ramus, Bacon, and Descartes to Hartley and de Condillac. "Then follows my own Organum verè Organum — which consists of a Σύστημα of all *possible* modes of true, probable, and false reasoning, arranged philosophically . . . The whole will conclude with considerations of the value of the work, and it's practical utility — in scientific Investigations . . . in the arts of healing . . . lastly, to the Senate, the Pulpit, and our Law courts."[22] And this is only introductory to a system! What this further elaboration was in Coleridge's mind at this time we can only infer from his plans after finishing the *Organum*: "I shall . . . set seriously to work . . . [on] my Investigations relative to the omne scibile of human Nature — *what* we *are*, and *how* we *become* what we are; so as to solve the two grand Problems, how, being acted upon, we shall act; how, acting, we shall be acted upon. But between me and this work there may be Death."[23]

A few days later he says that his *Organum* "is half-written *out*; and the *materials* of the other Half are all on paper — or rather, on papers — etc in my Hand."[24] None of this material has ever come to light, except a partially filled notebook containing an incomplete discussion of logic, which Miss Snyder assigns to 1803 as a part of the *Organum*.[25] Possibly Coleridge's plans were again changing. A notebook entry for September–October 1803 reveals an interesting point of view with respect to his speculations: "Seem to have made up my mind to write my metaphysical works, as *my Life*, and *in* my Life — intermixed with all the other events/ or history of the mind and fortunes of S.T. Coleridge."[26] He mentions the *Organum* again a month later in a list of prospective works, but this is the last notice of it for some time until it reappears as an essay on the Logos in 1814,

[22] *CL*, II, 947–948. June 4, 1803.
[23] *CL*, II, 948–949.
[24] *CL*, II, 952. June 10, 1803.
[25] "MS. A," *Coleridge on Logic and Learning: with Selections from the Unpublished Manuscripts*, ed. Alice D. Snyder (New Haven, 1929), pp. 52–53.
[26] *N* 1515.

marking a new direction in Coleridge's thought.[27] Instead Coleridge
begins to discuss plans for a work of practical psychology; he calls it
"Consolations and Comforts from the exercise and right application
of the Reason, the Imagination, and the moral Feelings, addressed
especially to those in Sickness, Adversity, or Distress of Mind, *from
speculative Gloom*, etc." [28] The abandonment of the plans for the
Organum and the system coincides roughly with the end of the years
of rigorous philosophizing. After 1804 "abstruse research" was employed more directly in immediate occupations such as the writing
of *The Friend* and in the various courses of lectures. The project of a
philosophical autobiography, however, emerged a few years later in the
Biographia Literaria, and in subsequent years the impetus toward a
great synthetic work took on new vigor and the attempt to explain
this system occupied most of Coleridge's energy.

The general features, then, of Coleridge's thought during this period
suggest a shift, in emphasis at least, from the political and religio-moral
concerns of the decade 1790–1800 to a greater interest in psychology
and epistemology and, for the first time, in poetic theory. These are
the distinctive characteristics of his philosophy in the years leading
up to the writing of the *Biographia*. In order to see this in detail we
must go back to 1801 and look at the first fruits of the Keswick speculations.

LOCKE AND THE RELATIONSHIP OF THOUGHTS TO THINGS

"I have been *thinking* vigorously during my Illness," Coleridge
wrote early in 1801. "The subject of my meditations has been the Relations of Thoughts to Things, in the language of Hume, of Ideas to
Impressions: I may be truly described in the words of Descartes. I
have been 'res cogitans, id est, dubitans, affirmans, negans, pauca in-
telligens, multa ignorans, volens, nolens, imaginans etiam et sen-
tiens — '." [29] The immediate result of these speculations was a series
of four lengthy letters written in February 1801. They were addressed

[27] N 1646.
[28] *CL*, II, 1036. January 15, 1804.
[29] *CL*, II, 671–672.

to Josiah Wedgwood, of the pottery family, so that he might convey
them opportunely to his invalid brother Thomas who was a philosopher
by avocation. It does not seem that the busy Josiah ever read the long
analyses of Locke and Descartes, or indeed that he was likely to have
done so. But Coleridge was writing for himself as much as for the
Wedgwoods, and the clarification of his long reflections was his primary purpose.[30]

The letters, Coleridge says, are a prelude to a communication on
"the result of *my* meditations on the relations of Thoughts to Things."
Since he has been reading Locke's *Essay on Human Understanding*,
however, he has been considering some errors "in the generally received *History* of metaphysical opinions." [31] These considerations form
the subject of his letters to Wedgwood. The general argument is that
Locke, contrary to contemporary interpretation, was not really the
critic of Descartes but rather depended on him for the substance of
his own metaphysics. The view is overstated, in the opinion of modern scholars, but Coleridge had the distinction of being among the
first, if not the first, to realize Locke's debt to Descartes.[32]

Coleridge's criticism of Locke is fairly straightforward. The analysis
of innate ideas by Locke, he says, is confused and immethodical.
Though Locke claims originality in attacking the innatism of older
authors, he does not name his predecessors or present their doctrines,
nor does he clarify the meaning of innate ideas.[33] The term "idea" is
itself the cause of confusion. Coleridge argues that Descartes eventually
discarded it as imprecise and preferred instead the periphrasis *quae-
cunque sub perceptionem nostram cadunt* or, in another place, that
he used ideas "pro omni eo quod immediate a mente percipitur." [34]
This, Coleridge points out, is the same meaning Locke gives to the
word. "He [Locke] would willingly change the Term 'Idea' for a
Better, if any one could help him to it. But he finds none that stands

[30] The letters can be found in *CL*, II, 677–703. The originals have been lost and we
know them now from copies made by Coleridge for Poole.
[31] *CL*, II, 678.
[32] *CL*, II, 678, headnote. Griggs cites the opinion of R. I. Aaron.
[33] *CL*, II, 679–680.
[34] "Whatever falls under our perception." *CL*, II, 692. "For everything that is immediately perceived by the mind," *CL*, II, 683.

so well *'for every immediate object of the mind in thinking, as Idea does.'* "[35]

As Descartes and Locke agree in their use of the term "idea," they also agree, Coleridge argues, in their explanations of the origin of ideas. "They both taught, nearly in the same words and wholly to the same Purpose, that the Objects of human Knowledge are either Ideas imprinted on the Senses, or else such as are perceived by attending to the passions and operations of the mind, or lastly Ideas formed by Help of Memory and Imagination, either compounding, dividing, or barely representing those originally perceived in the aforesaid Ways." [36] In Descartes' terms, these divisions are named adventitious, innate, and factitious. Locke would call the first "ideas of sensation," the second "ideas of reflection," and the third complex ideas formed by combining, comparing, or separating various simple ideas of sensation or of reflection.[37]

Coleridge's principal argument is that Locke, in asserting the originality of his criticism of innatism, misunderstood what Descartes had meant by innate ideas and was fighting a straw man. By confusing *innasci*, the word which Descartes chose "because it implied Birth and of course *Subsequence*, and at the same time pointed out the *place* of Birth," with *connasci*, "to be 'born *at the same time with*,'" Locke concluded that Descartes was among those who held "that there are in the Understanding certain Innate Principles, some primary notions, Κοιναὶ ἔννοιαι, characters as it were stamped upon the mind of Man, which the Soul receives in it's very first being, and brings into the World with it." [38] In fact, says Coleridge, the innate ideas of Descartes are exactly equal to Locke's ideas of reflection, while innate ideas in the sense in which Locke understands them were explicitly denied by Descartes.[39]

Coleridge charges Locke with other errors, among them attributing

[35] *CL*, II, 683.
[36] *CL*, II, 685–686.
[37] *An Essay Concerning Human Understanding*, ed. A. C. Fraser, 2 vols. (Oxford, 1894), II, 121–125; I, 148.
[38] *CL*, II, 691–692, 680.
[39] *CL*, II, 692.

the doctrine of "connate Principles and Ideas" to Aristotle, "whose expressions in reprobation of such a doctrine are even violent," and dealing sophistically with the Cartesian *Cogito* by supposing that it meant "that we are always *voluntarily* combining Ideas." [40] The number and complexity of the distinctions Locke has introduced in discussing the categories of ideas confuse rather than clarify. The *Essay* is thus "only a prolix Paraphrase on Des Cartes with foolish Interpolations of the Paraphrast's; the proper motto of which would be Nihil hic Novi, plurimum vero superflui." [41] The explanation of Locke's reputation is to be sought, among other sources, in the service he is supposed to have done Christianity by providing a defense against the materialism of Gassendus and Hobbes, in his alliance with Newton in the English "triumph" over the Cartesian philosophy, in the "common sense" answer his theories are thought to provide to Leibnitz, and in the general decline of metaphysics in contemporary England.[42]

More important than Coleridge's corrective of the history of philosophy with respect to Descartes and Locke is the meaning of this investigation for his own speculations. It has already been noted that the Wedgwood letters were only a prelude to an account of his reflections on the relations of thoughts to things. This larger problem had been in his mind since his return from Germany. It represented the crystallization of all his doubts about mechanical associationism, and was presumably at the heart of the metaphysical work for which he was preparing himself at Göttingen.

To see the context of this problem we must go back to the fall of 1800 and a lengthy passage in a letter to Godwin, one of the regular confidants of Coleridge on philosophical questions. Coleridge is urging him not to forsake entirely his speculations in order to write for the theater:

I wish you to write a book on the power of words, and the processes by which human feelings form affinities with them — in short, I wish you to *philosophize* Horn Tooke's System, and to solve the great Questions —

[40] *CL*, II, 693–694.
[41] *CL*, II, 699–700.
[42] *CL*, II, 701–703.

whether there be reason to hold, that an action bearing all the *semblance* of pre-designing Consciousness may yet be simply organic, and whether a *series* of such actions are possible — and close on the heels of this question would follow the old 'Is Logic the *Essence* of Thinking?' in other words — Is *thinking* impossible without arbitrary signs? and — how far is the word 'arbitrary' a misnomer? Are not words etc parts and germinations of the Plant? And what is the Law of their Growth? — In something of this order I would endeavor to destroy the old antithesis of *Words* and *Things*, elevating, as it were, words into Things, and living Things too. All the nonsense of vibrations etc you would of course dismiss.[43]

If we separate the strands of this thick-textured passage, we discover some apparently unrelated problems. First of all there is the question of what seems to be predesigning consciousness in contrast to a merely "organic," that is, mechanical, interpretation of human activity.[44] This can be rephrased, in the light of a notebook entry of contemporary date, as the problem of the difference between thinking of a thing and perceiving it; the former involves "a succession of perceptions accompanied by a sense of *nisus* and purpose." [45] The question seems to be whether a philosophy of mechanically received sense impressions can account for this teleological element in thought and action. Secondly, there is the problem of whether words are merely arbitrary signs or whether they have a power, beyond mere denotation, of affecting the mind's operation, and, if so, what the sources and laws of this power are.

The way in which Coleridge relates the word-feelings question to the problem of the source of the nisus in thought and then connects this with the influence of words on thought and concludes by saying that he would destroy the antithesis of words and things may leave us somewhat bewildered and wondering if he is speaking a new

[43] *CL*, I, 625–626. Horne Tooke was a contemporary philologist and nominalist philosopher.

[44] Coleridge attaches no special meaning to the term "organic" at this time. It seems to refer here simply to the physiological functioning of an organ, as in the Hartleyan system.

[45] *N* 886. Thomas Wedgwood objected to Coleridge's yoking of "Things and Thoughts" since "Thought always implies an act or *nisus* of mind." Coleridge responded that "*A Thought* and Thoughts are quite different words from *Thought*" (*N* 1077). But Coleridge did not always preserve the distinction of usage in his own writings.

philosophical language. Some reflection, however, will make clear that the problems are not so unconnected as a first glance might suggest.

The starting point is the relation of thought to things.[46] This was a natural way of putting the questions which occurred as the mechanical explanation of the mind's operations became less satisfactory. The rejection of "the nonsense of vibrations" suggests that this was the context in which the question arose. Apparently the principal inadequacy of a mechanical theory of mind was its inability to explain purposiveness. Probably the relation of feeling to thought arose independently; we have already seen in the last chapter the beginnings of Coleridge's discomfort with a system that gave so little place to emotion as a source of moral guidance. In this three-way problem of relating thought, feeling, and thing, word emerges as the point where all three meet, the bridge between thought and thing, and the vehicle of the feeling that is associated with thing and affects thought. Thus, the problem becomes one of asking whether thinking merely employs words as arbitrary signs, and this is immediately denied, or whether words do not exist, like things, with associations and capacities to affect our feelings and thoughts independently of our intentions.

The two problems we have extracted from Coleridge's comments here — that of the origin of purposiveness, and that of the objective content of words — suggest an ambivalence of outlook that seems to be fundamental to Coleridge's philosophy at this time. On the one hand he would defend the contribution of the mind to thought processes, in opposition to a passive mechanistic theory, but on the other hand he would argue for the reality of external existents and their independent influence on the perceiving mind. The positions are not irreconcilable, but the evidence of these years indicates that no ready solution was apparent to Coleridge. It was, indeed, the essential problem for some time to come.

[46] In epistolary references to his speculations this was the way he commonly stated the problem at this time. "The subject of my meditations has been the Relations of Thoughts to Things." *CL*, II, 672. "The relations of Thoughts to Things," *CL*, II, 678. Or a variation: "The affinites of the Feelings with Words and Ideas." *CL*, II, 671.

We can see evidence for the first side of the difficulty in the very purpose of the Wedgwood letters, the destruction of Locke's claim to originality. In undertaking this task Coleridge was going counter to most of the received opinion of his day, and to his own earlier positions as well. It was the end of his overt devotion to a purely empirical psychology. In the main arguments of the letters he tries to avoid intruding his own philosophical opinions, but in the third installment he comes out himself for a kind of innate idea, "even in Mr. Locke's sense of the Word." "What if instead of innate Ideas a philosopher had asserted the existence of *constituent* Ideas/ the metaphor would not be a whit more gross, nor the hypothesis involved more daring or unintelligible, than in the former phrases/ and I am sure, it would lead to more profitable Experiments and Analyses." [47] This innatism is not developed but it is clearly connected with his speculations on the subjective aspect of knowing. Possibly this was what drew him to Descartes in the first place, as the supposed opposite of Locke on the point. In the second letter, for instance, Coleridge gives a summary of Descartes' autobiography of his ideas, and he mentions that Descartes had to "turn his view inward upon his own frame and faculties in order to determine what share they had in the making up both of his Ideas and of his Judgments on them." [48] Though this leads to the innate ideas or, in Locke's terms, ideas of reflection, it is possible to see in Coleridge's language the beginning of his long struggles with the beguiling but somehow insubstantial theories of idealism.

In opposition to this subjectivism, however, there are in these letters expressions which show that Coleridge is as much aware of how an objective reality shapes our thoughts. In the discussion of Locke's terms clear, distinct, obscure, confused, and so forth, much use is made of the possibility of inadequately perceiving real existents.[49] Even clearer is Coleridge's insistence that all simple ideas (in Locke's usage) are not adequate ideas, since a simple idea cannot refer to any external

[47] *CL*, II, 696. What he means by "constituent" here he does not say. The term comes up later.

[48] *CL*, II, 688.

[49] *CL*, II, 689–690.

substance representatively, "for as Pythagoras said, nothing *exists* but in complexity." [50]

Predictably, in view of the context of the Wedgwood communications, the clearest instance of Coleridge's confidence in the complex influence of externals on our ideas is his concern for words. One of Coleridge's favorite texts is from Hobbes (he quotes it in smiting Locke for the *innasci-connasci* muddle): "Animadvertite quam sit ab improprietate verborum pronum hominibus prolabi in errores circa res." [51] Descartes' doctrine on words he makes his own:

Words (according to Des Cartes) are to be considered in three ways — they are themselves images and sounds; 2. they are connected with our Thoughts by associations with Images and Feelings; 3. with Feelings alone, and this too is the natural Tendency of Language. For as words are learnt by us in clusters, even those that most expressly refer to Images and other Impressions are not all learnt by us determinately; and tho' this should be wholly corrected by after experience, yet the Images and Impressions associated with the words become more and more dim, till at last as far as our consciousness extends they cease altogether; and Words act upon us immediately, exciting a mild current of Passion and Feeling without the regular intermediation of Images . . . Words therefore become a sort of Nature to us, and Nature is a sort of Words . . . Yet both Ideas and Words wherever they are different from or contrary to our Habits either surprize or deceive us; and both in these instances deceive where they do not surprize. [52]

Some three years later Coleridge answered a correspondent who had posed questions on God, the soul, the reason, and understanding. The response clarifies his doctrine on the relation of thoughts to things and the mediation of words, and shows the fundamentally realistic content of this area of his thought. He begins by saying that, since we are incapable of conceiving what God and the soul are, the most we can expect from our discourse is that we might express ourselves concerning them without inconsistency in our definitions, and with no falsehood felt during their enunciation, "which might war with our internal sense of their actuality." Thus he moves to the question of

[50] *CL*, II, 691.

[51] *CL*, II, 691. "It is but a short downhill passage from errors in words to errors in things."

[52] *CL*, II, 697–698.

"the difference or distinction between THING and THOUGHT." "In other words, what do we mean by REALITY?" He answers that "*Things* and *Realities*" possess "a *permanency*, and *expectability* so great, as to be capable of being contra-distinguished both by these, and by their *vividness*" from "our Thoughts, which therefore as appearing posterior and faint we deem the Images and imperfect Shadows of the former." He goes on to show by a fanciful etymology how language illustrates this process of our minds: the word thought is derived from the past participle of *reor* (*ratus*), while thing (*res*) is from the present participle and implies "actuality in full and immediate action." All our thoughts, of course, are inadequate to the whole of the things they represent. "I have a distinct Thought of a Rose-Tree; but what countless properties and goings-on of that plant are there, not included in my *Thought* of it?" [53]

By way of rounding off these remarks on thoughts and words, we might jump ahead some years, to the lectures of 1811–1812 and a passage that seems to complete the lines quoted above. Coleridge is defending Shakespeare's "conceits," and he insists that it be understood "that language is not, was not, and never will be, the mere vehicle of representing external objects or simple information." Horne Tooke's book, notes Coleridge's amanuensis J. Tomalin, was called *Epea Pteroenta*, "Winged Words." "In Coleridge's judgment it might have been much more fitly called *Verba Viventia*, or 'living words,' for words are the living products of the living mind and could not be a due medium between the thing and the mind unless they partook of both. [Recall the words of the letter of September 22, 1800: "elevating, as it were, words into Things, and living Things too."] The word was not to convey merely what a certain thing is, but the very passion and all the circumstances which were conceived as constituting the perception of the thing by the person who used the word." [54]

The subjective-objective dichotomy, if it can be called such without doing violence to the facts, reveals itself also in the confusion of Coleridge's philosophical idols at this time. Though he has rejected "the

---

[53] *CL*, II, 1193–1195.
[54] *ShC*, II, 104. The interpolation is mine.

nonsense of vibrations," Hartley still comes in for praise in several passages. In dismissing Locke from the popular pantheon, he suggests that the name of Newton should have "a more worthy associate"; the candidate is first Bacon but then, on consideration, Hartley.[55] In the last lines of the unfinished fourth letter he nominates as "the three greatest, nay, only three *great* Metaphysicians which this Country *has* produced," Berkeley, and Butler, "in whose company I place Hartley as a useful Writer." [56] Yet in the following month we find him saying, after intense study: "If I do not greatly delude myself, I have not only completely extricated the notions of Time, and Space; but have overthrown the doctrine of Association, as taught by Hartley, and with it all the irreligious metaphysics of modern Infidels — especially, the doctrine of Necessity." [57] And only a few weeks previously he had been critisizing Locke for his ignorance of the laws of association as they explained memory *and reasoning*! [58]

In a sense it is possible to say that the years following 1801 involved for Coleridge a succession of attempts to find a formula by which he could coexist with associationism, by distinguishing clearly what was corrupt and what was salvageable in the doctrines of his youth. It can also be said that the reconciliation of the subjective elements in knowledge with the existential demands of the known object is a major problem of the period. It illuminates the increasing concern of Coleridge with words as the medium between thought, feeling, and thing, and probably influenced the parallel interest, now for the first time, in the theory of poetry as mediator between mind and reality. Such were the fertile implications in the attempt to free himself from mechanism.

INDISTINCTNESS AND THE SUBCONSCIOUS

The discussion of the function of words in the relation between thoughts and things suggests certain features of the knowledge process

[55] *CL*, II, 686.
[56] *CL*, II, 703.
[57] *CL*, II, 706.
[58] *CL*, II, 694–695.

which are implied in the theory of language here expressed. Since ideas never adequately express the real existents to which they refer, a degree of indistinctness and obscurity seems to be an inevitable concomitant in true knowing. The question may be asked whether this indefiniteness is a handicap or a good insofar as we are concerned.

The problem has a certain currency in Coleridge scholarship as the result of a recent emendation of a much quoted notebook entry of Coleridge's. In the original *Anima Poetae* an early entry quoted the sentence: "Poetry gives most pleasure when only generally and not perfectly understood." [59] Miss Coburn's edition of the notebooks has restored the full text, which is given here with the important conditional qualification:

> The elder Languages fitter for Poetry because they expressed only prominent ideas with clearness, others but darkly — Therefore the French wholly unfit for Poetry; because is *clear* in their Language — i.e. — Feelings created by obscure ideas associate themselves with the one *clear* idea. When no criticism is pretended to, and the Mind in its simplicity gives itself up to a Poem as to a work of nature, Poetry gives most pleasure when only generally and not perfectly understood. It was so by me with Gray's *Bard*, and Collins' odes — *The Bard* once intoxicated me, and now I read it without pleasure. From this cause it is that what *I* call metaphysical Poetry gives me so much delight. — [60]

Miss Coburn thus interprets the emended passage: "The argument is not for obscurity but against it, for the superior discrimination of the imagination as compared with the mere logic of the conceptual understanding or the mere instinct of youthful enthusiasm." [61] Humphrey House extends this observation by remarking that "when criticism *is* pretended to, then the pleasure follows in proportion to the understanding. The sentence can no longer be enrolled to support a view of poetry as a kind of vague magic." [62]

"Vague magic" may not be exactly what Coleridge prized most in

[59] *Anima Poetae: From the Unpublished Notebooks of Samuel Taylor Coleridge*, ed. E. H. Coleridge (London, 1895), p. 5. Hereafter cited as *AP*.

[60] *N* 383. Perhaps a slip of Coleridge's pen omitted the word "everything" in the second sentence: "because [everything] is *clear* in their Language."

[61] *N* 383, note.

[62] House, *Coleridge*, p. 30.

poetry, but it does seem that the obscurity or indistinctness that House rejects is in fact an essential element in our mental apparatus and in the imaginative creation of poetry according to Coleridge. As evidence of this importance of the indefinite, we may examine some of the many passages in the letters and notebooks from this date through the period under discussion.

First, there are texts which show that indistinctness is a fundamental characteristic of our human way of knowing, the absence of which ought to be grounds for suspicion of the clarity and distinctness of the ideas which result. Thought cannot bear too much clarification, Coleridge seems to be saying, or it loses its power of capturing the complicated and irreducible reality. Thus in a notebook entry of 1801 he asks: "Whether or no the too great definiteness of Terms in any language may not consume too much of the vital and idea-creating force in distinct, clear, full made Images and so prevent originality — *original* thought as distinguished from positive thought." [63] On the other hand, Miss Coburn interprets Coleridge as saying that it is the function of mind to bring clarity out of this indefiniteness and dimness. A notebook entry made about this time records that he is considering translating part of J. J. Engel's *Der Philosoph für die Welt* (1775–1777) as an introduction to his "Essay on Locke." Engel had argued that inventiveness and originality must assist in bringing forth truths from their potential origin in nature. "The creative human mind," says Miss Coburn, "brings what is dim and unrealized into clarity." [64] Though this criticism of Locke's lack of creativity is doubtless one part of Coleridge's indictment, it does not necessarily exclude an equally forceful criticism of the truth-value of clarity and distinctness and an insistence on the necessity of some fertile indefiniteness in the process of knowing. In another notebook entry, for 1805, Coleridge supposes a conversation with "a Paleyan or Priestleyan," to whom he speaks of "my *mist*, my delving and difficulty," but gets back an answer that is "a set of parrot words, ⟨quite satisfied, clear as a pike-staff, — nothing *before* and *nothing behind* — a stupid peice of mock-knowledge, having no *root*

[63] *N* 1016.
[64] *N* 930 and note.

for then it would have feelings of dimness from *growth*, having no buds or twigs, for then it would have yearnings and strivings of obscurity from *growing* . . .⟩ acknowledging no sympathy with this delving, this feeling of wonder." [65] By 1805 "Paleyan" and "Priestleyan" are clearly pejorative terms for Coleridge.

Second, there is the correlation between indistinctness and strength of feeling. In explaining how, in the passage from "Tintern Abbey," by "the deep power of Joy/ We see into the *Life* of Things," Coleridge notes: "i.e.— By deep feeling we make our *Ideas dim*— and this is what we mean by our Life — ourselves." In thinking of the wall before me, I have a distinct image, but the idea and the thinking I are two distinct and opposite things. But in thinking of myself, "the Idea becomes dim whatever it be — so dim that I know not what it is — but the Feeling is deep and steady — and this I call *I*— identifying the Percipient and the Perceived —." Miss Coburn interprets this passage as implying that, though for the perfect creative sensibility rational understanding and strong feeling will merge directly ("Clear and distinct ideas we must have, but before they are assimilable in a poem they must merge with strong feeling"), in the normal sensibility thought and feeling will be successive.[66] But, in the context of his other remarks, Coleridge seems rather to be saying that the experiences which involve our deepest feelings (such as the transcendental identification of our own life with that of nature, percipient and perceived — "we are laid asleep in body and become a living soul" — which the poem describes) are those least clear to our understanding, "so dim that I know not what it is." The unity of thought and feeling is certainly part of the process; Coleridge says in another note on love that, unlike revenge and anger, the feeling is "of such intimate affinity with ideas, so as to modify them and become one with them." [67] However, it is precisely the strength of the feeling that is correlative to the obscurity of the

[65] *N* 2509. The angle brackets enclose a later addition by Coleridge. Miss Coburn comments on this passage: "*Dimness* is a favourite and an emotionally charged word, often associated with growth, change, the unknown processes of life, as well as with subjective feelings and efforts to explore them."

[66] *N* 921 and note.

[67] *N* 2441.

idea. "Our notions," he says, "resemble the index and hand of the dial; our feelings are the hidden springs which impel the machine, with this difference, that notions and feelings react on each other reciprocally. The veneration for the Supreme Being, sense of mysterious existence, is not to be profaned by the intrusion of clear notions." [68]

The last remark suggests another aspect of indistinctness, and a confirmation of the previous interpretation of Coleridge's words, the consideration of the power of strong feelings allied with indefinite ideas to influence moral and religious response. In this context, however, the reverse is often true, and clarity of notion in moral matters is to be preferred to the seductive appeal of the indistinct. For example, in a letter of July 1802 Coleridge strongly criticizes the moral content of a poem of Salamon Gessner's which he is translating for Sotheby. Not directly vulgar like the plain sense of Theocritus, Gessner's "refinement" instead "leads the imagination to Ideas without *expressing them*." If they were shaped and clothed the mind would merely turn away from them, "but in that shadowy half-being, that state of nascent Existence in the Twilight of Imagination, and just on the vestibule of Consciousness, they are far more incendiary, stir up a more lasting commotion, and leave a deeper stain." The reason for this is that "the Conceptions, as they *recede* from distinctness of *Idea, approximate* to the nature of *Feeling*, and gain thereby a closer and more immediate affinity with the appetites." [69] So in another note Coleridge discusses the superiority of a clear and distinct idea over a *schwankend* notion, that is, a fluctuating or vague one, when there is a question of a moral choice between an immediate pleasure (for example, wine) or a future general good(health). The clear image of the present good will prevail over the indistinct idea of a future benefit; thus the fallacy of teaching children virtue by immediate inducements, as do "Hartley, Priestley, and the Multitude." [70] So in the moral order indistinctness is a peril when strongly allied to feeling; but when present goods are weighed against future ones, it is likely that clearer conceptions of immediate

[68] *ShC*, II, 12. The exact words are not those of Coleridge, but in this case of H. C. Robinson reporting the lecture.
[69] *CL*, II, 814.
[70] *N* 1714, 1713.

pleasure will be more appealing than the indistinct possibilities of the distant future. Apparently indistinctness, when it cannot command feeling, is powerless. Perhaps we are also to conclude that the mind without feeling is at the mercy of clear and distinct conceptions. The distinctness of images of immediate good or pleasure is seductive only because of the absence of strong feeling toward other, higher values, the ideas of which are indefinite; thus the idea of the greatest of all goods, heaven, is "utterly indistinct and dim." [71] So feeling causes indistinctness when joined to an idea, but the converse is not necessarily true. Indistinct notions may of themselves remain merely confused.

Finally, this obscurity joined with feeling is said to be a particular characteristic of the operation of the imagination. It is for this argument especially that the emendation of the *Anima Poetae* passage does not seem to change its meaning substantially. Coleridge identifies imagination, at least in some of its operations, with indistinctness in our ideas. For example, a note of 1803 reads: "Mix up Truth and Imagination, so that the Imag. may spread its own indefiniteness over that which really happened, and Reality its sense of substance and distinctness to Imagination/." [72] Again, in another note he comments ironically on contemporary criticisms of Darwin: "and it is *Imagination*, forsooth, that misled him! too much *poetry* in his philosophy! — this abject deadness of all that sense of the Obscure and Indefinite, this superstitious Fetisch Worship of lazy or fascinated *Fancy!*" [73] For corroboration we may turn to a passage from the lectures of 1811–1812. Coleridge is discussing Shakespeare's "conceits" and explains a passage from *Romeo and Juliet* in which love and hate are variously juxtaposed by saying that when the mind cannot describe what it wishes to, but must reconcile opposites and qualify contradictions, its consequent middle state is more appropriate to imagination, as it wavers between images:

As soon as it is fixed on one image, it becomes understanding; but while it is unfixed and wavering between them, attaching itself permanently to

[71] N 1715.
[72] N 1541.
[73] N 2325.

none, it is imagination. Such is the fine description of Death in Milton: —
> The other shape,
> If shape it might be call'd, that shape had none . . .

The grandest efforts of poetry are where the imagination is called forth, not to produce a distinct form, but a strong working of the mind, still offering what is still repelled, and again creating what is again rejected; the result being what the poet wishes to impress, namely, the substitution of a sublime feeling of the unimaginable for a mere image.[74]

Thus the single image is rejected in favor of the multiple suggestiveness of the indistinct when coupled with a strong feeling. To be sure this is not Coleridge's complete doctrine on poetic expression, and the analysis is more suited to "the grandest efforts" than to other types of poetic expression. Kant's notion of the sublime as limitlessness apparently has some effect on Coleridge here.[75] There is no need to pursue the subject in detail because Coleridge's subsequent theories solve much of the problem; it is sufficient to see that indistinctness is closely related at this point in Coleridge's thought to the characteristic operation of the imagination.

Thus, Coleridge's qualification, "When no criticism is pretended to, and the Mind in its simplicity gives itself up to a Poem as to a work of nature," seems to mean exactly what it says: for critical evaluation of a poem perfect understanding of the employment of the poetic art is desirable, even requisite, while for uncritical enjoyment poetry is best only generally understood. The difference may turn on the distinction between the clarity of one's "understanding" of the poetic expression, of the precision of the use of poetic techniques, on the one hand, and the unanalytic receptivity to the fertile indistinctness of the images and ideas presented, on the other. This would recall the fundamental function of word in the relation of thought and thing. Mind inclines to abstraction, to clarity and distinctness in its ideas, while reality exists in a complex and imprecise way. The word which mediates between the two must possess the qualities of both; thus though its reference may be to indefinite things, it may be employed in relatively clear and analyzable techniques. This would fulfill the demands of both a

[74] *ShC*, II, 138.
[75] *ShC*, II, 138–139, note.

realistic epistemology and a poetic art, and allow the art to be the subject of discursive criticism while the noetic function of the poem — its knowledge relation to the referent — would be best achieved without discursive understanding. Thus the clarity of understanding involved in the critical judgment may destroy the capacity of an inferior poem to arouse pleasure. But there are poems which no amount of critical analysis can weaken because the ideas and the art are perfectly matched in them. Such is "metaphysical" poetry for Coleridge.[76] Furthermore, as we shall subsequently see, Coleridge certainly held a theory of poetry which required that the poem be approached as "a work of nature." Perhaps it is too much to say that Coleridge employed such a doctrine fully developed at this time. However, it seems more than consistent with the future direction of his poetic theory.

IMAGINATION

It would be no contribution to the understanding of Coleridge's intellectual development if this study gave the impression that his progress from tentative to more elaborated positions was by logical steps and clearly stated transitions. Still, in the mass of reflections, sugges-

---

[76] What exactly Coleridge means by "metaphysical poetry" is not clear. Possibly it is connected with the "metaphysical pathos" or "union of deep and subtle thought with sensibility" which is one of the excellences of Wordsworth's poetry and which, along with imagination "in the highest and strictest sense of the word," makes Wordsworth capable of producing "the first genuine philosophic poem." *BL*, II, 122–124, 129. The quality seems to be a kind of reflection. The "meditative pathos" of the *Biographia* is closely connected with "a sympathy with man as man; the sympathy indeed of a contemplator, rather than a fellow-sufferer or co-mate, (spectator, haud particeps) but of a contemplator, from whose view no difference of rank conceals the sameness of the nature." In *Table Talk* for July 21, 1832, Coleridge says that Wordsworth possessed more of the genius of a great philosophic poet than any man since Milton, but "he ought never to have abandoned the contemplative position, which is peculiarly — perhaps I might say exclusively — fitted for him. His proper title is *Spectator ab extra.*" *Specimens of the Table Talk of the Late Samuel Taylor Coleridge*, ed. H. N. Coleridge, 2 vols. (London, 1835), II, 71–72. But "metaphysical" poetry is not necessarily the same as "philosophical" poetry, and we are really left no clearer as to Coleridge's precise meaning. There may be another clue in a letter of May 13, 1796, to Thelwall: "But why so violent against *metaphysics* in poetry? Is not Akenside's a metaphysical poem? Perhaps, you do not like Akenside — well — *but I do* — and so do a great many others — Why pass an act of *Uniformity* against Poets?" The poem referred to seems to be *The Pleasures of Imagination* (1774). *CL*, I, 215.

tions, questions, and answers that fill the notebooks and letters, and in the occasional prose of his money-making ventures, there is a consistent development of ideas. Several germinal conceptions occur, independently or only loosely related. Coleridge develops one until he has exhausted its fertility, but then the relevance of another is recognized and it is brought in to continue the development, perhaps in a somewhat different area but always advancing the whole scheme. One important source of productive reflection was certainly the criticism of Lockean and Hartleyan empiricism and the attempt to understand the relation of thought, word, and thing. A second key concept must now be examined. It is the notion of the special activity of the mind to which Coleridge gave the name imagination.

The roots of the idea, as has been said, originate deep in Coleridge's dissatisfaction with associationist mechanism and in the persuasion that certain kinds of knowing demand an explanation that admits of subjective participation in the knowledge act. The earliest version of a distinction between two kinds of intellectual ability is the division of *genius* from *talent*, which first occurs in an unelaborated form in a notebook entry of 1800, genius apparently there being identified with his lost poetic ability, talent with what capacity he might have remaining to enable him to become at least a good lawyer.[77] Miss Coburn notes that the distinction becomes in later years practically the same as that between imagination and fancy. It occurs in almost the same form in a letter of 1802: "As to myself, all my poetic Genius, if ever I really possessed any *Genius*, and it was not rather a more general *aptitude* of Talent, and quickness in Imitation/ is gone." [78]

By September of the same year the distinction between imagination and fancy is fully stated in a letter to William Sotheby, a contemporary poet and translator, with lengthy preambles that clarify much of Coleridge's intended meaning. In commenting on the second volume of Bowles's poems Coleridge disapproves of the moralizing in them: "Never to see or describe any interesting appearance in nature, without connecting it by dim analogies with the moral world, proves faintness

[77] N 669.
[78] CL, II, 831. Incidentally, Coleridge gives first place among the reasons for the loss to "long and exceedingly severe Metaphysical Investigations."

of Impression. Nature has her proper interest; and he will know what it is, who believes and feels, that every Thing has a Life of it's own, and that we are all *one Life*. A Poet's *Heart* and *Intellect* should be *combined*, *intimately* combined and *unified*, with the great appearances in Nature — and not merely held in solution and loose mixture with them, in the shape of formal similes." These formal similes are not to be excluded from poetry, but they do not suit the highest kind of poetry; they are "Sermoni propiora." Bowles wants the passion of a great poet, "because he is not a Thinker." [79] This curious remark might seem at first incongruous, but it really summarizes what Coleridge is trying to say, that the highest conceptions require the most intense feelings and they both must be intimately unified in poetry. "Young somewhere in one of his prose works remarks that there is as profound a Logic in the most daring and dithyrambic parts of Pindar, as in the ʺOρyανον of Aristotle — the remark is a valuable one." By way of illustrating this idea Coleridge recounts an attempt he once made to associate with Sca Fell some sublime poetic expressions; thinking the native subject too humble for this treatment he revised the verses so as to describe the "grander external objects" of Chamouny, and he was consequently satisfied with the result.[80] Further, it occurs to him that the psalms show how untrue it is to say that there is a similarity between the Greek and Jewish conceptions of the divine:

It must occur to every Reader that the Greeks in their religious poems always address the Numina Loci, the Genii, the Dryads, the Naiads, etc etc — All natural Objects were *dead* — mere hollow Statues — but there was a Godkin or Goddessling *included* in each — In the Hebrew Poetry you find nothing of this poor Stuff — as poor in genuine Imagination, as it is mean in Intellect — / At best, it is but Fancy, or the aggregating Faculty of the mind — not *Imagination*, or the *modifying*, and *co-adunating* Faculty. This the Hebrew Poets appear to me to have possessed beyond all others — and next to them the English. In the Hebrew Poets each Thing has a Life of it's own, and yet they are all one Life. In God they move and live, and *have* their Being — not *had*, as the cold system of Newtonian Theology represents/ but *have*.[81]

[79] *CL*, II, 864.
[80] *CL*, II, 864, 865.
[81] *CL*, II, 865–866.

It is to be noted that in this statement the operation by which the imagination modifies and coadunates is posterior to and by virtue of the real existence of things in a unified way. Thus, both knowing and being are involved, and the latter is prior to and the source of the possibility of the former.

It may be asked what exactly the imagination unifies. The lengthy passage discussed above would suggest that the main work of the imagination is to fuse thought and feeling. Though this is true, it does not go far enough in specifying how the imagination operates as a mode of expression or communication, or even of knowing. In other words we must add making to the concepts of being and knowing. An important passage in a letter of 1804 clarifies this. Coleridge is discussing the achievement of Wordsworth. As a poet, he says, Wordsworth is original and no more like Shakespeare or Milton than they are like each other. His originality is that he is "the first and greatest philosophical Poet — the only man who has effected a compleat and constant synthesis of Thought and Feeling and combined them with Poetic Forms, with the music of pleasurable passion and with Imagination or the *modifying* Power in that highest sense of the word in which I have ventured to oppose it to Fancy, or the *aggregating* power — in that sense in which it is a dim Analogue of Creation, not all that we can *believe* but all that we can *conceive* of creation." [82]

The elements therefore which the imagination works on are thought, feeling, and poetic forms.[83] Prior to the imaginative act, there is the world of objects, not dead, as the Greeks conceived them, but possessing a being that actively (they *have* life, not *had*) participates in some way in the divine being. Our reaction to this world involves thought and feeling and, if artistic externalization is our aim, poetic form. When

[82] *CL*, II, 1034.

[83] "The music of pleasurable passion" can be omitted, as denoting the specific kind of poetry that is in the form of verse. (At this point Coleridge does not seem to insist that poetry be in verse. See the discussion of the definitions of poetry in the Shakespearean lectures below. Later he will argue that meter is a natural concomitant of poetry. See the criticism of Wordsworth's theories in *BL*, II, discussed in Chapter VII.) Thought, however, is a characteristic of all poetry, as Coleridge elsewhere says, and not merely of "philosophical" poetry. "A great Poet must be, implicitè, if not explicitè, a profound Metaphysician." *CL*, II, 810.

the mind merely aggregates these elements in a loose mixture, or a solution, so that the expression of our awareness of the external world is made in formal similes, Coleridge says the fancy is at work. The imagination, on the other hand, matches thought and feeling and arrays them in forms, the whole process being distinguished by a modification and coadunation of the elements. What this is precisely Coleridge does not really say here. He suggests that the operation of imagination is dimly analogous to divine creation (actually, though dim, the best analogue we have). What is at least implied is a totally new kind of existence which cannot conceivably be the result of the mere unity of the pre-existing elements, but rather connotes an informing act of the imagination.[84]

Coleridge's dissatisfaction with the doctrine of imagination as it stands in this form will issue in the attempt to clarify the whole matter in the *Biographia*. For the time being, it may be suggested that the rejection of "formal similes" as indicative of the lack of imagination points the way to the development of Coleridge's later notions of symbol. Coleridge had little more to say about imagination until 1815 or so. It seems that he had not fully distinguished the notions of being, knowing, and making, the first of which now begins to concern him predominantly.

FEELING AND THE VESTIGES OF ASSOCIATION THEORY

Before pursuing the concept of being that is involved in much of Coleridge's speculation after 1803, we must return to two or three ideas that have already been noticed and relate them to the general direction

[84] In a notebook entry some years later Coleridge gives another much quoted formula: "How excellently the German *Einbildungskraft* expresses this prime and loftiest faculty, the power of co-adunation, the faculty that forms the many into one — *In-eins-bildung*! Eisenoplasy, or esenoplastic power, is contradistinguished from fantasy, or the mirrorment, either catoptric or metoptric — repeating simply, or by transposition — and, again, involuntary [fantasy] as in dreams, or by an act of the will." *AP*, p. 236 (1810). The etymology of *Einbildungskraft* is mistaken; the prefix *ein* does not suggest unity, but rather the completeness or inward direction of the action. What exactly Coleridge meant by the unifying action which he always attributed to the imagination we shall have to inquire subsequently. The question of dreams will occur again also.

of Coleridge's thought. We have mentioned that Coleridge only reluctantly abandoned certain parts of the British association philosophy that
he learned so early in life. The basic premise of all associationist
theories, that some of the fundamental operations of the mind can be
explained by the similarity, contiguity, or contrast of mental impressions at the time they are first received, was too well verified by experience and reflection to be cast aside along with the mechanistic and
overly empirical superstructure built on this foundation by some
enthusiasts. Besides, the associationist philosophy provided the conceptual scheme in which Coleridge first began his speculations. Whatever could be saved consistent with his recent insights would buttress
novelty with a familiar and indeed traditional authority.

It is not surprising therefore that even after Coleridge announced
that he had overthrown Hartleyan associationism in 1801 the general
theory continued to interest him as an explanation of certain mental
phenomena. The difference was that he now began to think in terms of
the relationship of feeling to thought in the associational process. His
critical analysis of contemporary poets had shown him (in 1802) that
what Bowles lacked and Wordsworth possessed to a great degree was
the intimately unified combination of thought and feeling, but he had
not yet discovered the precise influence of feeling on thought. His own
experiences taught him. In January 1803 he wrote to his fellow philosopher Thomas Wedgwood about the turbulent state of his mind and
faculties when among powerful scenery and the objects of nature. In
particular he recalls the exaltation of climbing to great heights: "Life
seems to me then a universal spirit . . . In these moments it has been
my creed . . . that Feelings die by flowing into the mould of the
Intellect, and becoming Ideas; and that Ideas passing forth into action
re-instate themselves again in the world of Life. And I do believe, that
Truth lies inveloped in these loose generalizations." [85]

The vagueness is cleared up some seven months later. In a letter to
Southey he interrupts himself to tell of the "vivid recollection — indeed an ocular Spectrum," of a room they once shared, that overcame
him while writing the opening lines of the letter. It was the metaphor

[85] *CL*, II, 916.

he had been setting down that had reminded him of the time when in that room he used to compound "half-verbal, half-visual metaphors."

It argues, I am persuaded, a particular state of general feeling — and I hold, that association depends in a much greater degree on the recurrence of resembling states of Feeling, than on Trains of Ideas/ that the recollection of early childhood in latest old age depends on, and is explicable by this — and if this be true, Hartley's System totters . . . Look into Hartley's solution of the phenomena / how flat, how wretched! — Believe me, Southey! a metaphysical Solution, that does not instantly *tell* for something in the Heart, is grievously to be suspected as apocryphal, I almost think, that Ideas *never* recall Ideas, as far as they are Ideas — any more than Leaves in a forest create each other's motion — The Breeze it is that runs thro' them/ it is the Soul, the state of Feeling — . If I had said, no *one* Idea ever recalls another, I am confident that I could support the assertion.[86]

This is a particularly strong statement of the importance of feeling in the knowledge process, and it was really too extreme a position for Coleridge to maintain with consistency for long. As a corrective of mechanistic psychology it makes its point forcefully. Coleridge, however, was committed antecedently to an epistemology in which thought and feeling are proportioned to each other. He continued to speculate on the effect of emotional states on ideas, but the examples he chose usually had special determining circumstances. Thus in two notebook entries he considered, in the case of erotic dreams, how little power images have over feelings independently of the will, compared with the reverse influence, or how in acute physical suffering ideas are affected by the states of bodily feeling.[87]

What this assertion of association of ideas by means of feeling does signal is the distinct end of Hartley's influence. Hitherto Coleridge had been reluctant to reject him completely or to include him in his most severe excoriations of the mechanists. From now on, however, the name of Hartley occurs only four times in his letters through 1819, and then only in passing, as when he identifies the philosophy of "Locke, Hartley, and Condillac." Christian Philosophy is just as much Coleridge's interest now as it was in 1794, but no one is clearly its master

[86] *CL*, II, 961.
[87] *N* 2600, 2638.

as Hartley had once been. Perhaps by now Coleridge had decided that he himself would be the synthesizer of religion and philosophy.

WILL AND THE SELF

Near the end of the second chapter it was suggested that Coleridge's tendencies toward a more subjectively satisfying religious faith and his dissatisfaction with a psychology that denied feeling its evident importance could be summarized under the notion of an increasingly clear idea of the person as the subject of mental acts and emotional states. A similar conclusion suggests itself at this point, though of course the position now is a more advanced one, building as it does on some years of intense speculation. Beginning with the conviction, in the face of mechanism's failure, that mind is active, adding to it the analyses of the relation of idea to external object, the possibility and conditions of objectivity in the knowledge process, and the definition of the imaginative power, finally joining with these the remarks on the influence of feelings upon ideas, Coleridge's meditations on the knowing subject naturally come to a head in considerations about the unity of the self.

It seems to have been some reflections on will that led him to this topic. About December 1803 the notebooks are filled with lengthy extracts from Kant, several of which bear upon the nature of the will and its influence on the moral life. A brooding dissatisfaction with Kant's analyses, however, is apparent in most of the entries. For instance, Coleridge quotes a version of the categorical imperative: "It is not enough that we act in conformity to the Law of moral Reason — we must likewise *FOR THE SAKE* of that law." But he improves upon the formula by adding his own words: "it must not only be our Guide, but likewise our Impulse — Like a strong current, it must make a visible Road on the Sea, and drive us along that road gemäss — um desselben willen." [88] He complains constantly of Kant's deficiencies of psychological insight. Coleridge would prefer, in Miss Coburn's words, a more dynamic role for the imagination in the moral life, a criticism that was also made by Schiller. [89] Even the intellectual life is animated

[88] N 1705.
[89] N 1717, note.

by volition. "In all inevitable Truths," says Coleridge, "e.g. that the two sides of a [triangle] are greater than the third, I feel my will active: I seem to *will* the Truth, as well as to perceive it, Think of this! — "[90]

In the same note Coleridge comments on Kant's remark that the will is nothing other than the practical reason. He opposes to this conception his own self-reflection: "This I doubt/ My will and *I* seem perfect Synonimes — whatever does not apply to the first, I refuse to the latter/ — Any thing strictly of outward Force I refuse to acknowledge, as done *by* me/ it is done *with* me. Now I do not feel this perfect synonimousness in Reason and the Wille. I am sure, Kant cannot make it out. Again and again, he is a wretched Psychologist. Yet it is, doubtless, a most abstruse Subject." This concept of will as self and as efficient cause of the knowledge process is illustrated by a remark in a letter of the following month. In discussing the effects of illness he writes that his distresses "had taken away from me the connecting Link of voluntary power, which continually combines that Part of us by which we know ourselves to be, with that outward Picture or Hieroglyphic, by which we hold communion with our Like — between the Vital and the Organic — or what Berkeley, I suppose, would call — Mind and it's sensuous Language."[91]

A few months later the notion of the ego is first mentioned in connection with these speculations on epistemological problems in general. "Mem. To write to the Recluse [that is, Wordsworth] that he may insert something concerning *Ego*/ its metaphysical Sublimity — and intimate Synthesis with the principle of Co-adunation — without *it* every where all things were a waste — nothing, etc —."[92] Since imagination is not named as the "principle of Co-adunation" with which the ego is in intimate synthesis, it is possible that Coleridge is trying to distinguish a higher coadunating principle, of which imagination is properly only the agent for aesthetic creation, thus implying the later distinction of primary and secondary imagination. But this may be

---

[90] *N* 1717. In Coleridge's note the word "triangle" is represented by a drawing.
[91] *CL*, II, 1032. Note again the older meaning of "organic."
[92] *N* 2057.

reading too much into the text at this point. At any rate the ego is identified in a subsequent note with the will as prime mover in human conduct.[93] Coleridge, however, is far from certain about the matter, for he adds: "and what is Reason?" Though the whole drift of Coleridge's thought at this time seems to be toward elevating will over reason as the directive force in behavior, the problem did not take definite shape in his mind for some time, if indeed the speculations of the later years can be said to have decided the matter.

Confusion over the exact values to be placed on the functions of will and reason did not prevent the clarification of what was by far the more important principle for Coleridge's purpose, the unity of the knowing and acting subject. This unity is firmly stated but its sources and conditions are only confusedly explored at this time. In general it may be said that Coleridge was working toward a notion of substance that would satisfy the requirements of the individuality of the self while still providing for a universality of essence, and that would explain how created individuals participate in the divine being without necessitating a pantheistic monism. In many respects this is the same struggle that he had earlier carried on with certain tendencies in Berkeley and Boehme, and the outcome is much the same here insofar as Coleridge will not accept an answer that involves either thorough monism or solipsistic individualism. Thus in 1803 a notebook entry defends Spinoza's idea of substance as nonpantheistic, but the positive content of the notion of individual substance is not clear.[94]

There are several other entries of this period that bear on the same subject. In one Coleridge copies some passages from Scotus Erigena relating to God as the *esse* of all things. It may be doubted whether it is the *esse* of things that actually interests Coleridge, or rather the knowability of their essences, since most of the entry deals with the incomprehensibility of the substance or essence of a creature by the intellect, a quality which creatures share with God, and it concludes with the interesting statement: "For the essence which is known through quality, quantity, form, matter, or a certain differentia, place

[93] N 2058.
[94] N 1500 and note.

or time, is not the what (*quid*), but the that (*quia*)." [95] In any case
we should not assume the pantheism of Scotus Erigena's passage since,
as Gilson warns, these formulas, including this specific one (God as
the *esse* of all things), should always be read in the light of the meaning of participation for Erigena. This is best thought of as a distribution
of natures, or "to have being after," and as a consequence of, another
being — the figure often used by him is that of the sun and its radia-
tions.[96] In another entry shortly after this Coleridge says that the
Church of Rome does not seem to have decided between the Thomists
and the Scotists in the controversy "on the nature of the Being which
Creatures possess." [97] This seems to refer not to the school of Scotus
Erigena but to the followers of Duns Scotus, whom Coleridge mentions several times. It is easy to see how the doctrine of Duns Scotus
would interest Coleridge and further his thinking on the self. For
Scotus the problem of individuality meant, in addition to the principles
of specific essence and existence, the necessity of an individuating de-
termination or "thisness" ("hecceity") which constitutes the ultimate
actuality of a being.[98] Last among these notebook references of the
spring and summer of 1803 to the problem of substantial unity is an
entry which includes Erigena's explanation of creation "as only a
manifestation of the unity of God in forms — et fit et facit, et creat et
creatur." [99]

It does not seem that Coleridge's state of mind at this time can be
made thoroughly clear on the topic of individual substance and its
relation to divine being. Possibly some assistance can be got from a
contemporary letter in which he praises Abraham Tucker's *The Light
of Nature Pursued* (1768–1778), and indicates his intention of writing

[95] *N* 1369. The passage of Scotus Erigena is a translation from *De divisione naturae*
(Oxford, 1681), I, p. 3.

[96] Etienne Gilson, *History of Christian Philosophy in the Middle Ages* (New York,
1955), pp. 120–121.

[97] *N* 1379.

[98] Gilson, *Christian Philosophy*, pp. 461–462.

[99] *N* 1382. Coleridge had been reading rather extensively in the schoolmen and their
predecessors. Scotus Erigena, Duns Scotus, and Thomas Aquinas are mentioned several
times in the letters and notebooks between 1801 and 1803. *CL*, II, 746, 903, 949, 954,
1020. On November 25, 1803, he writes: "God bless the old Schoolmen! they have been
my best comforts, and most instructive Companions for the last two years." *CL*, II, 1020.

a preface for Hazlitt's projected one-volume abridgment of the work.[100] Tucker's work is a seven-volume treatise on the roles of reason and revelation in the conduct of life; it covers all the predictable divisions of mental faculties and moral virtues. One of its key ideas, and one of the points on which the author reluctantly corrects Locke, is Tucker's insistence on incommunicable substance, rather than the Lockean notion of consciousness, as the source of personal identity. His idea of substance involves not only the element of *substare*, of serving as the substrate of qualities, but also that of *subsistere*, of incommunicable existence. This is shown by self-reflection: "I may believe myself a conscient, not a consciousness; nor a continuation of thought, but a continual thinker; nor a perceptivity, but a perceptive spirit. Even God himself we do not apprehend to be a collection of attributes, but the I AM to whom they belong. In all these expressions there is an additional idea over and above the attributes or qualities: and this I call substance." [101] Whether or not Coleridge saw in Tucker support for his own speculations it is impossible to say. The passage quoted is from a chapter on "Word, or Logos" (chap. 22), a subject of perennial interest to Coleridge. It may also be noted that his intended preface to Hazlitt's redaction was to contain "the whole substance of the first Volume of Hartley, entirely defecated from all the corpuscular hypotheses." [102] If Tucker's system was an improvement on Hartley, it must have been in a direction which better explained the affective and intellectual unity of the human composite.[103]

That this is the main current in Coleridge's untidy speculations at this time can be seen in another notebook entry which can hardly be

---

[100] *CL*, II, 949. Coleridge actually speaks of "Search's Light of Nature." Tucker published four volumes of his work under the name Edward Search in 1768; three posthumous volumes appeared in 1778. Incidentally, this is the same letter mentioned just above in which he says that he is reading Scotus Erigena, and in which he outlines for the first time his *Organum Verè Organum*.

[101] *The Light of Nature Pursued*, 2nd. ed., revised and corrected, 7 vols. (London, 1805), VII, 21.

[102] *CL*, II, 949.

[103] Bate points out that in Tucker can also be found a concept of the imagination as the intensive and instinctive use of the total unconscious mind, which effects a "coalescence" of sensations or ideas into a new whole. This was all within the general framework of association aesthetics, but it illustrates the fertility of the English sources of Coleridge's thought. *From Classic to Romantic*, pp. 115–116, 118–122.

surpassed for compression of ideas, wide-ranging recapitulation of several common Coleridgean themes, and audacious word play. It is too long to quote in its entirety. Dated January 1, 1806, it begins with two Greek phrases which Miss Coburn translates as "body soul-shaped" and "soul body-shaping." Then follows the familiar Coleridgean etymology of *res*, thing, from the second person singular of the present indicative of "an obsolete Latin word," *reor*, think, so that think (like tank, Coleridge suggests) is the "Reservoir of what has been *thinged*." If this is correct, he says, the whole of German idealism is summed up in the derivation. "If so, it is the Iliad of Spinozo-Kantian, Kanto-Fichtian, Fichto-Schellingian Revival of Plato-Plotino-Proclian Idealism in a Nutshell *from* a Lilliput Hazel." The symbol of this doctrine Coleridge finds in the theta, $\odot$, in which the *kentron* or central point creates the circumference and both together create the infinite radii. "The Central point is primary Consciousness = living Action; the circumference = secondary Consciousness ⟨or Consc.: in the common sense of the word⟩ and the passing to and from the one to the other Thought, Things, necessary Possibilities, contingent Realities." The whole process suggests the interactivity of Father, Son, and Holy Ghost — "the Το Ον, Ο Λογος, η Σοφια." The center of the theta is I "which is the articulated Breath drawn inward, the O is the same sent outward, the $\odot$ or Theta expresses the syntheses and coinstantaneous reciprocation of the two Acts, the Dualism of *Thought* by *Distinctions*, the Unity of *Thing* by Indivisibility." By this time, however, Coleridge himself has had enough. "O Lord! what thousands of Threads in how large a Web may not a Metaphysical Spider spin out of the Dirt of his own Guts/ but alas! it is a net for his own super-ingenious Spidership alone!" [104]

His despair at coming to a satisfactory resolution of the difficulties does not blur the fact, as Miss Coburn notes here, that he is moving in the direction of the unity of the self. To see how close he will come in just a few months we may look at a letter of October 1806. This is the same letter cited above to show the clearest expression of his doctrine on the relation of thought to thing. Here he identifies the perfection

[104] *N* 2784, and note.

appropriate to each being with its progression in growth of consciousness, which is not Lockean consciousness but the "incommunicable attribute of self-comprehension." But it is not a mere quantum of possibility to which we can mechanically arrive; we can only approach it
by the kind of approximation that the geometricians call asymptotic,
as the curve approaches ever closer to the line though it never meets it.
In other words, constant growth toward an ideal perfection is involved.
This incommunicable self-consciousness in its highest state is an image
of the way in which past, present, and future are "co-adunated in the
adorable I AM." [105]

This conception of the self is the culmination of the psychology and
epistemology that formed the principal matter of Coleridge's speculations in the years 1800–1806. It emerges again as the motivating idea
behind much of the Shakespearean criticism in the lectures of 1808
and 1811–1814, and, of course, is a substantial influence in the religious
and philosophical inquiries of the *Biographia* period.

MODES OF BEING

Incommunicable self-subsistence is the kind of being proper to the
individual person. As Coleridge achieves some success in working out
this solution to the problem presented by Locke's and Hartley's psychology, the question arises of the being proper to other kinds of existents, in particular the ontological status of various "made" things, including the inanimate creatures of God's handiwork, but more especially the products of human creativity. The metaphysical links between
Nature and man were a problem that confronted Coleridge in his
youth; the solution then was not carried beyond the position that
physical nature is, in Berkeleyan terms, the language of God. More recent speculations on word, thing, and idea, and on the contributions of
mind to forming knowledge, raised the problem in a more sophisticated
form, and the question now involves the more precise ontology of this
relationship, together with that of the forms of communication we
create as a result of it. From 1804 on we find these topics occurring more
and more frequently in Coleridge's speculations.

[105] *CL*, II, 1196–1197.

A convenient starting place is a notebook entry for November of that year which sets down a tentative relationship between several of these entities:

Hard to express that sense of the analogy or likeness of a Thing which enables a Symbol to represent it, so that we think of the Thing itself — and yet knowing that the Thing is not present to us. — Surely, on this universal fact of words and images depends by more or less mediations the *imitation* instead of *copy* which is illustrated in very nature *shakespearianized/* — that Proteus Essence that could assume the very form, but yet known and felt not to be the Thing by that difference of the Substance which made every atom of the Form another thing/ — that likeness not identity — an exact web, every line of direction miraculously the same, but the one worsted, the other silk.[106]

Though all the essential terms can be found here that Coleridge later used in explaining his full theory of symbol as noetic medium between mind and nature, they are mixed up with concepts and illustrations that involve him in ambiguous contradictions.

There is first of all the question of the ontological status of symbol. This seems to be the link between earlier theories of the "one life" in us and in things, and later speculations about the nature and function of art. The general mediating office of language is the transitional notion: "Language and all *symbols* give *outness* to Thoughts/ and this the philosophical essence and purpose of Language." [107] The question then arises as to the nature of the likeness between symbol and thing, by virtue of which it has its representative capacity. Equivocity of meaning, of course, would rule out any representative potential, but the distinction must be preserved also between analogical and univocal relationships. This seems to be the value of the imitation-copy distinction. We are not deceived into thinking that the symbol is the existing thing, as we may be by an identical copy. Rather a symbol is an imitation; it has the very form of the original but it has its own incommunicable substance which makes every "atom" of the same "form" collectively yet a different thing. But is this really what Coleridge means, and in

---

[106] *N* 2274.
[107] *N* 1387. "Outness" is Berkeley's term for the externality we attribute to the causes of sense impressions. See *N* 1297, note, and 1307.

what sense can a representation be said to have the very form of the original, yet not be a copy of it, in the commonly understood meaning of the word?

A certain imprecision in the use of "form" here must be clarified. Coleridge is speaking from within the context of a representational theory of art, indeed of one that is narrowly — almost literally — interpreted as involving "things" and their made likenesses. The question is asked how the two differ ontologically. If the difference were only the individuated substantial form of each (in the Aristotelian sense: that principle which informs the matter and makes the result the kind of thing it is), then symbol and referent would only be as different as two individuals of the same species. This is clearly not the representation that art involves, in spite of Coleridge saying that the original and its likeness differ by reason of the substance of each. Does he mean that it is the material in which the form is expressed that accounts for the difference — the clay or paint or language the artist employs? This seems likely from the remark that follows — "an exact web, every line of direction miraculously the same, but the one worsted, the other silk." If so, then it is clear that his interpretation of the representing that art effects is limited to a very literal reproducing of the form of the original in another medium or "substance." The difficulty with this conception of art, aside from its intrinsic poverty, is that it makes the imitation-copy distinction practically meaningless, for what else could something be that reproduces "every line of direction miraculously the same" except a copy?

Perhaps the matter becomes clearer if we return to the notion of form that Coleridge employs and note that he insists that the relationship between symbol and referent is analogical, that is, partly the same and partly different.[108] Entities related analogously cannot, therefore, as has been said, be of the same species or possess a similar form considered

---

[108] They are necessarily different in kind, Coleridge says in a note, but there is a point of resemblance which is really the same in both. "Seeing and Touching are analogous senses with respect to magnitude, figure, &c — they would to a certain extent (and do) supply each others place. The air-vessels of Fish and of Insects are analogous to Lungs — the end the same, however different the means . . . but between light green and dark green, between a mole and a Lynceus there is a *gradation*, no analogy." *N* 2319. See also *N* 2320, and below, note 112.

as substantial principle. The meaning of form that Coleridge intends here then must be the equivalent of something like the idea of the thing, a vision of it that the artist abstracts from the thing — taking "abstracts," in an epistemological and not a logical sense, as "the way in which he sees it." This can be called an intelligible form and it is possible, though hardly satisfactory, to conceive of it being materially expressed in different mediums. What Coleridge does not clearly indicate here is a notion of this intelligible form which would express its dependence on the way in which the artist knows, thereby avoiding the implications of a form-and-medium approach to the problems of art. Only this further insight makes sense of the imitation-copy distinction, which must be seen as a distinction of degree and not of kind. For even the most literal rendering of reality necessarily involves the expression of an intelligible form in another medium and so constitutes art, albeit in Coleridge's terms only a copy.[109] But the vision which is an abstraction according to the medium to be employed, which is a knowing according to the artist's special capacities, results in an imitation that is much more a fusion of idea and medium, far more clearly a special way of seeing and making combined in one. There are indications that Coleridge had reached at least some of these conclusions, however incomplete his general theory of aesthetic representation was at this time. For instance there is a note in which he answers objections to the artificiality of certain forms such as opera by showing that the same supposed difficulties can be raised against tragedy and comedy and that all of them "proceed on the false principle that Theatrical representations are *Copies* of nature whereas they are imitations." [110] His meaning seems to be that drama and opera are representations of nature according to a special way of looking at nature — for example, in terms of the physical movements, facial expressions, the spoken or sung words of the players — and are not mere copies of what happens in our experience. Yet we must add that even the most realistic reproduc-

---

[109] "For the painter may say to himself, 'This is not a representation of a mountain, it *is* "mountain" under the form of paint.'" David Jones, *Epoch and Artist: Selected Writings*, ed. Harman Grisewood (London: Faber and Faber, 1959), p. 170. Jones uses "form" here to mean what Coleridge calls "substance" in the passage under discussion, that is, the medium in which the making takes place.

[110] *N* 2211.

tion of actual experience, a perfect copy, is still not the real life of men; it is that life re-expressed on a stage and therefore the product of artistic making. This confusion of the difference between representation and reality with the difference between a literal and a more abstract representation shows how narrowly Coleridge understood the imitative theory at this stage in his development.

Like many of the phrases he borrowed from other writers and other traditions, the imitation-copy distinction was only a partially successful addition to his own vocabulary. It is an ancient distinction, probably descended from Aristotle's defense of the noetic value of poetry against the imputation that the artist's creations were but imperfect copies of real things. So in the *Poetics* we find the notion of the ideal nature of art; it is the result of the abstractive capacity of the mind to perceive essential natures and then to re-present them through language and poetic techniques. Poetry is thus found to be a vehicle of truth as much as history is. The more immediate source that is sometimes suggested for Coleridge's version of the distinction is Schelling's *Philosophische Schriften*, though its use here antedates the publication of that work in 1809.[111] But the general obscurity of Coleridge's application of the distinction makes it rather futile to inquire after its provenance and exact meaning. It seems to rest here mainly on the idea of likeness conjoined with difference, or of formally similar but existentially diverse natures.[112]

The weakness of this sort of theory of imitation is that it hardly goes beyond this simple description of the imitation compared to the thing imitated. It says nothing about the being proper to the symbol itself. As such, it is really a theory of poetic illusion that Coleridge is analyzing, involving the effect of the imitation on an audience, that is, the extent to which it is or is not deceived. This is clear from another example he uses to illustrate the difference between imitation and copy.

[111] See Miss Coburn's remarks, *N* 2211, note.

[112] From the 1811–1812 lectures: "The word imitation itself means always a combination of a certain degree of dissimilitude with a certain degree of similitude." *ShC*, II, 80. "The distinction between imitation and likeness depends upon the admixture of circumstances of dissimilarity; an imitation is not a copy, precisely as likeness is not sameness, in that sense of the word 'likeness' which implies difference conjoined with sameness." *ShC*, II, 160.

"If it were merely the same as looking at a glass reflection, we should receive no pleasure. A waxen image after once it had been seen pleased no longer, or very little, but when the resmblance of a thing was given upon canvas or a flat surface, then we were delighted." [113] Therefore, where there is likeness but not so much that we are deceived, we are delighted with the work of art. As a theory of imitation this is quite elementary, compared with the later concept of the work of art as symbolic medium between mind and external reality.[114]

A subsequent notebook entry confirms that at this time Coleridge had a very imperfect idea of the mode of being (or of coming to be) of a work of art. He is discussing generation. After raising the question whether "the inducement of a Form on a pre-existing material" is a true definition of generation, Coleridge makes the distinction between generation and fabrication. The former must be "the inducement of a Form on pre-existing materials in consequence of the transmission of a *Life*, according to the kind of the living Transmitter, this principle of Life so transmitted being both the principle of the induction of the Form, and of the adduction of the pre-existing materials —." The difference is that in generation the form is *ab intra* and is evolved; in fabrication the form is *ab extra* and is impressed. A fabrication represents something other than itself, "and the more disparate that something is, the more admirable is the Form, (as in Painting it is more admirable than in solid Wax — in Iron or Bronze rather than Wax/ ⟨supposing the forms to be⟩ forms of Flesh — etc)." This will be recognized as the same principle of likeness but with necessary difference that is employed in the example of the waxen image and the canvas, just above. Though Coleridge is saying here that statuary and painting — and, by implication, all kinds of art — are fabrications, with a form impressed *ab extra* (which is the very opposite of his later theory of form in art), this distinction is still an important step toward the idea of aesthetic organic form insofar as it establishes clearly the difference between the two kinds of form. Blood in a bottle and water in a bottle, to return to Coleridge's note, have the same form impressed *ab extra*, but the micro-

[113] *ShC*, II, 80.

[114] For more material on the theory of dramatic illusion, see below, the section in Chapter IV, "A Kind of Illusion."

scope can detect "organization," form that is "permanent and organic," only in the former. When he later comes to see that poetry too has an organic form, the distinction is already established in his mind.[115]

It seems to have been under Schlegel's tutelage that Coleridge first distinguished between organic and mechanical form in art.[116] He acknowledges his indebtedness in a fragmentary lecture note, where he says that the idea comes from the writings of "a continental critic":

The form is mechanic when on any given material we impress a predetermined form, not necessarily arising out of the properties of the material, as when to a mass of wet clay we give whatever shape we wish it to retain when hardened. The organic form, on the other hand, is innate; it shapes as it develops itself from within, and the fullness of its development is one and the same with the perfection of its outward form. Such is the life, such the form. Nature, the prime genial artist, inexhaustible in diverse powers, is equally inexhaustible in forms. Each exterior is the physiognomy of the being within, its true image reflected and thrown out from the concave mirror. And even such is the appropriate excellence of her chosen poet, of our own Shakespeare, himself a nature humanized, a genial understanding directing self-consciously a power and an implicit wisdom deeper than consciousness.[117]

Though at first glance these remarks have the kind of "metaphysical

---

[115] N 2444.

[116] Reference has already been made to an earlier usage of "organic" to mean "mechanical" or "physical." See CL, I, 625; II, 1032. The note above (N 2444) is the first instance of the term with the newer meaning. It seems to antedate Coleridge's acquaintance with August Wilhelm von Schlegel's Vorlesungen über dramatische Kunst und Litteratur, delivered in Vienna in 1808 and published 1809–1811, and which Coleridge first saw after the eighth lecture of his 1811–1812 series, according to his own account. Anna von Helmholtz-Phelan, The Indebtedness of Samuel Taylor Coleridge to August Wilhelm von Schlegel, Bulletin of the University of Wisconsin, no. 163, Philology and Literature series, vol. 3, no. 4, pp. 273–370 (Madison, 1907), p. 294. James Benziger suggests that the notion came to Coleridge from Schlegel who got it from a little-known work of Karl Philipp Moritz, Über die bildende Nachahmung des Schönen (1788), where it had been inspired by the pantheistic monism of Leibnitz. Benziger thinks that Coleridge found Schelling's Natur-Philosophie attractive at first because of its pantheism but abandoned it when he realized that instead of spiritualizing matter it actually reduced spirit to matter, and that in rejecting monism he rejected organic unity as well. It is clear that Benziger sees no possibility of an organic viewpoint that is not pantheistic. Coleridge's organicism, however, seems to have been founded eventually on a theory of ontological analogy and participation. James Benziger, "Organic Unity: Leibniz to Coleridge," PMLA, 66 (1951): 24–48, esp. 27–33.

[117] ShC, I, 224. Raysor assigns no date to this fragment.

pathos," to use Muirhead's phrase, that suggests a penetrating insight into one of the essential romantic principles, a closer examination of them shows a great deal of confusion in Coleridge's mind. In fact, without the concluding sentence, which is not Schlegel's,[118] the distinction expressed here would seem like nothing more than a rephrasing of the definitions of fabrication and generation, a reopposing of art to nature. Yet Shakespeare is offered as an exemplar of the organic mode of creation. The actual distinction, furthermore, is curiously irrelevant to its context, which is a discussion of Shakespeare's conscious genius as opposed to interpretations which stress his inspired irregularity. Coleridge's argument is that Shakespeare possessed a native wisdom and insight which he yet consciously directed in creating his plays. The notion of the organic seems to be little more than an adventitious borrowing which instead of illuminating the thought actually interrupts and confuses it.

It is true that this passage exists only in a manuscript fragment and Coleridge can hardly be blamed for its imperfect state. Fortunately there is another statement of the distinction, in the ninth of the 1811–1812 lectures, which seems to clarify his understanding of the terms:

> Before I go further, I may take the opportunity of explaining what is meant by mechanic and organic regularity. In the former the copy must appear as if it had come out of the same mould with the original; in the latter there is a law which all the parts obey, conforming themselves to the outward symbols and manifestations of the essential principle. If we look to the growth of trees, for instance, we shall observe that trees of the same kind vary considerably, according to the circumstances of soil, air, or position; yet we are able to decide at once whether they are oaks, elms, or poplars.[119]

Three points are to be noted about these definitions. First, organic form is perceived in the *individual* thing. The development of the oak is influenced by the circumstances in which it grows; its essence is known as identical with that of other oaks by abstraction but it is known first and primarily in the way in which it actually exists, that is, with its essence immersed in the individuality which it has by reason

[118] Raysor's note, *ShC*, I, 224.
[119] *ShC*, II, 170.

of all its particular determinations. Second, this special form is characterized by organization of parts with respect to the whole. In Coleridge's terms, the parts are "outward symbols and manifestations of the essential principle." They are parts by virtue of the principle which organized them. Third, the unity of the work of art is like this organic unity. True organic unity is predicated of living things only; art imitates this unity. Just how this is accomplished requires some explanation.

The principle can perhaps be stated thus: the work of art imitates the individuation of essence that is especially characteristic of living beings. The operations are analogous rather than identical, and for Coleridge the basis of the analogy seems to be the unity which living things possess by reason of the principle of their growth. The "essential principle" evolves itself into a whole, the distinguishable parts of which have existence only in terms of the whole, while the whole itself exists only through its parts — which indeed are parts only by reason of our selective attention to them.

An artist can give a form to his work in two ways. He can copy the mere details of casual appearance, so that the result is mechanical unity. The imposition of a form on wet clay, in Coleridge's first text above, suggests the physical and unreflective way in which this mechanical unity can be achieved. Unfortunately the example also implies that wet clay could not be shaped with an organic form. Coleridge, trying to define organic form and not really caring to discuss mechanical unity in detail, is the victim of a hastily chosen illustration. The second way open to the artist is to give an organic unity, to give to the work of art an existence like that of a living thing. This is a necessity which seems to follow from the way in which the artist knows — knows the thing, mood, or event he is concerned with, according to the shape and material which gives it expression. For the moment this is a step beyond Coleridge's theory. He does not appear here to have discovered the kind of knowing on which the production of art depends. The concept, however, is implicit in what he is saying about organic unity and emerges in his later aesthetic. Furthermore, his use of the term "law," to describe that principle which all parts of the organic whole obey, anticipates the subsequent clarification of the notions of law and idea.

The former is the principle of the unity among and within external things and is correlative to idea or intellectual insight into this unity. Compare, for example, the relationship between the "powers" of our nature and the "shapes" of matter in the following passage from *The Friend* of 1809: "We can be subdued by that alone which is analogous in Kind to that by which we subdue, namely, by the invisible powers of our Nature, whose immediate presence is disclosed to our inner sense, and only as the Symbols and Language of which all shapes and modifications of matter become formidable to us." [120] Since a knowledge relationship is implied here, it seems worth some space to offer a possible explanation of the kind of knowing that art involves.

We may begin with the concrete knowledge of moods, things, and events as they actually occur in our experience. From these it is possible to abstract a discursive knowledge, formed in universal terms and expressed serially in propositions which individually specify aspects of the experience and together can approximately characterize the whole experience (the *OED* gives among other meanings for discursive: "passing from premises to conclusions, . . . ratiocinative"). This cannot be the kind of knowledge that is the basis of artistic creativity; to think so is to fall immediately into the dualism of idea and expression, a snare which is difficult enough to avoid in any case. What the artist seems to do is to experience things (or situations or emotions) functionally, that is, in terms of a specific way of expressing them. His knowledge of the experience is from the very beginning a shaped knowledge, a knowing according to the possibilities of making. Perhaps it is more exact to say that there is not first an experience and then a knowledge of it, but rather that the experience constitutes the knowledge. But if the structure of the artist's knowledge be rooted in the way in which he experiences, how are we to explain the temporal and even conceptual distance between experience and the finished work of art? What are the criteria of the value of the various possibilities that are encountered along the often long road of making? Are we not, after

---

[120] *The Friend* (Penrith, 1809–1810), p. 103. Hereafter cited as *Friend* (1809). Compare this with Coleridge's most elaborate clarifications of his "true and original realism" in the sixth and seventh chapters below.

all, forced to posit an "idea" for which the artist chooses experimentally among various modes of "expression" the one best suited to it? Perhaps we can escape this dichotomy by another route. Temporally speaking, the primary determinant of the final work of art is the initial experience of the artist. But this might be only a germ of the later shape the vision will take. What governs its development? Certainly a major influence, as T. S. Eliot has told us, is all of the artist's past experience, which at a given moment takes a certain shape and effects in dialogue with the present experience a new understanding of what he is doing. Furthermore, there are also at work, for better or worse, a great many discursively developed principles — philosophical, social, religious — of the kind that influence all human behavior. The process by which these principles interact with past and present experience must be conceived of as happening an almost infinite number of times in each making of a work of art, as often as the slightest possible adjustment is recognized, contemplated, effected or rejected. But there is never a time when the artist is in possession of two distinct things which he can label the idea and the material which is to contain it.

Coleridge calls the result an organic unity, a made thing with a kind of being analogously like that of living things, an individual existent whose parts exhibit the unifying power of an idea, an insight, an "essential principle." It is the inadequacy of language and the necessity of dealing with this subject discursively that leads us inevitably to interpose a conceptual gap between the knowing and the completion of the making, whereas the very point that Coleridge is struggling to make here, especially if the present discussion is seen in the light of the passage cited above from *The Friend*, is that what we perceive is always a function of the way in which we perceive, and, we may add, that the latter is influenced by a great many determinants — heredity, environment, training, conscious or unconscious purpose, to name only a few. But in the making of the work of art the various elements we have distinguished are only conceptually separable aspects of one single knowing-according-to-making. At no stage is there anything in the idea which is not contained in the material details; no part of the matter has any meaning except in virtue of the idea. There is no clear operative distinction, therefore, between the two moments in the creative process, knowing and making. Dialectically they complement one another, though criticism and speculation are more or less permanently exposed to the danger of separating the two. We shall see that Coleridge's later theory was complicated by the slight attention it gave to the problem of making.[121]

This analysis of the distinction between mechanical and organic unity receives some support from an examination of the context in which the passage occurs in the ninth lecture of the 1811–1812 series. First of all, Coleridge is discussing in the preceding paragraphs the idealizing aspect of Shakespeare's art, with special reference to his characters. Shakespeare has the gift of insight into the nature of man and of presenting this insight in individual persons that persuade us of their truth: "Shakespeare has evinced the power . . . of introducing the profoundest sentiments of wisdom, where they would be least expected, yet where they are most truly natural. One admirable secret of his art is, that separate speeches frequently do not appear to have been occasioned by those which preceded, and which are consequent upon each other, but to have arisen out of the peculiar character of the speaker." [122] Then follows the distinction of the mechanical from the organic, and this is followed by a long discussion of *The Tempest* in which Coleridge explains the relationship of each of the characters to the structure of the whole work, the individual credibility of the persons, and the judgment of Shakespeare in employing them in particular actions to further the theme of the entire play.[123]

[121] It is probably futile to have attempted to improve on Abrams' masterly explication of the notion of organic form, in *The Mirror and the Lamp*, pp. 167–177. He remarks on Coleridge's difficulties in avoiding the consequences of his own deliberate and indeliberate mechanism, pp. 173–176. For two early statements on the concrete unity of the poem, though without the organic implications, see *N* 983 (1801): "Universale in Particulari speculatur — which is the philosophy of Poetry"; and also *Friend* (1809), p. 251: "Paradoxical as it may sound, one of the essential properties of Geometry is not less essential to dramatic excellence, and (if I may mention his name without pedantry to a Lady) Aristotle has accordingly required of the Poet an involution of the universal in the individual. The chief differences are, that in Geometry it is the universal truth which is uppermost in the consciousness, in Poetry the individual form in which it is cloathed."

[122] *ShC*, II, 170.

[123] This analysis of *The Tempest* for its organic unity is one of the main supports for the contention of M. M. Badawi that Coleridge's Shakespearean criticism is concerned

That the artistic powers of Shakespeare depend on his capacity to know the condition of men and that this knowledge is not the abstract knowledge of science is clear from the last sentences of the lengthy analysis of *The Tempest*: "If Shakespeare be the wonder of the ignorant, he is, and ought to be, much more the wonder of the learned: not only from profundity of thought, but from his astonishing and intuitive knowledge of what man must be at all times, and under all circumstances, he is rather to be looked upon as a prophet than as a poet. Yet, with all those unbounded powers, with all this might and majesty of genius, he makes us feel as if he were unconscious of himself, and of his high destiny, disguising the half god in the simplicity of a child." [124] Finally there is a notebook entry of 1805 recording a reverie which touches on these subjects and suggests a unifying theme: "Saturday Night, April 14, 1805 — In looking at objects of Nature while I am thinking, as at yonder moon dim-glimmering thro' the dewy window-pane, I seem rather to be seeking, as it were *asking*, a symbolical language for something within me that already and forever exists, than observing anything new. Even when that latter is the case, yet still I have always an obscure feeling as if that new phaenomenon were the dim Awaking of a forgotten or hidden Truth of my inner Nature/ It is still interesting as a Word, a Symbol! It is Λογος, the Creator! ⟨and the Evolver!⟩." [125] There is no need for comment on this passage here; it will concern us quite enough in what follows.

---

with the formal structure of the plays as well as with the more usually noticed character studies. He remarks that the essence of organic form in the plays is their unity of action, but this does not mean, as in Johnson, the external arrangement of events, but rather "homogeneity, proportionateness, and totality of interest," a Coleridgean quotation which in its original source is immediately followed by a passage distinguishing between "mechanical talent" and "inspired genius," in the second of which "each part supposes a preconception of the whole in *some* mind" and "are effected by a single energy, modified *ab intra* in each component part." Then *Romeo and Juliet* is examined for its unity of structure, much as *The Tempest* was in the 1811–1812 series. The Coleridge text is an undated set of notes on *Romeo and Juliet*, *ShC*, I, 4–6. Badawi's article is "Coleridge's Formal Criticism of Shakespeare's Plays," *Essays in Criticism*, 10 (1960): 148–162, esp. 149 and 159–161.

[124] *ShC*, II, 181.
[125] *N* 2546.

REASON AND UNDERSTANDING

Lastly, we must include among the germinal ideas which occur in Coleridge's writings at this time the distinction of reason from understanding, not because it is of great importance to his thought during the period we are discussing, but because he later made much use of it in the *Biographia* and in subsequent works. It is first mentioned in a letter of October 13, 1806, the same one already twice quoted, in which he is asked by a correspondent to answer the questions: "What metaphysically the Spirit of God *is?* What the Soul? What the difference between the Reason, and the Understanding (νοῦς καὶ ἐπιστήμη: Vernunft, und Verstand) and how metaphysically we may explain St. Paul's assertion, that the Spirit of God bears witness to the Spirit of man?" [126] When he comes finally to the reason and understanding, he replies that understanding is the faculty of the soul "which apprehends and retains the mere notices of Experience, as for instance that such an object has a triangular figure, that it is of such or such a magnitude, and of such and such a color, and consistency, with the anticipation of meeting the same under the same circumstances, in other words, all the mere φαινόμενα of our nature." To the reason pertain all such notices as are characterized by universality and necessity, "as that every Triangle *must* in all places and at all times have it's two sides greater than it's third — and which are evidently not the effect of any Experience, but the condition of all Experience, and that indeed without which Experience itself would be inconceivable." Coleridge notes that this class of knowledge was called by the Ancients Νοούμενα in distinction from the former, or φαινόμενα. Reason is therefore most eminently the Revelation of an immortal soul, and it's best Synonime — it is the forma formans, which contains in itself the law of its own conceptions. Nay, it is highly probable, that the contemplation of essential Form as remaining the same thro' all varieties of color and magnitude and development, as in the acorn even as in the Oak, first gave to the Mind the ideas, by which it explained to itself those notices of it's Immortality revealed to it by it's conscience. [127]

[126] *CL*, II, 1193.
[127] *CL*, II, 1198.

Other references to the distinction of these two faculties are few. In a letter of December 14, 1808, Coleridge discusses the inauguration of *The Friend*: "My first Essay will be on the Nature and the Importance of *Principles* — i.e. of the pure REASON, which dictates unconditionally, in distinction from the prudential understanding, which employing it's mole Eyes in an impossible calculation of Consequences perverts and mutilates its own Being, untenanting the function which it is incapable of occupying." [128] Pursuing the same theme two weeks later he writes again of principles:

Are we not a union of Reason, Understanding, and Sense (i.e. the Senses)? As necessary as *Perceptions* are to the Senses, so necessary are *Rules* to the Understanding; and as necessary as *Rules* to the Understanding, so necessary are *Principles* to the Reason. For our sensuous nature would give us only Instinct, our Understanding could only superadd Cunning, or Prudence — in REASON lies the possibility of Virtue. The habit of realizing, as far as we can, the practical *Ideas* of Reason by availing ourselves of the powers of the *Understanding* and the *Sense* is human Wisdom.[129]

Lastly, there is the discussion begun in number 7 of *The Friend*, September 28, 1809, "On the Principles of Political Philosophy," in which Coleridge, while mentioning how institutions are justified by their expediency, adds a footnote to explain the meaning of sense, understanding (described in the text as "the faculty of suiting Measures to Circumstances"), and reason, as he employs them here. Sense is the passive or recipient element of our being, whereby "we perceive and imagine all things under the forms of Space and Time." Understanding is "the faculty of thinking and forming *judgements* on the notices furnished by the Sense, according to certain rules existing in itself, which rules constitute its distinct nature." Reason is "the power by which we become possessed of Principle, (the eternal Verities of Plato and Descartes) and of Ideas, (N.B. not images) as the ideas of a point, a line, a circle, in Mathematics; and of Justice, Holiness, Free-Will, etc. in Morals." [130]

The distinction of reason from understanding has been the subject

[128] *CL*, III, 146.
[129] *CL*, III, 152–153.
[130] *Friend* (1809), p. 106.

of much useless speculation in Coleridge studies. Four points need to be made. First, the distinction is one of the most venerable in Western thought. Plato gave different functions to νοῦς and διάνοια, Thomas Aquinas to *intellectus* and *ratio*, and Coleridge could have found the contrast between the intuitive and discursive faculties, whatever names are given to them, in Milton, Bacon, and the Cambridge Platonists.[131] Second, there can be little doubt that the immediate source of Coleridge's formulas for the distinction was Kant. To deny the echoes would be silly: *Vernunft, Verstand*, φαινόμενα, νοούμενα, the unconditional principles dictated by reason, the forms of the understanding which yield maxims at best prudential. These confirm the obvious conclusion from the notebooks that Coleridge was reading Kant at this time. Third, it is equally clear, or at any rate it will become so when Coleridge begins to use the distinction in a meaningful way, that he employs it not in its Kantian sense but rather more according to the traditional significance it has had since Plato's time. Coleridge was never prepared to admit that the deliverances of the reason had subjective value alone, nor that the reason was bereft of all contact with an external reality. This was why he ultimately sided with Plato against Kant; though that conclusion is not part of our study the sources of it will be clear (if they are not already) as we examine the requirements for the highest kind of knowledge in Coleridge's philosophy. Finally, at the moment the specific reason-understanding distinction is of little importance to us. Its influence on Coleridge's thought before 1816 or so has been greatly exaggerated. In the few places where it is mentioned in the early years it performs no very striking function. It seems at this time to be somewhat of an unassimilated novelty.[132]

In the years between 1800 and 1808, then, Coleridge gave a shape to his philosophy that was distinctively personal and no longer merely a

---

[131] Muirhead, *Coleridge as Philosopher*, p. 65.

[132] Gordon McKenzie to the contrary: "It is a distinction with which he was greatly concerned in his philosophical thought; from its formulation he derived the distinction between imagination and fancy as stated in the *Biographia*." *Organic Unity in Coleridge*, University of California Publications in English, vol. VII, no. 1 (Berkeley, 1939), p. 8. The first half of this sentence would certainly be true of the last years of Coleridge's life. For the second half I do not know what proof could be given, in view of the very early statements of Coleridge's imagination-fancy distinction.

derivative of associationist theories. He began negatively with a criticism of the wholly mechanical epistemology of Locke and Hartley, but even this position was grounded on the positive assumption of the creative activity of the mind in the knowledge process. As his thought formed it became increasingly existential and experiential, so that much of it had the same obscure shape and unclear credibility that concrete and particular knowledge always has. Speculations about the subconscious, imagination, the effect of emotion on knowing, led frequently to further confusion as often as to clarification. But the two fundamental principles of the activity of the mind and the objectivity of experience remained constant, and gradually Coleridge's speculations began to take a unified direction. The notion of the organic form of a work of art, with its implications of an explicable bond between mind, reality, and artifact, is perhaps the most striking achievement of these years but Coleridge's theories here mirror the state of his whole philosophy at this time: they are immensely suggestive but not thoroughly worked out, he has made a good beginning but has not followed his best insights through to any unified conclusions. He has come a long way from his dependence on the crudities of associationism but he has not yet sorted out his own best ideas to find the one capable of inspiring a whole philosophy of knowledge and of being. He did not attempt that until he came to write the *Biographia Literaria*, and he did not succeed even then.

CHAPTER IV

The Nature of Poetry:

The Lectures of 1811–1814

He [the poet] must have the *ear* of a wild Arab listening in
the silent Desart, the eye of a North American Indian tracing
the footsteps of an Enemy Upon the Leaves that strew the
Forest — ; the *Touch* of a Blind Man feeling the face of a
darling Child.

Letter of July 13, 1802

The year 1808 marks the end of a period mainly devoted to rustic
speculation, then to travel and public life, and the beginning of the
years when Coleridge became active once again in literary affairs.
Aside from miscellaneous journalism the first event of his renewed
literary life was the lecture series of the winter and spring of 1808.
In the following year he undertook the publication of *The Friend*, and
this project occupied him through the spring of 1810. Then from the
fall of 1811 he was occupied regularly in courses of lectures through
April 1814.[1] The lectures exist in various forms, largely in reports
of diarists and journalists or in the notes of amanuenses. Even in
their fragmentary state they are extremely valuable insofar as they
constitute the most extensive record we have of Coleridge's literary
criticism. When we reflect on the danger of interpreting Coleridge out

---

[1] Coleridge delivered courses of lectures in 1808 at the Royal Institution, London;
1811–1812 at Flower de Luce Court, London; 1812 at Willis' Rooms, London; 1812–
1813 at the Surrey Institution, London; 1813 at Bristol and at Clifton; 1814 at Bristol;
1818 at Flower de Luce Court again, for the London Philosophical Society; 1818–1819
at the Crown and Anchor. All but the last, which was devoted to the history of philosophy, were generally concerned with literary topics.

of a single work or a scattering of familiar texts, it becomes clear how useful it is for the reconstruction of his thought to have available a body of critical and speculative comment which in bulk exceeds that of the *Biographia* and also bridges what would otherwise be a chasm between the metaphysical interests of the years 1800–1808 and the years of rather productive literary effort 1815–1818. The earlier lectures are valuable, moreover, not only because they complete our knowledge of Coleridge's literary speculations, but precisely because they show the early application of his philosophy to literary topics. In so many ways they are an illustration of the development his thought underwent between 1800 and 1808, and thus they offer guidelines for understanding positions later taken in the *Biographia*.

Since the several lecture courses generally included Shakespearean criticism and discussions of the nature of poetry as their principal topics, there is much repetition from series to series, and this makes it difficult to treat them in a purely chronological fashion. It will be easier to perceive the structure of Coleridge's literary theory if we abstract the main themes and present them in relation to his earlier speculations on knowledge and existence. The central problems in his philosophy at this time might be summarized as: the kind of being which various beings possess, the conditions and qualifications of our knowledge of beings, and the self which is the subject of this knowledge. Paralleling these problems are the general divisions of his literary theorizing in the lectures: the nature of poetry and the circumstances which affect its existence, the conditions of our use of poetry, and the function of the creator of the poem.[2]

THE POEM AS HISTORICAL FACT

A great many of the problems that eighteenth-century literary criticism had studied and attempted to solve — the unities of dramatic poetry, literary genres, the nature of poetic diction, the governing function of wit — resulted from one or another assumptions about the nature of poetry which were derived from fixed philosophical prin-

[2] To treat the lectures this way may seem unbalanced, but our interest is primarily in the poetic theory they contain, not in their criticism of Shakespeare.

ciples. A great part of the effort of neoclassical criticism was devoted to adjusting the assumptions and the canons which flowed from them to the demands of concrete situations. Coleridge, however, was among the first who saw that aesthetic form is largely determined by historical context, and that the best clue to the explanation of literary artifacts is often the study of the circumstances in which they were created.[3]

There are traces of the growth of this idea long before the lectures of 1811–1812. For instance, in a letter written before his Malta sojourn, Coleridge discusses some essays which he plans to work on shortly, and he gives the methodology of the one on Shakespeare as typical of all of them. His approach will be wholly inductive. "Each scene of each play I read, as if it were the whole of Shakespeare's Works — the sole thing extant. I ask myself what are the characteristics [diction, meter, character, passion, moral, and so forth] . . . and when I have gone thro' the whole, I then shall . . . know . . . what proportion they bear to each other." And so on to plays by other authors of the Shakespearean period.[4] A second instance anticipating more directly the historical argument may be seen in a manuscript fragment assigned by Raysor to the lectures of 1808. It is a brief history of the theater from Greek to medieval times which attempts somewhat sketchily to explain the origin of classical comedy in mimicry and burlesque, the morality introduced by Christianity, and the instructional function of medieval drama. Lurking in the background of the discussion is the notion that the form of the drama in each age depended on its function and the circumstances of its employment, but the idea never emerges explicitly; the closest Coleridge comes to this position is the explanation of tragi-comedy as a modern development proceeding from the

[3] There is some reason for doubting that the conception was wholly original with Coleridge. Raysor, who surveys the evidence in the preface to his edition of the Shakespearean criticism, concludes that Herder is probably the source of the historical argument in defense of Shakespeare. Coleridge may have known Herder's *Von Deutscher Art und Kunst*, or have come in contact with his theories at Göttingen, where he attended the lectures of Herder's friend Heyne. *ShC*, I, xxviii–xxix, xliv–xlvi. However, the analysis of historical circumstances for its influence on poetry was a thoroughly consistent extension of Coleridge's earlier epistemological theories, as well as a constituent of his subsequent speculations on method.

[4] *CL*, II, 1054.

twin necessity of gratifying while teaching a people less docile than the ancients.[5]

The first clear use by Coleridge of a historical point of view in a literary analysis is in the defense of Shakespeare's "judgment," with particular reference to the dispute over the unities. The general proposition of this argument is that Sophocles and Shakespeare were both correct in their attitudes toward the unities because of the special circumstances in which each worked. The strictest formulations of neoclassical criticism, particularly among the French, had insisted on the minute adherence to the one place, the limits of a single day, and the unified action. "They hold, of course after Corneille and Racine, that Sophocles is the most perfect model for tragedy, and Aristotle its most infallible censor." [6] The first two unities had been attacked in eighteenth-century English criticism, and Lord Kames had explained them as due to the presence of the chorus in classical drama. Coleridge uses the same argument, though there is no other evidence that he knew the work of Kames.[7] The physical circumstances of the ancient theater, he says, account for the form of the drama and the importance of the unities. After dialogue was added to the original choral song and the size of the theater required the introduction of music in order that hearing might be artificially assisted, it became necessary to harmonize these elements,

and as the chorus was always present, it enforced the preservation of the unities, for it would have been too great an extravagation from nature to have had the same men and characters on the stage when the scene was totally different. As the chorus was always on the stage, there was no dropping of curtains; the same men could not be at the same time at Thebes and at Rome. It therefore became necessary that the same scene should be presented to the eye, constituting the *unity of place*, and that the piece should be acted nearly within the time that the events could have occurred in. And, lastly, they had what is common to all dramas, a *unity of interest and action*.[8]

[5] *SHC*, I, 189–196; also I, 176. Another fragment, which Raysor assigns to the same lecture of 1808, gives a history of the origin of tragedy and comedy. I, 183–187.

[6] *ShC*, II, 70.

[7] *ShC*, I, xix–xx. Raysor suggests, however, a possible link through Lessing.

[8] *ShC*, II, 82. For a more extended treatment of the unities, see *ShC*, II, 263–265.

Shakespeare observes this essential requirement. "He is not to be tried by ancient and classic rules, but by the standard of his age. That law of unity which has its foundation, not in factitious necessity of custom, but in nature herself, is instinctively observed by Shakespeare." [9] Coleridge calls this a unity of feeling or, revealingly, unity of character.

Coleridge develops this historical line of argument and uses it to show how the special circumstances of the theater in Shakespeare's day influenced his writing. The audience Shakespeare wrote for was a generally learned one, as a result of the religious controversies of the age, and with a taste trained by constant attendance at the theater. But there were also unlettered people in the audience who had no taste and came only for amusement. It was the excellence of the English drama that it satisfied both classes. Furthermore, the physical simplicity of the Elizabethan theater encouraged the imaginative capacities of both poet and audience; the drama was more a delight and employment for the intellect than an amusement for the senses.[10] The notion that the power of pleasing both the learned and the ignorant was characteristic of English drama is bound up with the idea that in the evolution of the English stage the crudities and humor associated with the vice and devils of the moralities were transformed into the reflections of the fools and clowns of a more advanced period. Coleridge makes it the special gift of Shakespeare to employ these low characters from contemporary theater-pieces in his tragic scenes with a unity of effect. He instances *King Lear* and the contrast of the Fool which "wonderfully heightens the colouring of some of the most painful situations." [11] Later he says that this conjunction of the highest and lowest characters is a kind of reconciliation of opposites.[12]

Aside from the subject of dramatic action, the most interesting use of the historical argument is Coleridge's defense of Shakespeare against the charge of indecency and immorality. It rests on a distinction be-

---

[9] *ShC*, II, 265.

[10] *ShC*, II, 84–86.

[11] *ShC*, II, 73–74.

[12] *ShC*, II, 169–170. However, Coleridge thought so little of the porter scene in *Macbeth* that he was willing to believe it an interpolation. *ShC*, I, 75, 77.

tween manners and morals. "By manners I mean what is dependent on the particular customs and fashions of the age. Even in a state of comparative barbarism as to manners, there may be, and there is, morality." Offenses against decency in manners can certainly be pointed out in Shakespeare, but they exist for the sake of merriment. "What he says is always calculated to raise a gust of laughter, that would, as it were, blow away all impure ideas, if it did not excite abhorrence of them." [13] The high moral level of Shakespeare's plays is a constant in Coleridge's criticism. In the lectures of 1808 he thought the union of morality and passion distinctive of Shakespeare, and in 1813 he was still saying that Shakespeare never deserted the high road of life, that he caused no excitement of passion for a faulty purpose, that with him vice never walked in twilight, that he never inverted the order of nature and propriety, that nothing was purposely out of place.[14]

The great principle behind these applications of a historical point of view to the subject of literature is expressed clearly, though in compressed form, in the announcement of the lectures of 1812–1813, nearly our whole record of the series. Under the topics for Lecture V we read: "The *Spirit* of Poetry common to all ages, and to *imitate* the Antients wisely, we should do as they did; that is, embody the Spirit in Forms adapted to all the Circumstances of Time, State of Society, etc." [15] The appreciation of the influence of time and place on poetry is thus not only the business of the critic who would understand the conditions of the poetry of the past and the present, but it also contains a fundamental precept for the poet himself. This bears on the nature of imitation — that striving not for identical similarity but for likeness which is partly the same but partly different, the same insofar as it embodies the spirit or essence of poetry, different insofar as the embodiment is always in the terms and details of the present age.[16] What the "spirit" of poetry is we may now inquire.

[13] *ShC*, II, 125–126.

[14] *ShC*, II, 268.

[15] *ShC*, II, 247. Raysor suggests Schlegel's *Vorlesungen* as the source. Coleridge mentions in a letter of October 25, 1813, that he used to take Schlegel's lectures with him to the Surrey Institution, that is, during the course of 1812–1813. *CL*, III, 446.

[16] The historical argument for the circumstantial derivation of literary forms has analogies with the central doctrine of Coleridge's subsequent poetic: if literary forms and

THE DEFINITION OF POETRY

Coleridge apparently gave the first of many "definitions" of poetry in the initial lecture of the 1808 series. Almost exactly the same discussion is presented more coherently in the report of the second lecture of 1811–1812, the version which will be considered here.[17] It is introduced by a discourse on the need for precision in thought and expression, not for the sake of pedantry but for understanding. "Men ought to endeavour to distinguish subtilely, that they may be able afterwards to assimilate truly."[18] The question is raised: what is meant by poetry? Various negative answers are given, but the point Coleridge wishes to make is that exactness in words is necessary. Words can be used in two ways: "in a sense that comprises everything called by that name," but also in a philosophic sense, "which must include a definition of what is essential to a thing." Two definitions of poetry follow:

It is an art (or whatever better term our language may afford) of representing, in words, external nature and human thoughts and affections, both relatively to human affections, by the production of as much immediate pleasure in parts, as is compatible with the largest sum of pleasure in the whole.

Or, to vary the words, in order to make the abstract idea more intelligible: —

It is the art of communicating whatever we wish to communicate, so as both to express and produce excitement, but for the purpose of immediate pleasure; and each part is fitted to afford as much pleasure, as is compatible with the largest sum in the whole.[19]

The definitions apparently are of poetry in the "philosophic sense."

_____

genres, the very shapes of the meaning in literature, are influenced in their development by a collective history of mind and culture, why should not the form of particular poem depend upon the way in which the individual creator knows and imagines?

[17] On the basis of external and internal evidence too complicated to discuss in detail, Raysor assigns to 1808 two ms. fragments, the first of which he completes from _Literary Remains_. The restored text of the first fragment contains in a less organized way the substance of the discussion and definition of poetry that we have in Collier's report of Lecture II of 1811–1812. The similarities are so striking between Raysor's fragment and Collier's report that it is tempting to deny the 1808 date to the former. Raysor's evidence seems unassailable, however. _ShC_, I, 163–167, 253–256.

[18] _ShC_, II, 65.

[19] _ShC_, II, 66–67.

The explanation of the terms which follows is exceedingly interesting for what it reveals of Coleridge's method of arriving at the "essential" element in poetry and for the implications of this method for theory and criticism. The first thing to be noticed is that it adheres to the inductive mode of analysis which he had announced earlier would be his procedure in studying such a subject as the sources of poetic pleasure — "in which without using the words bad or good, I simply endeavor to detect the causes and sources of the Pleasures, which different Styles etc have given in different ages, and then determining their comparative Worth, Permanency, and Compatibility with the nobler parts of our nature to establish in the utmost depths, to which I can delve, the characteristics of Good and Bad Poetry." [20] Coleridge's analysis here in the second lecture is actually an empirical description of what a poem is, combined with a separation of it from what it is not. Thus, he begins his explanation with the simplest element, the minimal classical assumption: "It is a representation of nature." To distinguish poetry from the works of the anatomist and the topographer he adds: "And of the human thoughts and affections." But this is likewise the domain of the metaphysician, so he subjoins: "It must be relative to the human affections." To clarify the difference between poetry and the novel or the history, he says: "And it must be done for the purpose of immediate pleasure." Since many prose writers have the same purpose, "The work must be so constructed as to produce in each part that highest quantity of pleasure, or a high quantity of pleasure." This is the justification of meter, where it is called for, and the source of the passion or continuous state of excitement. Finally, the pleasure of each part must be such "as is compatible with the greatest sum of pleasure in the whole," since the goal of the artist is to produce a total effect.[21]

Coleridge's analysis is not a priori, except insofar as it begins with what is undeniably an assumption, that the poem is a representation. Within the framework of this premise, which had been the starting point of most poetic theory since Plato and Aristotle — and whose

[20] *CL*, II, 1054.
[21] *ShC*, II, 67–68.

limitations Coleridge would later struggle to escape — he now proceeds to specify the restrictions, one by one, which empirical consideration of poems suggests as necessary. The "essential" element which he
arrives at and embodies in his definition responds only to the facts as
Coleridge observed them, and not to any prior philosophical position,
except in the general sense, which Coleridge himself would certainly
have insisted upon, that philosophical principles themselves influence
the arrangement of data. Notice also that the second definition quali-
fies even the primary assumption contained in the first: the representation must express and produce the excitement. Thus the being of the
poem is not merely heuristic, with a function of pointing to another
order of reality, or of indicating a conception of that reality which
exists in the writer's mind. It is rather itself poietic, in the etymological
sense that it is not just the result of a process of ποίησις, of making,
but that it also by its own proper power makes or produces the effect
intended by the artist.[22] This fundamental insight into the nature of
the poem becomes the basis for Coleridge's full theory of symbol.

Coleridge supplements these definitions by further observations. In
the next lecture he points out that poetry is not the antithesis of prose,
but rather that the opposite of poetry is science, and the opposite of
prose meter. "The immediate object of science was the communication
and acquirement of truth; the immediate object of poetry is the communication of pleasure." [23] So, though the most important moral truths
might be conveyed in poetry, its immediate object is pleasure. Yet what
distinguishes poetry from "animated Prose" which may convey all

[22] "The power of poetry is by a single word perhaps, to instil that energy into the
mind, which compels the imagination to produce the picture. Prospero tells Miranda,

> 'One midnight,
> Fated to the purpose, did Antonio open
> The gates of Milan; and i' the dead of darkness
> The ministers for the purpose hurried thence
> Me, and thy crying self.'

Here, by introducing a single happy epithet, 'crying,' in the last line, a complete picture is presented to the mind, and in the production of such pictures the power of genius
consists." ShC, II, 174.

[23] ShC, II, 75. Raysor points out that these distinctions are in Wordsworth's preface
to the Lyrical Ballads (1801), and that the probable source of both is an article by "En-
quirer" in the Monthly Magazine, 2 (1796): 453f, esp. p. 456, where verse is opposed to
prose and poetry to philosophy. ShC, I, 163, note.

the beauty and passion of natural and human life? The something extra: "It is that pleasurable emotion, that peculiar state and degree of excitement that arises in the poet himself in the act of composition." This is in consequence of his "more than ordinary sensibility, occasioning a more than ordinary sympathy with the objects of nature or the incidents of human life." And this is "united with a more than ordinary activity of the mind in general, but more particularly of those faculties of the mind we class under the names of fancy and imagination — faculties (I know not how I shall make myself intelligible) that are rather spontaneous than voluntary. They excite great activity, but such as is greatly beyond all proportion to the effects occasioned by them." [24]

This is summed up in another definition: "Poetry is a species of composition opposed to science as having intellectual pleasure for its object and not truth — and attaining that end by the language natural to all persons in a state of excitement." The final criterion must be a proportion between part and whole: "Is there more pleasure in the particular lines than is consistent with the whole? Is the sense of totality injured, or not injured, by the splendour of particular passages? For the great object of the poet must be to produce the great total effect." [25]

At the risk of repetitiveness, yet another version of the definition must be given, from the fourth lecture of 1811–1812. Tomalin, Coleridge's stenographer for some of these lectures, calls it a correction of the previous definition, and it does gather together several earlier comments, but in some respects it is inferior to the very first pair of definitions as an expression of the ontological status of poetry, stressing as it does more the knowledge-pleasure ratio:

It is that species of composition which, being together with some others opposed to science, as having for its immediate object the communication of pleasure, not of truth, is yet distinguished from all others by proposing to itself such a delight from the whole as is compatible with the distinct gratification from each component part, and thence enables us to place the perfection of a poem in the power of communicating the greatest degree of

[24] *ShC*, II, 77.
[25] *ShC*, II, 78–79.

pleasurable excitement from each part as is consistent with the largest possible portion of pleasurable excitement from the whole.[26]

Milton, says Coleridge, has summarized all of what he has been trying
to say by precise definition in three words: Poetry should be simple,
sensuous, passionate.[27] In the version of this comment which Raysor
assigns to 1808, simplicity connotes the absence of affectation and pecu-
liarity, the lack of effort required on the reader's part as opposed to
the arduousness of science; sensuousness is the "framework of objectivity, that definiteness and articulation of imagery, and that modification of the images themselves, without which poetry becomes flattened
into mere didactics of practice or evaporated into a hazy, unthoughtful,
day-dreaming"; and passion "provides that neither thought nor imagery shall be simply objective, but that the *passio vera* of humanity
shall warm and animate both." [28] In a later employment of this Mil-
tonic reference, the three terms are defined slightly differently: "*simple*,
that it may appeal to the elements and the primary laws of our nature;
sensuous, since it is only by sensuous images that we can elicit truth
as at a flash; *impassionate*, since images must be vivid, in order to
move our passions and awaken our affections." [29] Doubtless the intent
of these definitions is the same; still the inconcinnities show that Coleridge was perhaps at times inclined to use "plus" words in order to
suggest approbation without specifying very exactly what quality he
was approving.

At first glance the same tendency may seem to be at work in the
most elaborate description Coleridge gives of poetry, or rather of
"poetic genius" on which the adequate definition of poetry "in its
highest and most peculiar sense" must ultimately rest. Poetic genius
is that

which sustains and modifies the emotions, thoughts, and vivid representations of the poem by the energy without effort of the poet's own mind, —

[26] *ShC*, II, 98.
[27] As Raysor notes, the original use of these terms, in the essay "On Education," was
to distinguish poetry from rhetoric. It is "more simple, sensuous, and passionate" than
rhetoric. *ShC*, I, 165.
[28] *ShC*, I, 165–166.
[29] *ShC*, II, 260. Lecture I, 1813–1814.

by the spontaneous activity of his imagination and fancy, and by whatever else with these reveals itself in the balancing and reconciling of opposite or discordant qualities, sameness with difference, a sense of novelty and freshness with old or customary objects, a more than usual state of emotion with more than usual order, self-possession and judgment with enthusiasm and vehement feeling, — and which, while it blends and harmonizes the natural and the artificial, still subordinates art to nature, the manner to the matter, and our admiration of the poet to our sympathy with the images, passions, characters, and incidents of the poem.

This is followed by lines from Sir John Davies' *Nosce Teipsum* which apply to poetic genius the processes by which the spiritual soul turns bodies to spirit, as fire converts combustibles into flame and as we transmute food into our nature. So poetry abstracts from "individual states

> the universal kinds;
> Which then reclothed in diverse names and fates
> Steal access thro' our senses to our minds." [30]

Can distinguishable meanings be attached to the expressions in this extraordinary description of poetic genius, or is it merely a collection of all the favorable epithets in Coleridge's philosophical lexicon? Allowing for the rhetorical temptations of the lecture platform, it seems possible to discern here some of the basic principles in Coleridgean literary theory: the subjective activity of the poetic imagination, the objective function of poetic representation, the fusion of thought and emotion, the "disjunction conjunctive" of like but unlike qualities by the imaginative power, the old spirit in the forms of novelty and freshness, the intense emotion and yet greater precision of form, the final criterion of which is nature, substance, and the truth of the poem itself — the whole compared to the knowledge process by the fire-food metaphor of substantial change. That Coleridge's words here have more than vague meaning is confirmed by the close resemblance of this passage to a more famous one in the *Biographia Literaria* describing the ideal poet. The greater clarity and precision of expression of the latter text in explicating the function of imagination suggests that the ideas of

[30] *ShC*, I, 166–167.

the earlier version were important enough to Coleridge to retain and perfect as part of the formal exposition of his literary theory.[31]

Coleridge often spoke loosely, but these definitions of poetry do not seem to be examples of his carelessness. Their variations proceed from the circumstances of their use in different lectures, and from the diverse emphases Coleridge had in mind in individually formulating them. They represent the essence of poetry, what it is in itself, as Coleridge announced before he made the first of them. Within the context of the external, accidental, and historical circumstances already discussed, they form a coherent enough description of the complex entity that Coleridge conceived poetry to be.

A KIND OF ILLUSION

One natural consequence of asserting the historical origin of poetic form and the imitative quality of true poetry is the problem of the relationship between reader and poem, and of the conditions that govern the experiencing of the poem. There is no doubt that the audience of the poet is active in Coleridge's theory; this would follow if only as an extension of his general epistemology. In the fourth lecture of the 1811–1812 series this receptive creativity occurs in a discussion of the unified image and moral feeling that characterizes the poetic experi-

---

[31] The last lines of Davies' original version described the results of the abstractive knowledge process as:

"the universal kinds,
Which bodyless and immaterial are,
And can be only lodged within our minds."

See *BL*, II, 268. Coleridge's adaptation of the lines for the Shakespearean lectures illustrates both the objective and subjective elements in his theory, the form-discerning and form-giving operations of the poetic genius or, as he later called it when he repeated nearly the same passage in the *Biographia*, the imagination. And, incidentally, the image involved in the "reclothed" universals indicates as well as any example can the difficulties of avoiding the language of a dualistic, idea-and-expression theory of poetry.

Coleridge's second use of this passage is in *BL*, II, 12–13. It is discussed below in treating his critique of Wordsworth. The closeness between the two makes it difficult to see how the earlier one could have been written in 1808, as Raysor says, especially since a similar passage from the 1811–1812 series (*ShC*, II, 98) is so undeveloped, though this may be due to the compression of the Tomalin reports in general. Still, Raysor himself says of this latter passage that it is "developed and expanded" in the version of I, 166. It is difficult to see how this can be a development of something written three years later.

ence. The example is Shakespeare's Sonnet XXXIII, "Full many a glorious morning have I seen." "You behold," says Coleridge, "the sun the sovereign of the world, the elation of the high mountain flattered by a glance of his beams, and the activity of the poet's mind, which, in one image, has merged so many associations. You feel him to be a poet, inasmuch as, for a time, he has made you one — *an active creative being.*" [32]

This activity of the reader's mind, however, is still subject to the conditions which affect the poem as representation or expression. It is to this central problem that the discussion of the unities and especially that of imitation led Coleridge. In the period with which we are dealing his answers are somewhat tentative; moreover they are often confused, as we have seen, with the implications of the imitation-copy distinction and of the notion of the organic unity of a work of art. The theory of dramatic illusion that he later developed is hinted at in the lectures before 1815, but for the most part his reflections on the problem center around the notion of the ideal nature of poetry, and the observable fact that we voluntarily accept the illusion involved. For example, in the second lecture of the 1811–1812 course Coleridge takes up some of the conditions of stage illusion. By way of showing that even the Greeks did not observe the unities, Coleridge observes that their plays often included events which could not have taken place in so short a space of time. "This fact alone establishes, that all dramatic performances were then looked upon merely as ideal. It is the same with us: nobody supposes that a tragedian suffers real pain when he is stabbed or tortured; or that a comedian is in fact transported with delight when successful in pretended love." He then gives the argument, close to Schiller's, that if we want pain we can visit hospitals, and pleasure we can find in ballrooms: "It is the representation of it, not the reality, that we require, the imitation, and not the thing itself; and we pronounce it good or bad in proportion as the representation is an incorrect, or a correct imitation. The true pleasure we derive from theatrical performances arises from the fact that they are unreal and fictitious. If dying agonies were unfeigned, who, in these days of

[32] *ShC*, II, 93–94. Italics added.

civilisation, could derive gratification from beholding them?"[33] Coleridge persuades us well enough that we do not confuse poetic representation with reality, but he does not successfully pass beyond the
negative argument. He has not, it seems, fully assimilated his own
earlier observations on the analogical being of the symbol and the function of imagination.

A similar hesitancy can be seen in the treatment of the same topic
in the third lecture of the series. To suppose the unities of time and
place essential to the drama is "to suppose as evident a falsehood as
that the drama impresses with pleasure only as it is supposed to be
reality. The truth is, it is never believed to be real." The extreme form
of delusion, he says, is when we do not think about a thing's being
real or false but are affected only by the vividness of the impression.
The difference between reality and falsehood admits of many degrees
which do not involve delusion. On one end of the scale is "domestic
tragedy, which is too real to be compatible with pleasure." Shakespeare
represents the due medium and gratifies our senses from the imitation
of reality. At the other extreme from reality, but still no delusion, is
"the mere dance at an opera, which is yet capable of giving us the
highest pleasure, and which, with music and harmonious motions of
the body, can, by thus explaining some tale, deeply affect and delight
an audience."[34] Here Coleridge is dealing with examples which might
have led him to a full theory of mimetic art, particularly if he should
explain positively how the dance can be considered a representational
form.

A passage in which Coleridge anticipates an essential element of
his theory of illusion, the voluntary assistance given by the poet's
audience, occurs in the ninth lecture of this same series. He is speaking
of *The Tempest* and of how Shakespeare prepares the mind for the
introduction of such a fanciful and preternatural creature as Ariel.
The character tests the audience's willingness to cooperate in the
illusion, and the response is greater than to a real being because of the
anticipations by the poet. "Here, what is called poetic faith is required

[33] *ShC*, II, 72–73.
[34] *ShC*, II, 83–84.

and created, and our common notions of philosophy give way before it: this feeling may be said to be much stronger than historic faith, since for the exercise of poetic faith the mind is previously prepared." He promises to explain the distinction farther, but the promise is unfulfilled.[35]

The idealizing function of poetry leads to another aspect of the conditions under which poetry expresses being — the notion of the poem as prophecy. This is connected with the necessary disparity in art between experience and expression. Insofar as poetry is the formulation of our aspirations much of its pleasure is derived from the combination of mean object with ideal significance: "We take the purest parts and combine them with our own minds, with our own hopes, with our own inward yearnings after perfection, and, being frail and imperfect, we wish to have a shadow, a sort of prophetic existence present to us, which tells us what we are not, but yet, blending in us much that we are, promises great things of what we may be. It is the truth (and poetry results from that instinct — the effort of perfecting ourselves), the conceiving that which is imperfect to be perfect and blending the nobler mind with the meaner object." Thus Shakespeare, he says, who is often called a child of nature, is more accurately called a child of human nature and of the most important of human nature; his Protean ability enabled him to present not merely the resemblance of a character but the divinity that appeared in it.[36] This capacity for prophecy is not so much concerned with time as with insight. "While the poet registers what is past, he projects the future in a wonderful degree, and makes us feel, however slightly, and see, however dimly, that state of being in which there is neither past nor future, but all is permanent in the very energy of nature."[37] Shakespeare is of course the exemplar of this quality: "not only from profundity of thought, but from his astonishing and intuitive knowledge of what man must be at all times, and under all circumstances, he is rather to be looked upon as a prophet than as a poet."[38]

[35] ShC, II, 175.
[36] ShC, II, 80–81.
[37] ShC, II, 168.
[38] ShC, II, 181.

Two passages may be cited which show Coleridge penetrating somewhat deeper into the notion of illusion in art than he does in any of the remarks about imitation or about the ideal nature of poetry. The first is interesting because it associates the creative inspiration of poetry with the state of dreaming. It is a notebook entry of May 1804: "Poetry a rationalized dream dealing [?about] to manifold Forms our own Feelings, that never perhaps were attached by us consciously to our own personal Selves. — What is the Lear, the Othello, but a Divine Dream/ all Shakespeare, and nothing Shakespeare. — O there are Truths below the Surface in the subject of Sympathy, and how we *become* that which we understandably behold and hear, having, how much God perhaps only knows, created part even of the Form. — [?and so] good night — ." [39]

The emphasis here is on the creative side of the poetic process. For the correlative effect in the poet's audience, which becomes a basic theme in the explanation of poetic illusion in the *Biographia* and later, we have in the lectures before 1818 only one passage, which uses the ideas but imperfectly. Moreover, it is a manuscript fragment of uncertain date, though obviously between 1805 (the watermark) and 1814 (after which the analysis would be rather outmoded by the *Biographia* treatment). [40] The chief merit of the passage is twofold. First, it specifies that we willingly cooperate in the illusion (which is that of theater, the only context in which Coleridge discusses illusion until the *Biographia*). "These and all other stage presentations are to produce a sort of temporary half-faith, which the spectator encourages in himself and supports by a voluntary contribution on his own part, because he knows that it is at all times in his power to see the thing as it really is." Coleridge adds that it is a "suspension of the act of comparison, which permits this sort of negative belief." [41] Second, the discussion in this fragment juxtaposes the illusion of the stage and that credence we give to the reality of the objects in our dreams. The actual discussion is disappointing because Coleridge simply states that it is a mistaken opin-

[39] *N* 2086. Miss Coburn's square brackets indicate uncertain readings.
[40] Raysor discusses some reasons for an early date, but they are by no means compelling. *ShC*, I, 201.
[41] *ShC*, I, 200, 201–202.

ion that "in our *ordinary* dreams we judge the objects to be real." As
to nightmares, however, this opinion is considerably more just.[42] But
no comparison is made between the illusion of ordinary dreaming and
that of theatrical representation, and we are left to conjecture what
Coleridge's intention was in instituting the comparison. There is no
need to pursue the topic here, as it is taken up in far greater detail in
the Wordsworth criticism of the *Biographia*.

THE POET AS KNOWER

It has been suggested that the principal emphases of Coleridge's literary theory in the lectures we are discussing are correlative to the development of his philosophical speculations in the period 1800–1808.
Thus the elaboration of a theory of being can be considered similar to
the analysis of the historical and ontological conditions in which the
poem exists, and the knowledge theory suggests a relationship with the
epistemology of reader and poem. We may now consider a parallel to
the earlier theory of the self, in the discussion of the poet as the center
of the creative process.

Coleridge's main concern here is with the special capacity for insight,
the peculiar way of knowing and especially of knowing feelings,
which the poet seems to possess. This has been noted already in the
discussion of imitation where, at this stage of the development of the
concept, it is really knowledge of life and nature that Coleridge is
concerned with. It was also the basis of the analysis of the prophetic
function of the poet, again dependent on insight, and of the description
of the poet as being of more than ordinary sensibility, the result of
which is a more than ordinary sympathy with nature and human incidents. Only in passing and rather tentatively does Coleridge at this
time say anything about making as a function of the poet; the emphasis is generally on knowing.

What mostly concerns Coleridge in these reflections on the specific
power in the poet is a sympathy with human situations, or an empathy
(to preserve the contemporary distinction, though Coleridge does not

[42] *ShC*, I, 202.

use the term as yet) with natural objects, that borders on what we know more familiarly in Keats's term as "negative capability." [43] The idea is one that Coleridge may have become aware of from his own experience, or it may be related to the same sources as his early reflections on imagination. In any case there is a remarkable description of such a power in an early letter to Sotheby of July 13, 1802; it deserves to be quoted in full as it implies a great deal about the source of much of the later Shakespearean criticism and much about the union of philosophy and poetry in Coleridge's thought:

It is easy to cloathe Imaginary Beings with our own Thoughts and Feelings; but to send ourselves out of ourselves, to *think* ourselves into the Thoughts and Feelings of Beings in circumstances wholly and strangely different from our own/ hoc labor, hoc opus/ and who has atchieved it? Perhaps only Shakespeare. Metaphisics is a word, that you, my dear Sir! are no great Friend to/ but yet you will agree, that a great Poet must be, implicite if not explicite, a profound Metaphysician. He may not have it in logical coherence, in his Brain and Tongue; but he must have it by *Tact*/ for all sounds, and forms of human nature he must have the *ear* of a wild Arab listening in the silent Desart, the eye of a North American Indian tracing the footsteps of an Enemy upon the Leaves that strew the Forest — ; the *Touch* of a Blind Man feeling the face of a darling Child.[44]

This last sentence is, I think, possibly the most astute and persuasive observation on the kind of knowing proper to the artist that can be found in all of Coleridge's writings. The tactile mode of sense knowledge is proposed as a metaphor for the operation of poetic intuition and illustrated by three images which convey three elements requisite to this insight: the exquisite attention that must be given to the exact conditions of the experience, as the Arab centers his whole being on the expectancy of a distant sound in the stillness; the value that is to be placed on the slightest particle of significance, as the Indian searches for the least sign of his enemy's presence; and the total subordination

[43] Keats used Coleridge to exemplify the opposite of Shakespeare in regard to the possession of "negative capability." Barbara Hardy shows that their ideas at least were similar as to the nature of the observation and meditation of things which is proper to the poet. "Keats, Coleridge and Negative Capability," *Notes and Queries*, July 5, 1952, pp. 299–301.

[44] *CL*, II, 810.

to the limitations and the possibilities of the mode of knowing, as the blind man exhausts the power of touch in his desire to know and yet knows only according to touch. The result is a kind of knowing which calls art into existence in order to embody it. Nowhere else has Coleridge expressed so deftly the autonomous nature of poetic knowledge and its relationship to the existing world as well as to the abstracting mind. Coleridge afterwards devoted a great deal of effort to specifying the details of this intuition and its poetic incarnation but he hardly improved on the clarity of these stunning images to express both the essentially noetic function of poetry and the existential conditions and limitations of that function.

More common, in these Shakespearean lectures, are explanations of particular aspects of this poetic knowing. For instance, Coleridge speaks several times of the artist's sympathy with external things as resulting from meditation on the details of character and event. "Shakespeare has this advantage over all other dramatists — that he has availed himself of his psychological genius to develop all the minutiae of the human heart: shewing us the thing that, to common observers, he seems solely intent upon, he makes visible what we should not otherwise have seen: just as, after looking at distant objects through a telescope, when we behold them subsequently with the naked eye, we see them with greater distinctness, and in more detail, than we should otherwise have done." [45] This results not merely from observation on Shakespeare's part, especially not from that kind of observation which consists of gathering examples to confirm a previous theory, but rather it is as though he is "representing what he has observed, himself frequently unconscious of its worth, or its bearings," except of course that Shakespeare's judgment in the use of his details is unquestionable. It is plain, says Coleridge, that his characters were drawn "rather from meditation than from observation, or to speak correctly, more from observation, the child of meditation." [46] The Nurse is an example of Shakespeare's meditation-observation in the creation of characters. Every quality conceivable of such a person can be found in her — the

[45] ShC, II, 131–132.
[46] ShC, II, 132.

arrogance of ignorance, grossness, the garrulity and affection of old age, and in particular the way her memory works, by a collection of visual and temporal connections rather than by the cause-and-effect associations of a more philosophical person. "More is here brought into one portrait than could have been ascertained by one man's mere observation, and without the introduction of a single incongruous point." [47] This meditation shows itself too in the speech exactly appropriate to each character. He quotes Othello's lines on his honor from the second scene of the play: "I ask where was Shakespeare to observe such language as this? If he did observe it, it was with the inward eye of meditation upon his own nature: for the time, he became Othello, and spoke as Othello, in such circumstances, must have spoken." [48]

Sometimes the outward-going and objective nature of this capacity to observe is apparently confused with the inward-turning and subjective nature of meditation. "Shakespeare's characters, from Othello and Macbeth down to Dogberry and the Grave-digger, may be termed ideal realities. They are not the things themselves, so much as abstracts of the things, which a great mind takes into itself, and there naturalises them to its own conception." [49] Of course the answer is that both processes are correlative and interdependent. Once again, Coleridge seems to be touching on but not fully clarifying a theory of imagination as the agent of the coalescence of object and subject, and of the analogical nature of being as the metaphysical foundation of that activity.

Another way in which Coleridge specifies the capacity of the poet to perceive and record can be seen in his answer to the objection raised by many voices in earlier Shakespearean criticism, those who because they could not explain Shakespeare by their rules and would not censure his obvious abilities attributed his achievement to his irregular genius, saying, in Coleridge's words, "that he is now and then tasteful and touching, but generally incorrect; and, in short, that he was a mere child of nature, who did not know any better than to write as he had written." [50] Coleridge in his answer takes advantage of all the

[47] *ShC*, II, 135.
[48] *ShC*, II, 136.
[49] *ShC*, II, 162.
[50] *ShC*, II, 70.

qualifications which history might offer — "the condition of the stage, and the character of the times in which our great poet flourished, must first of all be taken into account, in considering the question as to his judgment" — but in the end he firmly asserts Shakespeare's intelligent art: "If it were possible to say which of his great powers and qualifications is more admirable than the rest, it unquestionably appears to me that his judgment is the most wonderful; and at this conviction I have arrived after a careful comparison of his productions with those of his best and greatest contemporaries." [51]

This is in many ways the central proposition of all of the Shakespearean lectures. The historical analysis of the conditions of the stage and of dramatic form in ancient and modern times is propaedeutic to the explanation of Shakespeare's art in terms of both genius and judgment. After the early espousal of the union of thought and feeling, and the development of the imagination as the faculty of this unity, it cannot be surprising that Coleridge would defend Shakespeare by exactly the same principles that he had used to analyze poetry. Thus all the character analyses, which reveal in the poet a combination of abstractive thought and sympathetic feeling; the definitions of poetry, which suppose that the end is pleasure as well as instruction; the descriptions of meditation joined with observation; and the account of the ideal and prophetic character of poetry — all tend toward a defense of Shakespeare as both philosopher and artist, indeed inseparably the two: "Conceive a profound metaphysician and a great poet, intensely occupied in thinking on all subjects, on the least as well as the greatest — on all the operations of nature and of man, and feeling the importance of all the subjects presented to him — conceive this philosophical part of his character combined with the poetic, the twofold energy constantly acting; the poet and the philosopher embracing, but, as it were, in a warm embrace, when if both had not been equal, one or the other must have been strangled. With this rule the reader might go through what was really Shakespeare's, and dis-

[51] *ShC*, II, 71. Raysor notes that this emphasis on Shakespeare's judgment, first expressed in Lecture II of 1811–1812, predates Coleridge's acquaintance with Schlegel. The argument is not new in English criticism, but Coleridge goes further than any of his predecessors. *ShC*, II, 71, note; see also Raysor's introduction.

tinguish him from every man that ever lived." [52] Clearly there is no opposition in Coleridge's mind at this point between the claims of metaphysics and of poetry.

Finally, the discussion of the poet may be concluded with a clutch of Coleridgean observations on some characteristics of the essential poet. The extent to which the poetic gift is natural and not artificial is mentioned in the fourth of the 1811–1812 lectures: "That gift of true Imagination, that capability of reducing a multitude into unity of effect, or by strong passion to modify a series of thoughts into one predominant thought or feeling — those were faculties which might be cultivated and improved, but could not be acquired. Only such a man as possessed them deserved the title of *poeta* who *nascitur non fit* — he was a child of Nature, and not the creature of his own efforts." [53] This is of course a variation on the imagination-fancy distinction, the genius-talent distinction, or the generation-fabrication distinction, the common note of all three being spontaneity *ab intra*. This is also the point of a later passage from the first of the 1813–1814 lectures: "One character attaches to all true poets: they write from a principle within, independent of everything without. The work of a true poet, in its form, its shapings and modifications, is distinguished from all other works that assume to belong to the class of poetry, as a natural from an artificial flower; or as the mimic garden of a child, from an enamelled meadow." The comparison, from Schlegel, is instructive. Genuine poetry is superior to poor verse, as the natural flower is to the artificial, and as the enameled garden (one product of art) is to the child's collection of real flowers broken from their stems and stuck into the ground. The child's garden will fade; the artist's creation has the gift of eternal freshness.[54]

A final quality of the poet's character, though the list could probably be extended indefinitely, is the holiness of his contemplation. If an undevout astronomer is mad, neither can the poet be without innocent awe: "The poet is one who carries the simplicity of childhood into the

[52] *ShC*, II, 86–87.
[53] *ShC*, II, 91.
[54] *ShC*, II, 261. See also Raysor's note on this passage.

powers of manhood; who, with a soul unsubdued by habit, unshackled by custom, contemplates all things with the freshness and the wonder of a child; and, connecting with it the inquisitive powers of riper years, adds, as far as he can find knowledge, admiration; and, where knowledge no longer permits admiration, gladly sinks back again into the childlike feeling of devout wonder." [55]

THE SELF AS CRITIC

As an addendum to the study of the poetic personality, some notes should be included on the critic, not because Coleridge makes any explicit comments on the art of criticism but because his own approaches to Shakespeare mirror so well his philosophical interest in the self and the adjuncts of a person-centered theory.[56]

The massive fact of Coleridge's nearly exclusive concern with either the personality of the poet or the characters of the drama must dominate any discussion of his Shakespearean lectures. The formal or structural aspects of dramatic art seem to have concerned him not at all.[57] This may have been due in part to his own method of introspection and to his natural interest in the person of the poet, but the state of critical theory in the period doubtless influenced his thinking as well. Thus the centrality of the dramatist's personality in Coleridge's criticism may have been the result of that emphasis on the unity of the self which grew up partly as a result of association theory, insofar as it aimed at an integral theory of mind, but more likely in opposition to that school, which failed to account for the full union of thought and feeling. As has already been noted, poetic theory broke loose from its genres, dictions, unities, and plots in general, and sought for the unifying element in a feeling or tone which was ultimately located in the poet. The latter emphasis, on character criticism, is frequently supposed to reflect the romantic cult of the hero, but probably interest in

[55] ShC, II, 148.

[56] In the first lecture of the 1811–1812 series there is a lengthy discussion of the causes of false criticism, and it tells us much about the actual state of literature and of reviewing in Coleridge's day. It does not, however, contribute anything to our understanding of the theoretical grounds of his own criticism. ShC, II, 57–63.

[57] For Badawi's opposite opinion, see previous chapter, note 123.

both character and hero is the natural result of the growth of a psychology of the self, especially since the traditional model for poetic criticism, Aristotle's analysis, was often discredited because of its assumed involvement with the mechanical details of genres and rules.

Raysor, in his introduction to the Shakespeare criticism, gives a brief history of the rise of character criticism in English letters, and shows that emphasis on Shakespeare's characters had never been absent even from extremely neoclassical criticism. William Richardson and Maurice Morgann are the most prominent of the critics who employed this method of analyzing Shakespeare's dramas; Richardson was the initiator of the mode, and Morgann, in his *Essay on the Dramatic Character of Falstaff* (1777), anticipated closely the method used by subsequent critics, including Coleridge.[58]

The most famous example of character analysis in Shakespearean criticism is Coleridge's discussion of Hamlet: it was an advance over anything previously attempted of this kind except Morgann's Falstaff, it gave an all but ineradicable coloring to Hamlet criticism, and it offers interesting evidence for any discussion of the psychology of the critical mind. Raysor notes that Coleridge, in attributing the delay of Hamlet's revenge to his weakness of will, had several predecessors, especially William Richardson, Henry Mackenzie, and Thomas Robertson.[59] However, he went beyond them in the general depth and vigor of his analysis, and in particular by assigning as the reason for Hamlet's vacillation the paralyzing excess of thought over action in his character. The first instance of Coleridge's use of this explanation is given in a memorandum by Crabb Robinson of a conversation of Coleridge's on December 23, 1810.[60] Of Hamlet Coleridge said: "He is a man whose *ideal* and internal images are so vivid that all real objects

---

[58] *ShC*, I, xxi–xxiv.

[59] Raysor cites: Richardson, *A Philosophical Analysis and Illustration of Some of Shakespeare's Remarkable Characters* (1774) and *Essays on Shakespeare's Dramatic Characters* (1784); Mackenzie, *Mirror*, nos. 99–100 (1780); Robertson, *Transactions of the Royal Society of Edinburgh*, II (1790), 251–267. For a summary of their views, see *ShC*, I, xxii–xxiii.

[60] Raysor notes that here also Coleridge's analysis antedates the publication of Schlegel's lecture on Hamlet (1811). Likewise it does not seem that Coleridge had yet read Goethe's *Wilhelm Meister*, where a similar but not identical discussion of Hamlet occurs. *ShC*, I, 18–19; II, 209 note.

are faint and dead to him. This we see in his soliloquies on the nature of man and his disregard of life. Hence also his vacillation and the purely convulsive energies he displayed. He acts only by fits and snatches. He manifests a strong inclination to suicide . . . Hamlet remains at last the helpless *un*practical being, tho' every inducement to activity is given which the very appearance of the spirit of his murdered father could bring with it." [61] The longest analysis of the character is given in the brilliant twelfth lecture of 1811–1812. One of the key observations Coleridge makes there is that "Hamlet beheld external things in the same way that a man of vivid imagination, who shuts his eyes, sees what has previously made an impression on his organs." Though he is not a coward and not unintelligent, he suffers "from that aversion to action, which prevails among such as have a world in themselves." "He is full of purpose, but void of that quality of mind which accomplishes purpose." In summary:

Shakespeare wished to impress upon us the truth, that action is the chief end of existence — that no faculties of intellect, however brilliant, can be considered valuable, or indeed otherwise than as misfortunes, if they withdraw us from, or render us repugnant to action, and lead us to think and think of doing, until the time has elapsed when we can do anything effectually. In enforcing this moral truth, Shakespeare has shown the fulness and force of his powers: all that is amiable and excellent in nature is combined in Hamlet, with the exception of one quality. He is a man living in meditation, called upon to act by every motive human and divine, but the great object of his life is defeated by continually resolving to do, yet doing nothing but resolve.[62]

It has long been obvious that Coleridge's Hamlet has more than a smack of Coleridge himself. The same personality that is described here can be discovered in a multitude of similar passages of self-analysis that fill his letters, and even Coleridge's friends gave currency to the resemblance. Robinson reports that at this lecture, "Somebody said to me, 'This is a satire on himself.' — 'No,' said I, 'it is an elegy.' A great many of his remarks on Hamlet were capable of a like application." [63]

[61] *ShC*, II, 209–210.
[62] *ShC*, II, 192, 193, 197, 197–198.
[63] Lecture of January 3, 1812. *ShC*, II, 229.

And yet Coleridge's interpretation is not so unlikely that it requires an autobiographical justification. If it were only that, it would not have so permanently altered the direction of Shakespearean studies. The persistent one-sidedness of romantic criticism in treating Shakespeare's dramas as though they were only character studies may well be due mainly to the influence of Coleridge's Hamlet, but the fault was not necessarily Coleridge's. He was following, as much as contributing to, a critical theory which distrusted genres and unities and subordinated plot to character as the source of dramatic coherence. At its best it was a criticism which sinned by omission — serious omission, it is true, but of a sort which the age could hardly have been expected to be conscious of. With our more elaborate historical perspective it is easy to see the weaknesses of romantic theory and of the Coleridgean Hamlet in particular. But Coleridge himself would have thought his insight only the result of that sympathetic identification with his object which he required of the poet and would presumably have extended to the critic as well. The critical evaluation no less than the poetic insight must take place in the inward eye, qualified and conditioned no less by the shape and limits of that eye. The weakness of Coleridge's theory at this point was that he had not yet learned how to express the relationship with the real that must ideally control the subjectivism implicit in this point of view. Had he explained this in his lectures his Hamlet might have been less of a target for clever friends and metahistorical critics.

In the lectures on poetry and on Shakespeare we find the first substantial embodiment of what we can call Coleridge's philosophy of literature. The speculations which began in 1800 with the refutation of Locke and Hartley soon expanded the narrow and negative epistemological base on which they rested into a metaphysics of being and a psychology of the perceptive and creative self. This philosophical structure was a necessary preliminary to any extensive literary analysis. The theory in the lectures corroborates weaknesses in the philosophy itself. The analogical mode of being is not fully developed and this limits the possibility of a more satisfactory theory of imitative representation and of dramatic illusion. The function of imagination is not clearly stated, and this uncertainty accounts for the diverse statements of what poetry does and what the essential characteristics of the poet are. The concept of art as activity, as making, is missing from the philosophical discussions, and this reduces the analysis of Shakespeare to an examination of character and feeling, with scarcely any mention made of plot, of structure, and particularly of the representative function of the drama as a whole. No assimilation is made of the reason-understanding distinction, so the moral status of poetry and its relationship to other human activities is not touched on.

With all these defects, it is still possible to say that the lectures from 1808 to 1814 apply the philosophy and especially the literary philosophy that Coleridge had been working on since 1800. Raysor's contention that Coleridge's best criticism had little to do with his philosophy as such can hardly stand the test of a detailed comparison of both. He calls Coleridge's aesthetic speculations "derivative," "mediocre," and "fragmentary." [64] It seems fairer to say that they are derivative only in the sense that Coleridge learned from others many of the principles that he worked into his own theoretical structure, mediocre only if we misconceive the originality of Coleridge's purpose or forget the historical limitations that any speculative effort has to overcome, and fragmentary only insofar as Coleridge's system was constantly growing before and after the Shakespearean lectures and indeed never did reach the perfection of shape that he wanted for it. As they stand the lectures before 1814 reflect accurately the status of his literary philosophy at the time.

[64] *ShC*, I, xlviii.

CHAPTER V

Interim, 1814

My morning Hours, as the longest and most important Division,
I keep sacred to my most important Work . . . The Title is:
Christianity the one true Philosophy . . . The Evenings I have
employed in composing a series of Essays on the Principles of
genial criticism concerning the Fine Arts.

Letter of September 12, 1814

Two things are notable about the year of quiet which separated the
last of the 1811–1814 lecture series from the writing of the *Biographia
Literaria* in 1815. Coleridge began to plan a new and more complicated
synthesis of his thought, and he wrote a group of essays on aesthetics.
Neither effort was in the long run successful. He tinkered with the
outline of the synthesis for some time but, except for stray references,
it exists only in the notebook entries of his last years. The papers on
art are uneven and the theory in them has little to do with Coleridge's
most typical and interesting speculations. Nevertheless, perhaps because they were unsuccessful, these two ventures deserve our attention.
System building, here as in 1800, seems to be a sign of shifting progress
in Coleridge's intellectual development, and his failures define this
progress as much as his successes. The essays on art also offer a system
manqué, within the limited sphere of aesthetics, and thereby constitute
an interesting preliminary to a much more important Coleridge failure, the *Biographia Literaria*.

LOGOSOPHIA

The magnum opus which Coleridge envisioned this time was not
the *Organum* which he had discussed so often in the years after 1800,

but a much more comprehensive work, perhaps the "system" to which that earlier will-o'-the-wisp was conceived as merely introductory. In any case the *Organum* was to have been a work on the history and true modes of logical reasoning. The new *summa* is to be nothing less than a unification of science, philosophy, and theology. The first mention of it occurs in a letter to Cottle in April 1814, in the midst of a discussion of the Trinity: "I have in my head some floating ideas on the *Logos*, which I hope, hereafter, to mould into a consistent form." [1] The project was publicly announced in the third of the essays "On the Principles of Genial Criticism Concerning the Fine Arts," in the summer of the same year. While discussing certain special meanings which he had given to the terms he was using, Coleridge observes that he need not go into detail at the moment "because I am about to put to the press a large volume on the LOGOS, or the communicative intelligence in nature and in man, together with, and as preliminary to, a Commentary on the Gospel of St. John," one of the purposes of which would be "to give real and adequate definitions of all the component faculties of our moral and intellectual being, exhibiting constructively the origin, development, and destined functions of each." [2]

The plan developed so rapidly that in September of the same year Coleridge was able to give an elaborate outline of the work. This was the first of at least three schematic descriptions of the great work that Coleridge gave in his letters between 1814 and 1816. There are some differences in the three but the basic plan is the same. [3] "The title is: Christianity the one true Philosophy — or 5 Treatises on the Logos, or communicative Intelligence, Natural, Human, and Divine" (1814). The name *Logosophia* occurs in the 1815 version and in miscellaneous references to the work. In the first outline the five treatises are preceded by an "Essay on the Laws and Limits of Toleration and Liberality illustrated by fragments of *Auto*-biography." [4] In the 1815 outline

---

[1] *CL*, III, 480.

[2] *BL*, II, 230.

[3] The three outlines are to be found in *CL*, III, 533–534 (September 12, 1814), *CL*, IV, 591–592 (October 7, 1815), and *CL*, IV, 687 (September 25, 1816).

[4] Chambers has suggested that the *Biographia* grew out of these fragments, *Coleridge*, p. 270. Coleridge later remarked that the "*Autobiography*" would be "an important Pioneer to the great Work on the *Logos*, Divine and Human, on which I have set my

there are six treatises, the first of which is a "philosophic Compendium of the History of Philosophy from Pythagoras to the present Day, with miscellaneous Investigations on Toleration, and the obstacles to just reasoning."[5] Aside from this varying conception of the introduction, the rest of the outline is substantially the same in the three versions, and the small variations serve to amplify our understanding of the content and purpose of each treatise.

The first treatise is called "Logos propaideuticos — or the science of systematic Thinking in ordinary life" (1814), or "The science of connected reasoning (with the History of Logic from Aristotle to Condillac) . . . applied to the purposes of real life — the Bar, the Pulpit, the Senate, and rational Conversation" (1815), or simply the "Organum verè organum" (1816). The second treatise is "Logos architectonicus, or an attempt to apply the constructive, or mathematical, Process to Metaphysics and Natural Theology" (1814), or "the Science of Premises, or transcendental Philosophy — i.e. the examination of the Premises, which in ordinary and practical reasoning are taken for granted" (1815), or "the principles of the Dynamic or Constructive Philosophy as opposed to the Mechanic" (1816). The third treatise," ὁ Λόγος ὁ θεάνθρωπος (the divine Logos incarnate)" (1814), is in all three outlines a commentary on the gospel of St. John. In the 1815 version Coleridge adds that this third treatise, to which the preceding one is introductory, is intended to prove "that Christianity is true Philosophy, and of course that all true Philosophy is Christianity." The fourth is "on Spinoza, and Spinozism with a Life of B. Spinoza — this entitled, Logos Agonistes" (1814), or, in a fuller version, "on the Mystics and Pantheists, with the Lives of Giordano Bruno, Jacob Behmen, George Fox, and Benedict Spinoza, with an analysis of their systems" (1815 and much the same, with Fox missing, in 1816). The last treatise is "Logos alogos, (i.e. logos illogicus) or on modern Unitarianism, it's causes and effects" (1814), or on "modern *Unicism* ab-

---

Heart and hope to ground my ultimate reputation." *CL*, IV, 585 (September 17, 1815).

    [5] "No such work exists, at least in our language," Coleridge added. In 1818 he gave the same reason as one of his motives in preparing the philosophical lectures. He also contemplated using them as an introduction to his magnum opus, which he was then dictating, he said, to Green. *CL*, IV, 917 (January 31, 1819).

surdly called Unitarianism" (1816). The purpose of the whole work, Coleridge says in the 1814 discussion, is to present "a philosophical Defence of the Articles of the Church." [6]

To sum up, the work was to consist of an introductory essay and four treatises. When Coleridge conceived of a preface on toleration and liberty of expression he was probably thinking of the essay in *The Friend* (1809) on this subject.[7] Undoubtedly he came to see that the topic could be subsumed in a general discussion of the conditions of right reasoning, and that a history of philosophy would be a better introduction to his work. The first treatise after the introduction would be the familiar *Organum*, a purely formal analysis of logic and the reasoning process in order to establish the rules of procedure. The second treatise would be the philosophical heart of the work, proposing the Dynamic or Constructive Philosophy which Coleridge was then evolving after Bruno, Schelling, Fichte, and so forth. The third part would be theological, taking up the dynamic philosophy into the theology of the Logos or communicative intelligence analogously present in nature, man, and God. The last two treatises would be critical evaluations of defective philosophical and theological systems.

It is extremely doubtful that the perfection of the *Logosophia* design

[6] I have ignored here the numbering of the "six" treatises in the 1815 version. As Coleridge gives them, they are: (1) history of philosophy, (2) science of reasoning, (3) transcendental philosophy, (4) commentary on St. John's gospel, (5) mystics and pantheists, (6) Unitarianism. Their numbering is worth noting only because there are several references to the *Logosophia* in *BL* and it is to this version that they refer. For example, *BL*, I, 179; 182, note. A much simpler version of the whole system is envisioned in an unpublished notebook entry. The date is impossible to ascertain since the notebook contains entries from 1804 to 1819 (on the other hand Coleridge does not use the name "Logosophia" elsewhere before 1815). The entry reads: "Logosophia or the System and the Method by S. T. Coleridge: in four parts consisting of Discourses and Dialogues concerning Science, Philosophy and Religion" (Notebook 21½, p. 64r, Br. Mus. Add. MS. 47519). The four parts are more imaginatively conceived in another note from the same manuscript: "The System conveyed in Discourses and Dialogues concerning Science, Philosophy and Religion. In Four Parts By S. T. Coleridge. Part the first — entitled The Library. Part 2nd — entitled The Holly Grove in the Winter Garden. Part 3rd — entitled The Cavern on the Sea-shore. Part 4th — entitled Travel Talk in Autumn: or Dialogues among the Lakes and Mountains" (p. 29v).

[7] "On the Communication of Truth and the Rightful Liberty of the Press in Connection with It," *Friend* (1809), pp. 33–89. In this discussion of the conditions which allow the dissemination of right but inadequate notions there is a germinal theory of method in investigation and communication.

was ever completely clear to Coleridge when he was making these outlines. He knew well enough what he wanted of an *Organum* as far back as 1803 (though it must be remembered that all of his copious writing on the specific topic of method was still in the future at this point), and he had fairly clear notions of the deficiencies of Unitarianism and, perhaps less clearly, of Boehmian mysticism and Spinozistic pantheism. The positive content of his projected work, however, was far from certain. His Dynamic Philosophy was very much in flux during these years, and his speculations on the Logos were equally imperfect. It seems likely that these outlines for the *Logosophia* represent an aspiration, an attempt on Coleridge's part to inspire a "mental initiative" which would make the scheme work out.

Perhaps the best way to take these plans is as a formulation of the central problem of philosophy as Coleridge could define it at the moment. In an earlier time he had conceived the work of philosophy as clarification of terminology preparatory to a solution of epistemological problems. This was the spirit of his letters to Josiah Wedgwood on Locke, and of the attempts to find an *Organum* which would be propaedeutic to a system, though it was never clear just what the system would require. As his speculations became more epistemological and then metaphysical, Coleridge's interest in an *Organum* waned. Indeed there are no references to a magnum opus from 1804 on until the problem of philosophy is redefined in 1814–1815 as the elucidation of the communicative intelligence, and the relationship of philosophy to religion. This more elaborate version of the problem represents a confident step forward in Coleridge's speculations. On the ruins of mechanism, idealism, pantheism, and Unitarianism, he would now erect a philosophy of dynamism and "realism," subsumed under a trinitarian religion by reason of the creative Logos which mediates between God and man. For the contents of this Dynamic Philosophy and the theology which is relevant to it we must look to the *Biographia* and subsequent writings. But even this fertile scheme, though it was an advance in the direction of a unified philosophy and theology, was not to last for more than a few years. The elaboration of the plan for the *Logosophia* apparently suggested the need for a more subtle instrument of investigation and orderly procedure, for we find Coleridge turning shortly after the *Lay Sermons* to the study of method in itself. And his speculations on this theme subvert his logosophic plan, so that in 1819 he is planning a newer structure, the basis and introduction to which will be the essays on methods.[8]

The publications of this period ahead are by no means to be considered parts of the *Logosophia* (though Coleridge hints occasionally that such is the case, the magnum opus is described in detail only in Coleridge's letters, not in any of the works themselves), but like all his writings they exhibit the stages of his intellectual development, and each is in some way a speculative advance, whatever the specific and immediate purposes of the work. Whether these works veer toward or away from Kant, whether they praise or criticize Schelling, whether the topic is the defects of Wordsworth's theories or the concept of "idea," the problem in the background is much the same one that was tentatively explored in the previous decade, the resolution of the demands of subject and object. Philosophically, what Coleridge accomplishes in the period 1814–1818 is the exposition of the grounds for a theory of knowledge. In literature the correlative advance lies in the statement, however confused, of the function of imagination, and of art as the mediator and reconciler of man and nature. Above all, in theology there is the unifying notion of the divine creativity. As before, literary theory cannot be studied apart from philosophy, and now philosophy is seen to be dependent on religion. The convergence of Coleridge's thought becomes clearer, even though the details are not always free from obscurity.

THE BEAUTIFUL: THE ESSAYS ON GENIAL CRITICISM, 1814

In August and September of 1814 Coleridge published three essays "On the Principles of Genial Criticism Concerning the Fine Arts, More Especially Those of Statuary and Painting, Deduced from the Laws and Impulses Which Guide the True Artist in the Production

---

[8] *The Friend: A Series of Essays in Three Volumes, To Aid in the Formation of Fixed Principles in Politics, Morals, and Religion, with Literary Amusements Interspersed*, 3 vols. (London, 1818), III, 129. Hereafter cited as *Friend*.

of His Works." [9] The occasion for the writing and for the place of
publication, Bristol, was an exhibition of paintings by Coleridge's
American friend Washington Allston, whom he had met in Rome
when returning from Malta some years before, and whose exhibition
he hoped to advertise by these articles. This also explains the attention
to painting announced in the title but not exactly pursued in the text.
In fact the essays have little to do with Allston's work except for two
or three trivial references.

The essays are important, however, as Coleridge's only venture into
general aesthetics before the thirteenth lecture of 1818. His purpose was
to establish a unified theory of pleasure in artistic representation, based
on an analysis of the beautiful. As Shawcross points out, however,
there is a certain amount of confusion between the subjective conception of the psychological requirements of beauty in the mind of the
artist and the objective notion of the beauty present in the aesthetic
creation.[10] The ambivalence of terminology occasionally results in
muddied theoretical waters. The title of the essays indicates the subjective aspect, promising that the theoretical analysis will be deduced
from the practice of the artist, but at least as much attention is given
to the aesthetic effect in the response of the audience to the work.

The theory of the essays is rather unrelated to the themes of Coleridge's speculations elsewhere. In later years he thought highly of
these works, and regretted that he had no copy of them, possibly because they formed almost his only completed utterance on the subject,
possibly because they do stand apart from more personal works which
by then might have seemed hopelessly inadequate as expressions of his
outlook.[11] As evidences of his chronological development, however,
the essays are valuable to us because they show Coleridge attempting
a general aesthetic theory before he had elaborated a relatively complete theory of imagination, and, consequently, when his notions of
symbol and of the mediating function of art were largely inchoate.
Insofar as he attempts to delineate the nature of beauty as a disinter-

[9] They were printed in *Felix Farley's Bristol Journal.* They can be found in the Shawcross edition of *BL,* II, 219–246.
[10] *BL,* II, 305, 308.
[11] *Table Talk,* II, 280, January 1, 1834.

ested balance of manifold and form, he is working toward later ideas. The insistence on pleasure as the purpose of art has already been noted and the interest in clarifying notions by "desynonymizing" words is thoroughly Coleridgean. The heavily Kantian spirit of the theory here is important as it marks the effective beginning of the protracted wrestling match with the critical philosophy that occupied so much of Coleridge's speculative energy to the end of his life. Before this there had been some relatively unassimilated borrowing of the reason-understanding distinctions, and a fairly extensive use of the ethical philosophy, but not much of the true transcendental criticism. From now on the body of Kant is behind a good many arrases, usually with a wound or two and sometimes missing distinctive limbs or even unrecognizably defaced, but always at hand for scholars to lug out and display.

The introductory essay states the general relationship between the fine arts. They can all be considered as species of poetry, differentiated by the senses through which the common spirit manifests itself: poetry of language, poetry of the ear or music, and poetry of the eye, which is either plastic (statuary) or graphic (painting).[12] "The common essence of all consists in the excitement of emotion for the immediate purpose of pleasure through the medium of beauty; herein contradistinguishing poetry from science, the immediate object and primary purpose of which is truth and possible utility."[13] The rest of the essays form an extended comment on this definition and on the problem central to it, the meaning of the term "beauty" and the question of its universal validity. Before he begins his disquisition proper, Coleridge justifies a new treatment of this topic by criticizing the contributions of associationist critics, and of Archibald Alison in particular. Their basic principle, he says, is too vague for practical guidance. "Associa-

---

[12] A distinction founded on the specific media of the arts might have been more satisfactory. "Language" is not a "sense," and the precise difference between sculpture and painting lies in their respective media. Kant distinguishes the fine arts according to modes of expression: word, gesture, and tone, resulting in the arts of speech (poetry and rhetoric), of sensuous intuition (plastic art and painting), and of the beautiful play of sensations (music and the art of color). *Kant's Critique of Aesthetic Judgment*, trans. J. C. Meredith (Oxford, 1911), pp. 183–184f.

[13] *BL*, II, 221.

tion in philosophy is like the term stimulus in medicine; explaining every thing, it explains nothing; and above all, leaves itself unexplained. It is an excellent charm to enable a man to talk *about* and *about* any thing he likes, and to make himself and his hearers as wise as before." [14] In addition Coleridge makes two postulates: "The first, that the reader would steadily look into his own mind to know whether the principles stated are ideally true; the second, to look at the works or parts of the works mentioned, as illustrating or exemplifying the principle, to judge whether or how far it has been realized." [15] The injunctions sound like an early version of the functions of idea (or hypothesis) and of inductive testing in the acquisition of knowledge, both of which topics are of great importance in the later essays on method.

The argument opens in the second essay with a favorite Coleridgean distinction, between the method of mathematics and that of other branches of learning, here of philosophy. The distinction is usually formulated to show that in mathematics the definition creates the concept, whereas in existential sciences the concept must be drawn at least in part from empirical evidence. The inspiration is Kantian and comes from the distinction between the mathematical method of synthesis where the objects of the mind are constructed by the mind, and the analytic method of natural philosophy where sense experience results in indistinct and confused notions which must be progressively clarified if they are to be useful. [16] Coleridge employs the differentiation

[14] *BL*, II, 222.
[15] *BL*, II, 223.
[16] "The relation of a trillion to unity is very distinctly understood, while philosophers have not yet been able to make the concept of freedom intelligible from its unities, i.e., its simple and familiar concepts. That is, the qualities which make up the proper object of philosophy are infinitely many, and to distinguish between them is extraordinarily demanding; moreover, it is far more difficult to resolve complicated cognitions by analysis than to combine given simple cognitions by synthesis and to reach conclusions in this way . . . Metaphysics is without doubt the most difficult of all human insights." Immanuel Kant, *An Inquiry into the Distinctness of the Principles of Natural Theology and Morals*, in *Critique of Practical Reason and Other Writings in Moral Philosophy*, trans. and ed. Lewis White Beck (Chicago, 1949), p. 268. The distinction between the methods of synthesis and analysis is described in *An Inquiry*, pp. 262–268, and in *Immanuel Kant's Critique of Pure Reason*, trans. Norman Kemp Smith (London, 1933), A. (1781 version) 712–736, B. (1787 version) 740–764, pp. 576–591.

here to point out that in mathematics the definition precedes the demonstration and even the axioms and postulates, whereas in philosophy the definition comes only after the facts and inferences. Where the definition is first it is so only as a faint outline which directs the reader's attention whither he must go. So in the discussion of poetry here the definition given, though open to no logical attack, presumes conceptions which may not consciously or distinctly exist. Thus the need for a certain amount of explication.[17]

The first clarification involves the term "immediate" (poetry is "the excitement of emotion for the immediate purpose of pleasure through the medium of beauty"). By this Coleridge intends to distinguish aesthetic pleasure from the satisfaction of mere animal appetites. An accurate synonym would be "disinterested": "All objects of mere desire constitute an interest (i.e. aliquid quod est inter hoc et aliud, or that which is between the agent and his motive), and which is therefore valued only as the means to the end. To take a trivial but unexceptionable instance, the venison is agreeable because it gives pleasure; while the Apollo Belvedere is not beautiful because it pleases, but it

---

[17] "The definition of poetry, in the preliminary Essay, as the regulative idea of all the Fine Arts, appears to me . . . liable to no just *logical* reversion." *BL*, II, 223–224. This use of "regulative" is part of a very important distinction for Coleridge, that of constitutive and regulative principles or ideas. This is in origin purely Kantian. The ideas of reason go beyond appearances in two ways: as regulative principles, in which they direct (show the way for, in Coleridge's usage) the understanding into more consistent and comprehensive syntheses of phenomena by providing maxims of thought for its guidance; or as constitutive principles, in which they mistake these maxims of pure thought (which refer directly to understanding, not to objects) for autonomous maxims of real knowledge, thus "constituting" so-called real objects, and leading to metaphysical illusion. *Critique of Pure Reason*, A. 508–510, 616–620, 671f, B. 536–538, 644–648, 699f; Smith ed., pp. 450–451, 515–518, 550f. The distinction lies dormant in Coleridge's thought for some time, but emerges again in a central position but with different meanings, in 1818, in the essays on method. The changed meanings of the later usage offer an illustration of how erratic can be Coleridge's employment of ideas borrowed from other philosophers. The distinction of constitutive and regulative ideas is obviously related to that of the method of synthesis and the method of analysis, discussed above. It is interesting that this latter distinction was a part of Kant's early, precritical speculations, when he had not yet in effect denied the possibility of a metaphysics, and the knowability of the material world had not been restricted to the knowledge provided by the forms of the understanding. Possibly this sympathy of Coleridge with the early Kantian viewpoint suggests the fundamental realism which constantly emerges in Coleridge's most transcendental moments and is at the bottom of his inability to accept the basic principle of the critical philosophy.

pleases us because it is beautiful." [18] In a later note Coleridge adds that when an object is agreeable the sensation of pleasure always precedes and causes the judgment. "We *find* it agreeable." But in the case of beauty, the contemplation or intuition precedes the feeling of complacency, in the order of nature at least, and in instances of great depression may exist without it.[19]

"Pleasure" is another term that requires clarification, since it is so comprehensive as to be often equivocal. "Complacency" would better express the intellectual nature of the enjoyment of the beautiful, but it seems to preclude all emotion. "Delight" does not indicate the kind of pleasurable emotion, which a general definition must do. Therefore the words were added "through the medium of beauty." But this is merely to remove the problem once more without solving it, for "beauty" is equally unclear.[20] These reflections lead Coleridge to consider the question of establishing distinctions between words often confounded in use: agreeable, beautiful, picturesque, grand, and sublime. This is a necessary preparation for understanding the nature of aesthetic enjoyment. In fact, he says, on the essential difference between the beautiful and the agreeable rests the whole question of whether great works of art (the *Iliad*, the poems of Shakespeare and Milton, Michelangelo's Sistine Chapel, and so forth) please us by accident of local association, the way a man might prefer a black pudding to a sirloin of beef, "or whether there exists in the constitution of the human soul a sense, and a regulative principle, which may indeed be

[18] *BL*, II, 224. The Kantian notion of disinterestedness is not wholly satisfactory here. For Kant interest is the delight connected with the representation of the real existence of an object, and is always related to the faculty of desire. With respect to the beautiful, however, there is no reference to our concern for the real existence of the thing, only to the estimate we form of it by contemplation. *Critique of Aesthetic Judgment*, pp. 42–44. Shawcross observes, however, that though we are satisfied with the object as represented, we have a decided interest in the representation itself as a real object. *BL*, II, 307. Coleridge seems to accept the exclusion of desire from the contemplation of the beautiful but is indifferent to denying our concern for the real existence of the thing. See the example of the golden wheel (below, in the discussion of "multeity in unity"), where real existence seems to be an added perfection beyond the beauty of the form.

[19] *BL*, II, 241.

[20] *BL*, II, 224–225. Here Coleridge tells one of his most frequently repeated anecdotes to illustrate the careless use of words and concepts. It concerns a lady who remarked, on viewing an immense waterfall, that it was not only sublime but beautiful and even *pretty*.

stifled and latent in some, and be perverted and denaturalized in others, yet is nevertheless universal in a given state of intellectual and moral culture," independent of temporary circumstances and dependent only on the degree of development of the faculties of the mind.[21]

This central question of the essays he defers to the final number, asking the reader's indulgence for so much attention to preliminaries. It is of the nature of the subject, however. Since " TASTE is the intermediate faculty which connects the active with the passive powers of our nature, the intellect with the senses; and its appointed function is to elevate the *images* of the latter, while it realizes the *ideas* of the former," we must learn what is peculiar to each before we can understand that "third something" which is formed by a harmony of both.[22] Here the function of mediating and uniting image and idea is given the name taste. This is a change from Coleridge's earlier use of the term. In the fragmentary "Essay on Taste" of 1810 the central point in the definition of taste in the appreciation of the fine arts was the union of intellectual perception of an object with a distinct reference to our own sensibility of pain or pleasure, in other words the combining and uniting of "a sense of immediate pleasure in ourselves with the perception of external arrangement." [23] As late as 1802 Coleridge had given the term an associationist implication by his use of the electrometer as an image for the operation of taste.[24] Now he damns "an English critic" as a "taste-meter to the fashionable world" because he understands the term literally and thinks the taste for venison the same thing as the taste for Virgil.[25] But not only does Coleridge remove the mechanical and wholly instinctive connotation of taste, now he gives it the same function that imagination had earlier, that of mediating the active powers of intellect with the passive powers of sense, joining image and idea, which is a considerably broader function than unifying perception and the sense of pleasure or dislike. Furthermore, where use of the term imagination was confined to discussions of

---

[21] *BL*, II, 226–227.

[22] *BL*, II, 227.

[23] *BL*, II, 248. This fragment was published posthumously, in the *Literary Remains* of 1836.

[24] *CL*, II, 877.

[25] *BL*, II, 225–226. Shawcross thinks that this must be Francis Jeffrey. *BL*, II, 308.

poetry earlier, the term taste is here used with reference to all the fine arts. Since this universal aesthetic function was ultimately assigned to imagination again in the *Biographia*, it seems that the transition from early to later definitions of imagination was made by way of the general aesthetic function assigned to taste in these essays.

The third essay proceeds to the analysis of the agreeable and the beautiful. There are two senses in which the former term is used: for what is naturally suited to our senses by reason of a pre-established harmony between the organs and their appointed objects, and for what habit or association has made pleasing to us. The color green is naturally agreeable to the eye; tobacco and "the crutch that had supported a revered parent" are pleasing by custom and association.[26]

Coleridge defines the beautiful quite simply, but devotes considerable effort to explaining his definition. "The BEAUTIFUL, contemplated in its essentials, that is, in *kind* and not in *degree*, is that in which the *many*, still seen as many, becomes one." Another formula that expresses this requirement is: "Multëity in Unity."[27] Coleridge defends the use of such "hard words" from the old schoolmen because he wants to convey the notion of the many as simply contradistinguished from the one, and the word "multitude" has the disadvantage of suggesting the notion of "a *great* many."[28] The whole idea here is not entirely new. The formula multeity in unity is an advance in succinctness, but the notion of the pleasure from each part consistent with the pleasure from the whole was a feature of the definition stated earlier in the Shakespearean lectures of 1808 and 1811–1812.

The conception of multeity in unity places the essence of beauty in the conjunction of the formal and the material elements of art. This is clear from Coleridge's various examples. Even an old coach wheel shows through its tar and dirt the abstract figure in which the radii, center, and circumference are related as parts in one harmonious whole. But when content is perfectly matched to form the delight is even greater: "Imagine the polished golden wheel of the chariot of the Sun, as the poets have described it: then the figure, and the real

[26] *BL*, II, 231.
[27] *BL*, II, 232.
[28] *BL*, II, 230.

thing so figured, exactly coincide. There is nothing heterogeneous, nothing to abstract from: by its perfect smoothness and circularity in width, each part is (if I may borrow a metaphor from a sister sense) as perfect a melody, as the whole is a complete harmony." [29] The definition of the kind, Coleridge had said before, is likewise the definition of the highest degree of that kind. The example of the golden wheel is apparently intended to show that the formal element predominates in the form-and-matter union of art, and that the highest degree of the kind is achieved when the material is perfectly appropriate to the form and there is nothing to abstract from. A subsequent image illustrates the same point. The form must realize itself in something, but the material elements must in the least possible degree distract the attention, "in the least possible degree obscure the idea, of which they (composed into outline and surface) are the symbol." Compare a pure crystal with a transparent body such as the air, on the one hand, and with an opaque or cloudy mass on the other. "The crystal is lost in the light, which yet it contains, embodies, and gives a shape to; but which passes shapeless through the air, and, in the ruder body, is either quenched or dissipated." [30]

Summing up these remarks on multeity in unity, Coleridge draws three conclusions: "First, that beauty is harmony, and subsists only in composition, and secondly, that the first species of the Agreeable can alone be a component part of the beautiful, that namely which is naturally consonant with our senses by the pre-established harmony between nature and the human mind; and thirdly, that even of this species, those objects only can be admitted (according to rule the first) which belong to the eye and the ear, because they alone are susceptible of distinction of parts." [31] "The result, then, of the whole is that the shapely (i.e. *formosus*) joined with the naturally agreeable, constitutes what, speaking accurately, we mean by the word beautiful (i.e. *pulcher*)." [32] As Shawcross notes, Coleridge's attempts to discriminate functions sometimes get him into unfortunate locutions;

[29] BL, II, 233.
[30] BL, II, 238.
[31] BL, II, 233.
[32] BL, II, 234.

here he seems to be attributing the perception of shapeliness to the form and the pleasurable sensation to the material, which, if true, would involve again an inescapable dualism.[33]

There are some further remarks which, if anything, confuse the notion of form already achieved. Life and free will are superior, Coleridge says, to the highest impressions of sense. Therefore to the formally beautiful ought to be added the perception of life and spontaneous action, so that "the latter only shall be the object of our conscious *perception*, while the former merely acts, and yet does effectively act, on our feelings." The notion of life here, suggestive of later Coleridgean themes such as organic unity, is not explained at all; the desirable effect of its addition to the idea of the beautiful is illustrated instead by reference to a painting of Allston's, "Dead Man reviving from the touch of the bones of the Prophet Elisha," apparently the literal source of the life metaphor. The excellence of Raphael's "Galatea" is attributed to the reconciliation of the "conflicting principles of the FREE LIFE, and of the confining FORM! How entirely is the stiffness that would have resulted from the obvious regularity of the latter, *fused* and (if I may hazard so bold a metaphor) almost *volatilized* by the interpenetration and electrical flashes of the former." Having made form the correlative of at least three kinds of principles (material images, objects naturally agreeable to our nature, and "free life"), Coleridge wisely drops the subject altogether as prematurely supposing later material which he cannot explain here. He moves on to a recapitulation.[34]

There are three principles to be drawn from these considerations. The first is that what is agreeable to us not by its own nature but by habit or association is neither beautiful nor capable of being a component part of beauty, though it may increase the sum of our pleasure or even detract from it. The rose is not more beautiful when given by the hand of the woman we love. The associationist school of aesthetics is thus eliminated from consideration. The second principle states that the naturally agreeable, the pleasure from which is contained in the immediate impression, cannot properly speaking be called beautiful,

[33] *BL*, II, 311.
[34] *BL*, II, 234–235.

but one among the component parts of beauty, wherever it can exist as a part of a whole. This, according to Shawcross, is directed against the physiological definition of beauty which identifies it with the naturally agreeable.[35] The third principle states the main conclusion of the essays:

The safest definition, then, of Beauty, as well as the oldest, is that of Pythagoras: THE REDUCTION OF MANY TO ONE — or, as finely expressed by the sublime disciple of Ammonius, τὸ ἄμερες ὄν, ἐν πολλοῖς φανταζόμενον, of which the following may be offered as both paraphrase and corollary. *The sense of beauty subsists in simultaneous intuition of the relation of parts, each to each, and of all to a whole: exciting an immediate and absolute complacency, without intervenence, therefore, of any interest, sensual or intellectual.*[36] The BEAUTIFUL is thus at once distinguished both from the AGREEABLE which is beneath it, and from the GOOD, which is above it: for both these have an interest necessarily attached to them: both act on the WILL, and excite a desire for the actual existence of the image or idea contemplated: while the sense of beauty rests gratified in the mere contemplation or intuition, regardless whether it be a fictitious Apollo, or a real Antinous.[37]

The third essay ends with a dialogue between Milton and a stern and prejudiced Puritan, concerning the front of York Cathedral, intended to illustrate once again the disinterestedness of the Beautiful in comparison with the necessary instrumentality by which we define the Good. The final summation is in strictly Kantian terms: "The GOOD consists in the congruity of a thing with the laws of the reason and the nature of the will, and in its fitness to determine the latter to actualize the former: and it is always discursive [that is, referred to a conception previously existing in the mind]. The Beautiful arises from the perceived harmony of an object, whether sight or sound, with the inborn and constitutive rules of the judgement and imagination: and it is always intuitive. As light to the eye, even such is beauty to the mind, which cannot but have complacency in whatever is perceived

[35] *BL*, II, 312.

[36] Coleridge had earlier in these essays defined the sense in which he was using "intuition," in Hooker's words: "a direct and immediate beholding or presentation of an object to the mind through the senses or the imagination." *BL*, II, 230.

[37] *BL*, II, 238–239.

as pre-configured to its living faculties." He ends with another clever
but wholly fanciful etymology: "Hence the Greeks called a beautiful
object καλόν quasi καλοῦν, i.e. *calling on* the soul, which receives
instantly, and welcomes it as something connatural." [38]

These essays on criticism offer a mixed bag of contributions to aesthetic theory. The denial of the accidental in producing beauty, and
the insistence on the artist's purpose in creating according to a form or
idea are all to the good. The statement of the multeity in unity which
constitutes beauty is an important key to later theories. And the position that beauty is contemplated for its own sake contributes to the
autonomy of art. On the other hand, some of the key notions on which
the essays depend are confusingly presented: aesthetic disinterestedness is made to seem too much like absence of all relation to actual
existence or to truth value, and form is too mechanically separated
from content in some of the very formulas which are proposed to
indicate their unity.

Unquestionably the gravest defect of the essays is the heavily formal
conception of beauty and aesthetic pleasure that is the basis for most
of the theory. To see beauty primarily as arrangement limits the possibilities of explanation to all but the most general propositions about
relations of parts. This may be satisfactory enough as an expression of
the purely abstract requirements of aesthetic arrangement, but it leaves
untouched large areas which a richer poetic ontology ought to include:
emotion, volition, external nature, the ethical, and the true. Perhaps
this is too heavy a demand to lay on Coleridge when he was undertaking so modest a subject. But Coleridge's method never was to propose narrow aims for himself; there is scarcely one of his completed
prose works which does not send out probing tendrils in every direction and suggest relations on the widest scale with most of the central

[38] *BL*, II, 243. The bracketed explanation of "discursive" is the one given by Shawcross in his note on the passage. In an appendix Coleridge dismisses utilitarian aesthetics
by denying that proportion alone or suitability of means to end can constitute the beautiful. The swan's neck is disproportionate to its body, while the neck of the ostrich is in
exact proportion to its height and of great utility in grazing, but no one would confuse
the beautiful and the ugly between them. A final remark notes that the Good that he
has been discussing is, of course, the relatively good, and not the Absolutely Good which
must await another occasion for explanation. *BL*, II, 245–246.

areas of thought from theology to physiology. Hardly anything from these essays survives to flourish again in Coleridge's later works, except the potentially important notion of multeity in unity, and the implications of the imaginative faculty found in the notion of taste. It seems reasonable to conclude that Coleridge found it too constricting to work within such narrow assumptions as he chose for himself here when he limited his problem to the distinction of terms between the agreeable and the beautiful. He needed an existentially more opulent object for his speculations, and he went back to the poem itself for inspiration.

CHAPTER VI

The Argument of the First Part
of the *Biographia*, 1815

One long passage [in the intended "preface" to an edition of
the poems] — a disquisition on the powers of association, with
the History of the Opinions on this subject from Aristotle
to Hartley, and on the generic difference between the faculties of Fancy and Imagination . . . I certainly extended and
elaborated . . . as laying the foundation Stones of the Constructive or Dynamic Philosophy in opposition to the merely
mechanic —.

Letter of July 29, 1815

Between the end of May and the end of September 1815 Coleridge
wrote the twenty-two chapters that form the substance of his *Biographia Literaria; or Biographical Sketches of My Literary Life and
Opinions*.[1] The book which was to become, in the twentieth century
at least, his best known work was the result of little planning and
foresight. As late as the thirtieth of May 1815 Coleridge still considered
it as a preface, on the principles of philosophic criticism in the fine
arts and in poetry especially, for a two-volume edition of his poems.
In slightly over three months, then, this central document in English
literary history was begun and finished. The result was a remarkable
failure, an important fragment. As an autobiography, even an intellectual autobiography, the work is at best sketchy and is detailed only
in covering the earliest years of Coleridge's life. The philosophical

---

[1] The *Biographia* was published at London, July 1817. The most recent version of
the mutations which the work underwent and the trials of its author in connection with
it is given by Griggs in the introduction to volume III of *CL*, xlvii–liii. See also the
relevant letters.

parts are extremely diffuse. As for literary speculation, there is the celebrated and enigmatic discussion of imagination, but this is broken off just as it approaches explanation and it is obvious that the fragment offered is a slender contribution to literary theory without supplements from the other writings of Coleridge. Only the history and refutation of association philosophy and the criticism of Wordsworth's poetic theory are more or less completely treated, and to many readers these are the least interesting parts of the book. Coleridge himself called the work an "immethodical miscellany," and in this case he was not speaking with atypical modesty.[2]

The value of the *Biographia*, however, lies precisely in the image it gives of the drama of Coleridge struggling to impose order on the recalcitrant elements of his earlier philosophy. The speed with which it was written guarantees that the work is primarily a record, not of Coleridge's youthful search for a literary theory, but of the state of his mind in the summer of 1815. Moreover this is Coleridge's first attempt to come to terms with his speculations in a work of any size. If we do not look at it as an exposition of a philosophy or even as a biographical sketch of literary opinions, but instead as the vehicle of Coleridge's own immediate deliberations on his theories, an attempt to argue out to conclusions some of his most personal ideas about the nature of literature, we can see much more clearly what he accomplished and where he failed. This position implies necessarily that the book can only be understood as a part of his whole intellectual career, and indeed in terms of what followed the failure of the *Biographia* as much as by what preceded it. Like most of Coleridge's works it is a fragment, and much of the confusion over its interpretation and value in the recent history of literary criticism has resulted from reading it out of context.

STATUS QUAESTIONIS

The *Biographia* is too rich a jumble of opinions, queries, asides, irrelevant anecdotes and isolated critical insights to allow a detailed

[2] *BL*, I, 64.

summary of it here. Still there is a pattern to be found among all the
acrobatics of Coleridge's lively mind. With the most obvious of its
digressions and padding eliminated (certainly the letters from Coleridge's German tour and the review of Maturin's *Bertram*), the *Biographia* falls roughly into two parts: what appears to be a long digressive review of the genesis of Coleridge's literary philosophy, beginning
in his school days and culminating in the attempt to provide the
promised theory of imagination, and then in the second volume the
elaborate criticism of Wordsworth's poetical principles and practice.
Behind this superficial division, the book has the structure of an
argument, an attempt by Coleridge to convince himself of the unity
of his literary philosophy. The two volumes are in some respects two
separate versions of the argument, the second a final effort to succeed
on different grounds from these where the first failed. Let us look at
the details more closely.

The opening chapters form the *status quaestionis* of Coleridge's
argument. They describe several "facts," conclusions about the true
nature of poetry which Coleridge had arrived at before his philosophical studies began, and which an adequate theory of literature must
explain. They form, in a manner of speaking, the evidence that must
be considered, and they center on three names important to Coleridge.
The first is that of his master at Christ's Hospital, James Boyer. This
wise teacher gave him models of excellence drawn from great writers
of the past: Demosthenes, Homer, Theocritus, Terence, Catullus,
Shakespeare, and Milton (on the last two he was a particularly hard
taskmaster). But the great lesson he taught was the unity of the poem:

> I learnt from him, that Poetry, even that of the loftiest and, seemingly,
> that of the wildest odes, had a logic of its own, as severe as that of science;
> and more difficult, because more subtle, more complex, and dependent on
> more, and more fugitive causes. In the truly great poets, he would say, there
> is a reason assignable, not only for every word, but for the position of every
> word; and I well remember that, availing himself of the synonimes to the
> Homer of Didymus, he made us attempt to show, with regard to each,
> *why* it would not have have answered the same purpose; and *wherein* con-
> sisted the peculiar fitness of the word in the original text.[3]

[3] *BL*, I, 4–5.

Coleridge is insisting here again on the formal demands of poetry as an autonomous activity, on the poem as a unity whose intelligibility is of a special kind proper to poetry and not the intelligibility of discursive writing structured by a proposition that is translatable into varying grammatical and verbal shapes. He does not say in what this unique unity consists, only that it is dependent on subtle, complex, and fugitive causes. It is a fact, and he must shortly attempt to explain it.

However, Coleridge goes on, the great works of past ages fail to move a young man in the way that productions of contemporary genius can. It was the poetry of William Lisle Bowles that first spoke to him with a convincing modern voice. He records two obligations. The first was the awakening of the introverted and speculative youth to the possibility of a poetry which expressed genuine emotion in a credible way. The "tender and yet so manly, so natural and real, and yet so dignified and harmonious" style of Bowles's sonnets rescued him from the bewilderment of "metaphysicks" and theological controversy to which he was susceptible even as a schoolboy.[4] His reaction to the poems of Bowles was not to a purely idiosyncratic quality but a response to a change in style of the poetry of the age. The older masters, from Donne to Cowley, expressed exotic and fantastic ideas "but in the most pure and genuine and mother English," whereas the moderns clothe the most obvious thoughts "in language the most fantastic and arbitrary." Whereas before passion was scanted in favor of wit and subtlety of intellect, the fashionable poetry of Coleridge's childhood subordinated both passion and intellect to an artificial diction and ornamentation that was half image and half abstract meaning. (He recalls a couplet "of a young tradesman": "No more will I endure love's pleasing pain,/ Or round my *heart's leg* tie his galling chain.") "The one sacrificed the heart to the head; the other both heart and head to point and drapery."[5] The poems of Bowles and of Cowper, however, avoided these faults and restored the traditional balance. They were "the first who combined natural thoughts with natural diction; the first who reconciled the heart with the head."[6] Yet, Cole-

[4] *BL*, I, 9–10.
[5] *BL*, I, 15.
[6] *BL*, I, 16.

ridge notes perceptively, they suffered the fate of those who succeed in improving the taste and judgment of their contemporaries: their own original genius now seems less striking by comparison.

The second obligation he owed to Bowles was the impulse to examine critically the poetic theories of those who followed Pope or, more generally, "that school of French poetry, condensed and invigorated by English understanding, which had predominated from the last century." The excellence of the kind of poetry represented by this tradition "consisted in just and acute observations on men and manners in an artificial state of society, as its matter and substance: and in logic of wit, conveyed in smooth and strong epigrammatic couplets, as its *form*." Even in the best of this poetry, "The Rape of the Lock," "The Essay on Man," or Pope's *Iliad*, "a *point* was looked for at the end of each second line," and the overall impression is of a sorites of epigrams, an artificial unity. Further, the matter and diction was "characterized not so much by poetic thoughts, as by thoughts *translated* into the language of poetry." [7] Whether or not, as Coleridge suggests, it was the schoolroom custom of composing Latin verses out of a *Gradus ad Parnassum* that perpetuated or even originated this kind of poetry, these "translations of prose thoughts into poetic language," the practice certainly did violence to Coleridge's concept of the requirements of poetry as a formally distinct literary kind.[8] In attacking the couplet and the unnatural and bookish language of the poetry of the age, Coleridge tells us, he constantly appealed to the earliest Greek verse and to English poets from Chaucer to Milton; his ultimate argument was that "no authority could avail in opposition to TRUTH, NATURE, LOGIC, and the LAWS OF UNIVERSAL GRAMMAR." [9] The impulse to universalize his principles and to find an absolute standard of judgment was evident early in his youth.

The third and most important of Coleridge's insights into the nature of poetry was the result of his acquaintance with Wordsworth.[10] Cole-

---

[7] *BL*, I, 11.
[8] *BL*, I, 12–13.
[9] *BL*, I, 14.
[10] No attempt is being made here to touch on all the literary matters in the *Biographia*. The remarks on men of genius, the nearsighted evaluation of Southey, and the

ridge first came to know Wordsworth's poetry, in particular the *Descriptive Sketches* (1793), when he was an undergraduate. "Seldom, if ever, was the emergence of an original poetic genius above the literary horizon more evidently announced." In the form and style of the poems "harshness and acerbity connected and combined with words and images all a-glow." The language was peculiar, strong, and contorted "as if by its own impatient strength." The "struggling crowd of images" demanded a closeness of attention greater than descriptive poetry has a right to claim, and was not seldom obscure.[11]

But, Coleridge adds, "it is remarkable how soon genius clears and purifies itself from the faults and errors of its earliest products." When he came to meet Wordsworth in person in 1795, the poet's work was a revelation to the young Coleridge. "I was in my twenty-fourth year, when I had the happiness of knowing Mr. Wordsworth personally, and while memory lasts, I shall hardly forget the sudden effect produced on my mind by his recitation of a manuscript poem."[12] What he found so remarkable was the lack of strained thought, forced diction, and crowded imagery; the human association and manly interest that was given to natural objects; the imperceptible fusion of style and manner. However, it was not only the freedom from false taste that so impressed him. "It was the union of deep feeling with profound thought; the fine balance of truth in observing, with the imaginative faculty in modifying the objects observed; and above all the original gift of spreading the tone, the *atmosphere*, and with it the depth and height of the ideal world around forms, incidents, and situations, of which, for the common view, custom had bedimmed all the lustre, had

---

defense of Southey and Wordsworth from the charge of forming a "school" — the substance of the second and third chapters — all count as digressions here as they contribute little to the account of Coleridge's literary education. There is also a long note at the end of chapter III in which Coleridge acknowledges the immense moral influence of Southey on his own character. *BL*, I, 49.

[11] *BL*, I, 56.

[12] *BL*, I, 57, 58. The reading seems to have been from "The Female Vagrant." See Shawcross' note, *BL*, I, 224. Coleridge and Wordsworth met in the autumn of 1795 at Bristol, according to a letter of Wordsworth's, but the acquaintance did not become an intimate one until the spring of 1797. *CL*, I, 215–216, note; 319, note; and 325, note. Coleridge, who was born on October 21, 1772, regularly confused the date and even the year of his birth. Chambers, *Coleridge*, p. 1.

dried up the sparkle and the dew drops." [13] This gift, he says, quoting from *The Friend* (1809), is one of the marks which distinguish genius from talent, the ability to represent familiar objects with freshness and novelty.[14]

Coleridge's reflections on this characteristic of Wordsworth's poetry are the beginning of his theory of the imagination. "Repeated meditations led me first to suspect, (and a more intimate analysis of the human faculties, their appropriate marks, functions, and effects matured my conjecture into full conviction,) that fancy and imagination were two distinct and widely different faculties, instead of being, according to the general belief, either two names with one meaning, or, at furthest, the lower and higher degree of one and the same power." [15] What is the justification for desynonymizing the meanings of these two terms? To begin with, the adjectival forms are certainly used differently, even in common critical terminology: "Milton had a highly *imaginative*, Cowley a very *fanciful* mind." If the powers to which these terms refer could be actually distinguished, and if the division be no less grounded in nature than that of delirium from mania, or the difference between Otway's line "Lutes, lobsters, seas of milk, and ships of amber" and Shakespeare's "What! have his daughters brought him to this pass?" then the theory of fine art could not but be illuminated as a result, and the philosophic critic and even the poet himself be furnished with a torch of guidance.[16]

This distinction Coleridge does not immediately propose to delineate. Somewhat self-consciously admitting his passion for metaphysics and psychology, he points out that in making the division in kind between imagination and fancy he had a different purpose from that of Wordsworth in his preface to the 1815 edition of *Lyrical Ballads and Other Poems*. Wordsworth aimed at classifying the effects of the different faculties as they were manifest in poems. Coleridge's object was to in-

---

[13] *BL*, I, 59.

[14] *Friend* (1809), pp. 76–77.

[15] *BL*, I, 60–61.

[16] *BL*, I, 62. Coleridge uses the mania-delirium distinction in several places. Mania seems to be the derangement of the imagination or, alternatively, of the reasoning faculty, while delirium results from the derangement of the fancy or of the understanding. See the citations given by Shawcross, *BL*, I, 225–226.

vestigate the seminal principle. Wordsworth has given the foliage and the "poetic fruitage" of the tree; Coleridge aims to add the trunk and even the roots as far as they are visible to our common consciousness. In other words, Coleridge is about to take the laborious route of explaining the philosophical foundations of his theory of imagination.[17]

As preliminaries to the central philosophical argument of the *Biographia*, the first four chapters thus present us with three experienced facts about poetry which are now felt as convictions. Together they originate in Coleridge's mind the whole question of the possibility of the imagination as a special faculty in the creation of poetry, and therefore they are the primary evidence which any subsequent philosophic theory will have to consider and explain. From Boyer he absorbed the lesson that poetry is a mode of utterance formally distinct from other kinds of writing, with a logic of its own. Bowles showed him that emotion and natural diction could be combined in convincing and effective verse, and provided him with a perspective by which to criticize the "prose thoughts translated into poetic language" that characterized the fashionable verse of the eighteenth century. Wordsworth gave him the most important insight of all, but one which was difficult to define precisely. It was an awareness of the unity of thought and feeling, of style and manner in Wordsworth's poetry, of a power of idealizing the commonplace, a sense of oneness with the world of nature experienced. In its fundamental notion of the unity of the poetic intuition and of its expression, this last insight of Coleridge's summarizes and completes the first two, and implies an activity so unique as a creative communication that a special faculty of the mind must be distinguished as its source. Perhaps for the very reason that he could not put this overwhelming insight into words, Coleridge was driven to theorize at length about the philosophical implications of imagination.

THE FAILURE OF ASSOCIATIONISM

Having set out the evidence that he wishes to take account of and explain, Coleridge begins his elaborate explication of the concept of

[17] *BL*, I, 63–64.

imagination. His general procedure is autobiographical; he follows the course of his own youthful speculations and his own philosophical enthusiasms. Thus he begins where his own systematic thinking in fact began, with a criticism of associationism. But his first task is to define the problem clearly, to phrase it in arguable terms. Since his explanation proceeds through several stages in the course of the first volume of the *Biographia*, Coleridge actually gives several different statements of the problem, narrowing its dimensions and specifying more exactly the question at issue with each successive step of the argument.

The first of these is in conjunction with the refutation of associationist psychology. Coleridge poses the problem in terms of what he calls "the natural difference of *things* and *thoughts*," and the resulting conjectures concerning the way in which our perceptions originate. "In the former, the cause appeared wholly external, while in the latter, sometimes our will interfered as the producing or determining cause, and sometimes our nature seemed to act by mechanism of its own, without any conscious effort of the will, or even against it. Our inward experiences were thus arranged in three separate classes, the passive sense, or what the school-men call the merely receptive quality of the mind; the voluntary; and the spontaneous, which holds the middle place between both." [18] When experimental research was still in its infancy, metaphysicians gave such thorough explanations of our passive and voluntary perceptions that for many centuries it has been difficult to advance a new truth or even a new error in the philosophy of intellect or of morals. But it has been the claim of modern philosophers, especially the British, to have discovered a theory of the third category, the so-called spontaneous movements of thought.[19] Coleridge means, of course, the partisans of associationist psychology, and he makes it his first task in the exposition of a theory of imagination to refute this particular explanation of the nonvoluntary yet not wholly receptive acts of the mind.

No less an authority than Sir James Mackintosh, says Coleridge, asserted "that the law of association as established in the contemporaneity

[18] *BL*, I, 66.
[19] *BL*, I, 66–67.

of the original impressions, formed the basis of all true psychology; and any ontological or metaphysical science, not contained in such (i.e. empirical) psychology, was but a web of abstractions and generalizations." [20] Hobbes, according to Mackintosh, was the discoverer of this law, and Hartley the systematizer of the insight. Coleridge dissents on the question of Hobbes's originality with respect to the modern principle of association, and assigns to Descartes the distinction of having first proposed the mechanical recall of contemporaneous impressions and the construction of general ideas from simple ones. The dispute sets Coleridge to reviewing the history of the associationist principle.

The beginning of the doctrine can be found in Aristotle. He very wisely, says Coleridge, proposed no successive particles propagating motion like billiard balls (which Coleridge says Hobbes did), nor animal spirits which become fluids and etch engravings on the brain (as did the followers of Descartes), nor any oscillating ether to vibrate the fibers of the nerves and brain (as in Hartley), nor any of the recent theories of chemical or electric affections in the brain. Aristotle was content to propose a theory without pretending to a hypothesis, by which Coleridge means that Aristotle gave a comprehensive survey of the facts and their relations to each other but did not offer suppositions in explanation of the facts. The general law of association which Coleridge finds in Aristotle is this: "Ideas by having been together acquire a power of recalling each other; or every partial representation awakes the total representation of which it had been a part." In practice there are five occasioning causes of this phenomenon: connection in time, connection in space, causal connection, likeness, and contrast. "In association then consists the whole mechanism of the reproduction of impressions, in the Aristotelian Psychology. It is the universal law of the *passive* fancy and *mechanical* memory; that which supplies to all other faculties their objects, to all thought the elements of its materials." [21]

Coleridge proceeds to show how Hartley differs from Aristotle, and

[20] *BL*, I, 67.
[21] *BL*, I, 71–73.

that he differs only to err. The "hypothetical vibrations" in the "hypothetical oscillating ether of the nerves" Coleridge dismisses out of
hand, remarking that under the despotism of the eye we are restless
because invisible things are not the subject of the vision, and thus metaphysical systems become popular "in proportion as they attribute to
causes a susceptibility of being *seen*, if only our visual organs were sufficiently powerful." Without the material hypothesis of Hartley's system, however, other parts of it lose their main support and reason for
existence. "Thus the principle of *contemporaneity*, which Aristotle had
made the common *condition* of all the laws of association, Hartley was
constrained to represent as being itself the sole law. For to what law
can the action of *material* atoms be subject, but that of proximity in
place? And to what law can their *motions* be subjected, but that of
time?" This leads inevitably to the position that the will, reason, judgment, and understanding, instead of being the determining causes of
association, are represented as its creatures and among its mechanical
effects. "The consequence would have been, that our whole life would
be divided between the despotism of outward impressions, and that of
senseless and passive memory." [22] This "law" amounts to a subordination of final causes to efficient causes, and the soul becomes nothing
more than an *ens logicum*. "The sum total of my moral and intellectual
intercourse, dissolved into its elements, is reduced to *extension, motion,
degrees of velocity*, and those diminished *copies* of configurative motion,
which form what we call notions, and notions of notions." The existence
of an infinite spirit according to these principles must be "mere articulated motions of the air." [23] Coleridge does not impugn Hartley's religious spirit, to be sure, but he charges him with an unbridgeable
dichotomy between the philosophy of the first book of his *Observations*
and the theology of the second part. This coexistence of associationist
psychology with a genuine religious spirit, however, does not render
the former any less pernicious.[24]

The basic error of the Hartleyan philosophy is reducible to one
sophism: "the mistaking the *conditions* of a thing for its *causes* and

[22] *BL*, I, 74, 76, 77.
[23] *BL*, I, 81, 82, 83.
[24] *BL*, I, 84.

essence; and the process, by which we arrive at the knowledge of a faculty, for the faculty itself. The air I breathe is the *condition* of my life, nor its cause. We could never have learnt that we had eyes but by the process of seeing; yet having seen we know that the eyes must have pre-existed in order to render the process of sight possible." Thus contemporaneity is the limit and condition of the laws of our minds; at most it is to thought as the law of gravitation is to loco-motion. When we move voluntarily we first counteract gravitation and then take advantage of its reaction to assist us.[25] The law is thus the limit and condition of our actions. A water insect moves by alter-nate pulses of resistance to the current and then cooperation with it. "This is no unapt emblem of the mind's self-experience in the act of thinking. There are evidently two powers at work, which relatively to each other are active and passive; and this is not possible without an intermediate faculty, which is at once both active and passive." [26] The opportunity of seizing upon this attractive emblem takes Coleridge rather far ahead of his argument here, for he has mentioned nothing heretofore of a synthesizing faculty to mediate between the active and passive powers, though of course it is implicit in his refutation of the mechanical explanation of knowledge. He says that in philosophical language we must call this faculty the imagination.[27] With these somewhat digressive remarks out of the way, Coleridge returns to his final observations about the association of ideas. The "true prac-tical general law" of association can be stated thus: "Whatever makes certain parts of a total impression more vivid or distinct than the rest,

[25] *BL*, I, 85. Mackintosh had said, according to Coleridge, that Hartley, the systema-tizer of associationism, stood in the same relation to Hobbes as Newton to Kepler, "the law of associationism being that to the mind, which gravitation is to matter." *BL*, I, 67.

[26] *BL*, I, 85–86.

[27] The rest of Coleridge's parenthetical remark is interesting with respect to the goal of this whole discussion: "In philosophical language, we must denominate this inter-mediate faculty in all its degrees and determinations, the IMAGINATION. But, in common language, and especially on the subject of poetry, we appropriate the name to a superior degree of the faculty, joined to a superior voluntary control over it." *BL*, I, 86. This seems to be a form of the distinction between primary and secondary imagination. Both have the mediating function between active and passive powers of the mind, but it is the higher degree or the secondary imagination that we particularly appropriate to poetry, as in common usage we do not much attend to the mediating operation of the primary imagination.

will determine the mind to recall these in preference to others equally
linked together by the common condition of contemporaneity, or
(what I deem a more appropriate and philosophical term) of *con-
tinuity*." And this emphasis may be furnished by the will itself arbitrarily giving vividness or distinctness to any object whatsoever.[28]

THE FAILURE OF MATERIALISM

At the beginning of the eighth chapter Coleridge redefines the problem that he is attempting to solve. The context now is Cartesian dualism, and the difficulty that of explaining the interaction of the soul
as a "*thinking* substance" and the body as a "*space-filling* substance."
Their action on each other is apparent and yet so also is the principle
that causality is possible only between things that are in some way
homogeneous.[29] The doctrine of pre-established harmony violates
common sense, and the thesis of hylozoism, maintaining that each
atom of matter has its own principle of life, merely multiplies the
difficulty. Coleridge's response to these problems is to challenge the
whole framework in which they are proposed, the very possibility
of discussing the epistemological problem as a gap that must be
bridged between body and soul. "A close analysis evinced it to be
no less absurd than the question whether a man's affection for his
wife, lay North-east, or South-west of the love he bore towards his
child." [30] How the *esse* can ever unite itself with the *scire*, or being
transform itself into knowing, once they are assumed to be originally
distinct, "becomes conceivable on one only condition; namely, if it
can be shown that the *vis representativa*, or the Sentient, is itself a
species of being; i.e. either as a property or attribute, or as an hypostasis or self subsistence." [31]

The first possibility, that the knowing subject is itself a property
or attribute of being, is the answer of materialism, which would be an
extremely persuasive system if it could fulfill what it promises. But

[28] *BL*, I, 87.
[29] *BL*, I, 88.
[30] *BL*, I, 89.
[31] *BL*, I, 89–90. This formulation of the problem, and the refutation of materialism
that follows, is drawn from Schelling. See Shawcross' note, *BL*, I, 239.

if the physical object could act on the conscious self as on a consubstantial object, it could produce in it only effects homogeneous with itself, that is, movements of particles describable in terms of time and space. And it would be the impact of the physical object on the percipient, and not the object itself, that would be so described. Coleridge opposes to this what he later calls the "true and original realism": we are irrevocably persuaded that it is not the impressions or the ideas of objects that we know, but the objects themselves that are somehow in us. Nor is it the conclusion of a syllogism based on physical data that we know. "The transition, into the percipient, of the object itself, from which the impulse proceeded, assumes a power that can permeate and wholly possess the soul," and in the face of this fact the consistent dogmatic materialist has no choice but to fall back "into the common rank of *soul-and-bodyists*; to affect the mysterious, and declare the whole process a revelation *given*, and not to be *understood*, which it would be profane to examine too closely." But, says Coleridge, "a revelation unconfirmed by miracles, and a faith not commanded by the conscience, a philosopher may venture to pass by, without suspecting himself of any irreligious tendency." [32]

Coleridge's refutation of the materialist hypothesis is satisfactory, at least to those of his readers who will accept the validity of his conclusions from experience. Logically the next step in his argument should be an explanation of the second way in which the conscious self can be considered a species of being homogeneous with the object of knowledge, that is, "as an hypostasis or self subsistence." Otherwise the positive content of his entire argument is wanting, and the meaning of his challenge to the whole Cartesian formulation of the epistemological problem is left uncertain. Yet this is exactly what happens. In an ominous foreshadowing of the technique he later uses to get out of his difficulties with the Schellingian Absolute and the imagination, Coleridge simply announces here that he will not "dilate further on this subject," since he means to treat of it fully and systematically "in a work, which I have many years been preparing, on the PRODUCTIVE LOGOS human and divine; with, and as the introduction to,

[32] *BL*, I, 91.

a full commentary of the Gospel of St. John." [33] We are left only with three observations on the subject of associationism and the materialist hypothesis generally: first, that all association presupposes the existence of the thoughts and images to be associated; second, that the hypothesis of an external world exactly correspondent to those images or modifications of our own being which alone we behold is as thorough an idealism as Berkeley's; third, that this hypothesis neither explains nor denies the necessity "of a mechanism and co-adequate forces in the percipient, which at the more than magic touch of the impulse from without is to create anew for itself the correspondent object." [34] The description in the last phrases, though it carefully preserves intact the facts and assumptions that Coleridge wishes to explain — the external object of knowledge, the homogeneity of knower and known, the formative activity of the percipient — still tells us nothing of how these requirements are to be intelligibly unified in the operation of the imagination.

This redefinition of the problem of the imagination suggests, I think, one of the principal reasons for the ultimate failure of Coleridge to explain his theories satisfactorily, even to himself. The first statement of the problem had proposed that a special faculty was necessary to explain the "spontaneous" acts of the mind. Here in the second formulation the scope of the problem is considerably widened: no longer aimed at explaining one kind of mental act, the faculty in question is now the source of the unity of being and knowing in every act of knowledge. I do not wish to say that the imagination cannot be the agent of this unity, nor do I wish to force Coleridge's words to bear more meaning than he intended them to at this stage of the discussion, but I think that the confusion here becomes a pattern for the rest of his analysis of the imagination, and the reason why it ultimately fails: Coleridge gradually sets up requirements for the imagination which it cannot possibly fulfill in terms of its original conception. The subsequent development of Coleridge's argument makes this clear.

[33] *BL*, I, 91–92.
[34] *BL*, I, 92.

THE CONTRIBUTION OF IDEALISMS

After he had successively studied in the schools of Locke, Berkeley, Leibnitz, and Hartley, Coleridge says, and could find no resting place, he began to ask if a system of philosophy, apart from a mere history and classification of theories, were even possible. A negative answer seemed contrary to human nature. Yet if the principle "nothing is in the intellect that was not first in the senses" be taken in its strictest sense, and if Leibnitz' additional qualification "except the intellect itself" be interpreted for all of Kant's categories in the same narrow way that Hume had done for cause and effect, what is left to us? "How can we make bricks without straw? or build without cement?" It is apparent that we learn all things "by occasion of experience," but the quality of this experience and the inability of the materialist theories to explain it "force us inward on the antecedents, that must be pre-supposed in order to render experience itself possible." [35] Thus Coleridge takes up the idealist position, and the ninth chapter is an autobiographical review of various versions of idealism which contributed to his conception of the imagination.

He begins with a general statement of the common denominator of these theories, though he does not call it such: philosophy can be defined as "an affectionate seeking after the truth," and "Truth is the correlative of Being." "This again is no way conceivable, but by assuming as a postulate, that both are *ab initio*, identical and coinherent; that intelligence and being are reciprocally each other's substrate." [36] This will be recognized as a restatement in metaphysical terms of the *esse-scire* identity of the previous chapter. He refers in passing to the historical popularity of the notion of God as completely pure act without any potentiality, which is the basis of the ontological argument, as a justification for his position. In one long sentence he acknowledges his debts to Plato and Plotinus, Marsilio Ficino, Proclus, Gemistus Pletho, and Giordano Bruno, all of whom prepared him to appreciate the *Cogito* of Descartes.

[35] *BL*, I, 94.
[36] *BL*, I, 94.

This rapid summary of the history of his dealings with the tradition of idealism is interrupted by a long encomium of the humble learning of Boehme and the simple fervor of George Fox and William Law, men whose writings kept his mind "from being imprisoned within the outline of any single dogmatic system." He invokes them against the antecedent limitations that any "dogmatic" system sets up for our knowledge, in particular the limitations of the understandings: "They contributed to keep alive the *heart* in the *head*; gave me an indistinct, yet stirring and working presentiment, that all the products of the mere *reflective* faculty partook of DEATH, and were as the rattling twigs and sprays in winter, into which a sap was yet to be propelled from some root to which I had not penetrated, if they were to afford my soul either food or shelter." [37]

He says of Spinoza only that he doubts that his system is an irreligious pantheism, incompatible with both natural and revealed religion. The discussion of Kant is almost as disappointing, in view of the light that might have been shed on the theory of imagination by a more detailed analysis. He says that the writings of Kant, more than any other work, invigorated and disciplined his understanding; their "clearness" and "evidence" delight him still after fifteen years' acquaintance. He makes the interesting comment that the apparent contradictions in Kant are due to the two different starting points of his *Critique of Pure Reason* and his *Critique of Judgment*; the former is an analysis not of human nature *in toto*, but of the speculative intellect alone, and it therefore begins at "the point of *reflection*, or natural consciousness," while the second critique, containing the moral system, is able to begin on higher ground, the autonomy of the will deduced from the unconditional command or categorical imperative of the conscience. Coleridge expresses two doubts about Kant's philosophy, one of which is predictable but the second rather surprising. The first is disbelief that Kant could have meant no more by his *noumenon*, or "thing in itself," than his words express, "or that in his own conception he confined the whole *plastic* power to the form of the intellect, leaving for the external cause, for the *materiale* of our sensations a

[37] *BL*, I, 98.

matter without form, which is doubtless inconceivable." Coleridge had insisted before, even when speaking of Kant, on the external reality of the object of knowledge precisely as it is known by us. He goes on to express a doubt also that Kant had laid all the stress on the moral postulates that he seemed to, and, in view of Coleridge's early and late views on the importance of the will even in the knowledge-act, this is somewhat unexpected.[38]

Fichte and Schelling are the last two names in this litany of Coleridge's intellectual progenitors. Fichte led him to see that the point of departure of metaphysics ought to be an act rather than a substance or thing, but in his system this insight was overbuilt with arbitrary notions and the whole degenerated into a crude egoism and a hostility to Nature, while his religion recognized a deity that was a mere Ordo Ordinans, and his ethics consisted of a monkish mortification of the natural passions and desires.[39]

It was Schelling in whose thought Coleridge first found a resemblance to his own. They were both students of Kant and of the "polar logic and dynamic philosophy" of Giordano Bruno, and both revered the mystical writings of Boehme. Coleridge praises Schelling as the founder of "the Philosophy of Nature" and the improver of "the Dynamic System" which Bruno began and Kant purified and clarified.[40] Whatever in the *Biographia* or in his future works resembles the doctrine of Schelling, Coleridge wants attributed to his German master, even though, as he had just said a page or two earlier, identity of thought or even similarity of phrase does not necessarily argue that the material has been borrowed. "In this instance, as in the dramatic lectures of Schlegel to which I have before alluded, from the same motive of self-defence against the charge of plagiarism, many of the most striking resemblances, indeed all the main and fundamental ideas, were born and matured in my mind before I had ever seen a single page of the German Philosopher."[41] Mere questions of source and influence never interested Coleridge personally, though he was quite

[38] *BL*, I, 99–100.
[39] *BL*, I, 101–102.
[40] *BL*, I, 103–104.
[41] *BL*, I, 102.

sensitive, as these remarks show, to imputations of plagiarism. The use to which these borrowed ideas and phrases could be put was far more important to him. "I regard truth as a divine ventriloquist: I care not from whose mouth the sounds are supposed to proceed, if only the words are audible and intelligible." [42] With these few notes on Schelling Coleridge ends the history of his intellectual development.

This ninth chapter disappoints the reader who hopes to find in the *Biographia* some clue to the extent of the idealist influence on Coleridge's thinking. What he gives by way of comment amounts to not much more than a hasty outline, a cartoon that will not do where a finished painting is demanded. Yet Coleridge's approach here is curiously revealing of his state of mind and suggests a partial answer to the much larger question of the meaning of the whole argument of the *Biographia*. The fact is that Coleridge devotes most of four chapters to a long and very circumstantial refutation of associationist psychology, but only one short chapter to the influence of the whole idealist tradition on his thought. Even this one chapter is not much more than a quick tour of idealism which makes only the predictable and obvious criticisms and approbations, and nowhere gives any of the solid philosophical arguments that characterize the chapter on associationism. The imbalance in the division of Coleridge's labors here seems to indicate something about his own conception of his philosophy of knowledge — namely, that it was, whether explicitly or implicitly, primarily an answer to associationism, basically a refutation of that system's pretensions to explain mechanically things which Coleridge knew from his own experience were more than material and automatic.

If Coleridge's epistemology had this fundamentally negative motivation, then perhaps it becomes clearer why he was finally so unprepared to deal — in the last chapters of the first part of the *Biographia* — with all the claims that Schelling made for the imagination as an organ of knowledge, and why ultimately he fell into silence on the topic. What explanation there is of the imagination in the latter part of the work comes almost entirely from Schelling. Nearly the whole

philosophical discussion in the first volume, therefore, is divided between association psychology and Schelling's metaphysics. All the
other idealist influences from Plato to Kant and Fichte, usually thought
so important for Coleridge's thought, are crowded into a short intermediate chapter. I am not suggesting that these figures are not important for Coleridge's philosophy, but it seems that, when he was
engaged in writing the *Biographia*, Coleridge conceived the answer
to his epistemological problem to lie in a choice between the extremes
of associationism and Schellingian idealism. He rejected the first, of
course, and for very sound reasons; but then he discovered that in
the second he had more than he wanted, not only a faculty to explain
the affective and noetic unity of the work of art in itself and in relation to the world of experience, but also a faculty which was the source
and guarantee of universal and absolute truth. Coleridge could not
really give that importance to imagination, and finding no medium
between the two views he ended in confusion. If this seems a bold
explanation of Coleridge's difficulties, I hope it will seem less so after
some more of the evidence for it is examined.

FURTHER PRELIMINARIES

The next two chapters are devoted to "digression and anecdotes,"
mainly on the subject of his literary ventures, and on his opinions in
religion and politics, with the entire eleventh chapter devoted to an
"exhortation to those who in early life feel themselves disposed to
become authors." The discussion of imagination resumes in the twelfth
chapter. Coleridge's uneasiness about a straightforward presentation
of his theories is evident in the title: "A Chapter of requests and
premonitions concerning the perusal or omission of the chapter that
follows." [43] He must make certain that the reader understands all the

---

[43] *BL*, I, 160. In the chapters not discussed here there are some interesting remarks
about words. Though it is pedantry, Coleridge says, to use words unsuitable to the time,
place, and company, where a new sense must be conveyed a new word is allowable. Thus
he coins the term *esemplastic* as a modifier of "imagination," from the Greek εἰς ἓν
πλάττειν, to shape into one, in order to avoid confusion with the usual meaning of
imagination (presumably Coleridge is thinking of the usage which signifies the associative fancy based on memory, common to the eighteenth century). Other words which

conditions and qualifications and preparatory cautions that apply to his explanation of the imagination.

Coleridge first pleads for a sympathetic hearing from his auditors, who should understand the total context of his remarks. He invokes one of his favorite maxims: "Until you understand a writer's ignorance, presume yourself ignorant of his understanding." He cheerfully admits that this "golden rule" of his resembles those of Pythagoras in its obscurity rather than in its depth, but he tries to explain his meaning by an example: "I have now before me a treatise of a religious fanatic, full of dreams and supernatural *experiences*. I see clearly the writer's grounds, and their hollowness. I have a complete insight into the causes, which through the medium of his body has acted on his mind; and by application of received and ascertained laws I can satisfactorily explain to my own reason all the strange incidents, which the writer records of himself. And this I can do without suspecting him of any intentional falsehood . . . I UNDERSTAND HIS IGNORANCE." [44] It is this kind of contextual understanding that Coleridge asks of his readers. Though in one sense it is no more than any writer deserves, looked at in another way it introduces a kind of *appellatio ad tenebras* into the process of interpretation, a wholly idiosyncratic last-refuge in which an author can disclaim the responsibility of fully explaining his theories. In any case it shows Coleridge very much in doubt about his ability to make clear the forthcoming theory of imagination.

He goes on to request that his readers will either pass over the following chapter altogether, or read the whole connectedly. To ask for a completely unprejudiced reader would be unrealistic, but Coleridge puts down one criterion by which the reader might discover whether he would lose his time or his temper studying the treatise which follows. "If a man receives as fundamental facts, and therefore of course indemonstrable and incapable of further analysis, the general notions of matter, spirit, soul, body, action, passiveness, time, space, cause, and

---

Coleridge says he will use in a special sense include sensuous, employed (as in Milton) to avoid the morally pejorative sensual; intuition, to designate the immediateness of any act or object of knowledge; objective and subjective, to distinguish the *percipere* from the *percipi*; and reason and understanding, which are not defined. BL, I, 107–109.

[44] BL, I, 160–161.

effect, consciousness, perception, memory and habit; if he feels his mind completely at rest concerning all these, and is satisfied, if only he can analyse all other notions into some one or more of these supposed elements with plausible subordination and apt arrangement: to such a mind I would as courteously as possible convey the hint, that for him the chapter was not written." [45] Such a person may be successful at the kind of philosophical legerdemain that consists in the subordination and arrangement of terms, but he is not ready for the science of ultimate truths, the *scientia scientiarum*, for which the analysis of terms is only a preparative, though an indispensable one.

The plain fact is that all men cannot be philosophers. "There is a *philosophic* (and inasmuch as it is actualized by an effort of freedom, an *artificial*) *consciousness*, which lies beneath or (as it were) *behind* the spontaneous consciousness natural to all reflecting beings." All the objects of human knowledge can be divided into those on this side and those on the other side of spontaneous consciousness. The latter is the domain of pure philosophy and is properly called transcendental, to distinguish it from mere reflection and re-presentation on the one hand, and "on the other from those flights of lawless speculation which, abandoned by *all* distinct consciousness, because transgressing the bounds and purposes of our intellectual faculties, are justly condemned, as *transcendent*." [46]

Coleridge's seemingly general warnings about the care with which his remarks are to be interpreted thus lead him to delimit rather sharply the number of his potential readers, and then to define explicitly the power which these few possess. He does this by means of a striking metaphor:

The first range of hills, that encircles the scanty vale of human life, is the horizon for the majority of its inhabitants. On *its* ridges the common sun is born and departs. From *them* the stars rise, and touching *them* they vanish. By the many, even this range, the natural limit and bulwark of the vale, is but imperfectly known. Its higher ascents are too often hidden by mists and clouds from uncultivated swamps, which few have courage and curiosity to penetrate. To the multitude below these vapors appear, now as the

[45] *BL*, I, 162–163.
[46] *BL*, I, 164. Kant, *Critique of Pure Reason*, A. 296, B. 352–353, Smith ed., p. 299.

dark haunts of terrific agents, on which none may intrude with impunity; and now all *a-glow*, with colors not their own, they are gazed at as the splendid palaces of happiness and power. But in all ages there have been a few, who measuring and sounding the rivers of the vale at the feet of their furthest inaccessible falls have learned, that the sources must be far higher and far inward; a few, who even in the level streams have detected elements, which neither the vale itself or the surrounding mountains contained or could supply. How and whence to these thoughts, these strong probabilities, the ascertaining vision, the intuitive knowledge may finally supervene, can be learnt only by the fact.[47]

Coleridge thus appeals to experience to confirm the difference between the spontaneous and the philosophic consciousness. The capacity for the higher kind of knowledge is not to be acquired by labor and searching but, he quotes Plotinus, by watching "in quiet till it suddenly shines upon us; preparing ourselves for the blessed spectacle as the eyes waits patiently for the rising sun." [48] In the figures he uses Coleridge emphasizes the natural teleology of this process, and the reciprocal influence of active and passive elements: "They and they only can acquire the philosophic imagination, the sacred power of self-intuition, who within themselves can interpret and understand the symbol, that the wings of the air-sylph are forming within the skin of the caterpillar . . . They know and feel, that the *potential* works *in* them, even as the *actual* works on them!" He also insists upon the connaturality of subject and object: "All the organs of sense are framed for a corresponding world of sense . . . All the organs of spirit are framed for a corresponding world of spirit: though the latter organs are not developed in all alike." [49]

What more precisely is the specific power which these descriptions attempt to suggest? The key word seems to be intuition, that is, intellectual intuition, the capacity to know truths without a medium.[50]

---

[47] *BL*, I, 164–166.
[48] *BL*, I, 167.
[49] *BL*, I, 167.
[50] This is the meaning Coleridge gives to intuition in a note a few pages later. He says that, though for Kant the term is confined exclusively to that which can be represented in space and time, and thus for Kant intellectual intuitions are impossible, he himself prefers to follow "our elder theologians and metaphysicians" and consider that intellectual intuitions comprehend "all truths known to us without a medium." *BL*, I, 190.

Coleridge's explanation of the significance of this power takes him through a complex series of arguments, based almost entirely on Schelling.[51] From the experienced fact of this higher knowledge (indicated in the descriptions already quoted) he moves to the question of the initiative of this knowledge, the act of the will that calls it into being. This requires a discussion of postulates in philosophy, and of the fundamental question of the primary postulate that determines the operation of the "inner sense," a term which seems to mean the same as "intellectual intuition" for Coleridge. It is while discussing this last problem that Coleridge breaks off once again and promises that the matter will be treated at length in his *Logosophia*.

Unsatisfactory though the outcome is, we must still recapitulate the substance of his argument here, for the light it sheds on the failure of his theory of imagination. The essential elements of that failure can be seen already in the descriptions of the "philosophic imagination" as the faculty of "transcendental" knowledge, of "pure" philosophy — a far greater dignity than any of Coleridge's speculations had ever conferred on the imagination before the *Biographia*, and in direct contradiction to claims he would make subsequently for the reason.

The ultimate question in Coleridge's (or Schelling's) argument here has to do with the premises of all philosophy. "All knowledge rests on the coincidence of an object with a subject . . . For we can *know* that only which is true: and the truth is universally placed in the coincidence of the thought with the thing, of the representation with the object represented." All that is objective Coleridge calls nature, in its passive and material sense, the phenomena by which its active existence is made known to us. All that is subjective he calls the self or intelligence. In all acts of knowledge there is a reciprocal and instantaneous concurrence of conscious intelligence and unconscious nature. The problem is to explain this concurrence, and to do so we must separate what in the act of knowledge is unified and discuss the objective and subjective as though capable of separation.[52]

He proposes two possibilities. (1) "Either the Objective is taken as

---

[51] Shawcross gives references in his notes to the appropriate passages.
[52] *BL*, I, 174.

the first, and then we have to account for the supervention of the subjective, which coalesces with it." If all knowledge has two poles reciprocally required and presupposed, says Coleridge, then all sciences must proceed from one or the other and tend toward the opposite as far as the equatorial point in which both are reconciled and become identical. The movement of natural philosophy is therefore from nature to intelligence, and thus we instinctively introduce theory into our views of natural phenomena. "The highest perfection of natural philosophy would consist in the perfect spiritualization of all the laws of nature into laws of intuition and intellect," and nature would then be identical with consciousness.[53]

(2) "Or the subjective is taken as the first, and the problem then is, how there supervenes to it a coincident objective." The success of every science depends on a faithful adherence to its own principles and the exclusion of the subjective, as for instance, arbitrary suppositions, occult qualities, spiritual agents, and the substitution of final for efficient causes; likewise, the transcendental philosopher avoids the intrusion of the objective, "as for instance the assumption of impressions or configurations in the brain, correspondent to miniature pictures on the retina painted by rays of light from supposed originals, which are not the immediate and real objects of vision, but deductions from it for the purposes of explanation." This purification of the mind is effected by a scientific skepticism, the objects of which are not the ordinary prejudices arising from education and circumstance but the original and innate prejudices natural to all men. These are reducible to one fundamental presumption, that there exist things without us. Because it does not originate in arguments and is proof against them, this conviction lays claim to immediate certainty, indemonstrable and irresistible, and yet, since it refers to something essentially different from and even in opposition to ourselves, we cannot conceive how it could possibly become a part of our immediate consciousness.[54] There is another position which claims immediate certainty, that *I am*, but this cannot properly be called a prejudice because it is itself the ground

[53] *BL*, I, 175–176.
[54] *BL*, I, 176–178.

of all other certainty. The apparent contradiction, that the existence of things without us should be affirmed as certainly as we affirm our own existence, though both are equally independent of all possibility of demonstration, can be solved by the transcendental philosopher only by supposing that the former is unconsciously involved in the latter, "that it is not only coherent but identical, and one and the same thing with our own immediate self-consciousness." [55]

In support of this position Coleridge appeals once again to the lesson of experience. "If it be said, that this is Idealism, let it be remembered that it is only so far idealism, as it is at the same time, and on that very account, the truest and most binding realism." Does the realism of the common man consist in affirming that there exists a something outside him which in some way occasions the objects of his perceptions? This explanation, Coleridge says, is neither connatural nor universal. It is a schoolroom explanation, "skimmed from the mere surface of mechanical philosophy." In its place Coleridge offers "the true and original realism." "This believes and requires neither more nor less, than the object which it beholds or presents to itself, is the real and very object." And in this sense we are collectively born idealists and therefore at the same time realists.[56]

Coleridge's paradox is fascinating. He solves with apparent ease the central problem of several centuries of philosophy. Can his words be intelligibly interpreted, or is there here only more "metaphysical pathos?" There seems to be no way of answering. Here again, at the crux of his argument, he defers his explanations to the third treatise of his forthcoming *Logosophia*. There the "demonstrations and constructions of the Dynamic Philosophy" will be presented. The system, he says, will be none other than that of Pythagoras and of Plato revived and purified from corrupting influences. In the meantime — until the whole structure can be set down — he takes from mathematics the maxim that a rule may be useful in practical applications, where its truth is judged by its result, even before it has been fully demonstrated. To this purpose he gives ten theses which are to outline

[55] *BL*, I, 178.
[56] *BL*, I, 178–179.

the Dynamic Philosophy, and which will be applied in the following chapter, he says, "to the deduction of the Imagination, and with it the principles of production and of genial criticism in the fine arts." [57]

The theses depend in substance on Schelling.[58] There is no need to go into each of them in detail; they repeat in categorical form much of the material already discussed as preamble to the imagination theory, but now clothed with the doctrine and even the exact words of Schelling's Absolute Idealism. Truth is correlative to being (I). It is either mediate or immediate, and the latter is absolute (II). We need to discover a truth self-grounded, unconditional, and known by its own light (III), and there can be but one such principle (IV). Such a principle cannot be any thing or object, which is what it is in virtue of some other thing; furthermore an object is inconceivable without a subject as its antithesis. Nor can a subject as subject be this principle, but only that which is neither object nor subject exclusively, but which is the identity of both (V). This principle manifests itself in the *Sum* or *I Am*, hereafter called Spirit, self, self-consciousness. "It is a subject which becomes a subject by the act of constructing itself objectively to itself; but which never is an object except for itself, and only so far as by the very same act it becomes a subject" (VI). There is no other predicate of self except self-consciousness; the essence of a spirit is to be self-representative; it must therefore be an act, which requires a will, and therefore freedom must be assumed as a ground of philosophy and can never be deduced from it (VII). The spirit with its object is neither infinite nor finite but a union of both, in the reconciling and recurrence of which contradiction consists the process and mystery of production and life (VIII). This will or primary act is the immediate principle of the ultimate science, transcendental philosophy, alone, since these theses refer solely to the science which begins in and confines itself solely to the subjective. We are not investigating an absolute *principium essendi*, but an absolute *principium cognoscendi* (IX). The principle of our knowing is sought within the sphere of our knowing; it is asserted only that the act of self-consciousness is for

[57] *BL*, I, 179–180.
[58] Shawcross, *BL*, I, 269–270.

us the source and principle of all our possible knowledge — not a kind of being for us, but the highest kind of knowing. Even if we begin with the objective, we could never pass beyond the principle of self-consciousness because we must either choose an infinite series of grounds, or affirm an absolute that is of itself cause and effect (causa sui), subject and object, or rather the identity of both. So even as natural philosophers we arrive at a self-consciousness in which the *principium essendi* does not stand to the *principium cognoscendi* as cause to effect but both the one and the other are coinherent and identical, the Absolute (X).[59]

Bearing in mind, says Coleridge, that intelligence is a self-development, we may conceive an indestructible power with two opposite and counteracting forces. The metaphor which expresses these is that of centrifugal and centripetal forces, borrowed from astronomy. In the one the intelligence tends to objectize itself, in the other to know itself in the object. "It will be hereafter my business," he says with persistent obscurity, "to construct by a series of intuitions the progressive schemes, that must follow from such a power with such forces, till I arrive at the fulness of the *human* intelligence." For now, he will assume this power as a principle from which he will in the following chapter deduce the faculty of imagination.[60]

Not content with the cautionary remarks he has already made, Coleridge devotes several pages to further preliminary observations on the difficulties of philosophical terminology and the general disrepute of metaphysics. Finally, at the chapter's end, he announces that he will now "proceed to the nature and genesis of the imagination."[61]

What is the significance of all the backing and filling in this untidy twelfth chapter? Can the interpretative injunctions to the reader and the qualifications of Coleridge's meaning indicate anything other than his own confusion as he prepares at last to define his theory of imagination? It is often supposed that the lengthy, sometimes word-for-word extracts from Schelling in this part of the *Biographia* are a proof

[59] *BL*, I, 180–188.
[60] *BL*, I, 188.
[61] *BL*, I, 193.

of Coleridge's enthusiasm, at least in 1815, for Schelling's system. It seems just as reasonable to think that his dependence on Schelling at this point is a sign of the weakness of his own argument, and that the sometimes unaltered paragraphs borrowed from the *Transcendental Idealism* and other works were intended to bolster a not very satisfactory theory which he had obligated himself to explain. Time and again in these chapters, when faced with the necessity of clarifying the crucial points of his dynamic philosophy, Coleridge falls back upon experience, the common persuasion of the "true and original realism," as his best argument, and announces that the theoretical account of this experience will be given in a future work. The tactic suggests that his insight into the fact of imagination still lacks a theory to explain that fact, and that the Schellingian paraphernalia here is a hopeful attempt to force a solution to the problem. The question of why it failed may be postponed a moment, until we have Coleridge's final words on the imagination.

THE IMAGINATION

The long awaited analysis of imagination which is to complete the argument of the first volume of the *Biographia* is almost a total disappointment. The thirteenth chapter, with the title "On the imagination, or esemplastic power," contains only a few more introductory remarks and then the much-quoted definitions. It begins with a distinction taken from Kant between logical opposites which are absolutely incompatible, and real but not contradictory opposites. As an example of the latter Coleridge cites different motory forces in a body which yet result in rest. This leads him to restate the Schellingian concept of the two essentially opposite infinite forces which the transcendental philosophy demands. Having described and outlined these two forces by means of discursive reasoning, Coleridge says, "it will then remain for us to elevate the Thesis from notional to actual, by contemplating intuitively this one power with its two inherent indestructible yet counteracting forces, and the results or generations to which their inter-peneration gives existence, in the living principle and in the process of our own self-consciousness." This intuition which elevates our knowledge from the notional to the actual is of course not within the power of everyone, says Coleridge in one final warning that the reader may not understand his argument. "There is a philosophic no less than a poetic genius, which is differenced from the highest perfection of talent, not by degree but by kind." Returning to the opposition of the infinite forces, Coleridge observes that rest or neutralization cannot be the result, but that the product must be "a tertium quid, or finite generation," which is "an inter-penetration of the counteracting powers, partaking of both." [62]

It is at this point that Coleridge breaks in with the "letter from a friend" urging him to postpone these novel and incomprehensible arguments until he can publish them in full in the treatise on the *Logos.* It is of course his own letter, "addressed to myself as from a friend," as he writes to his published Curtis.[63] The difficulty is that Coleridge has been obliged, so his fictitious correspondent says, to omit so many of the links of his argument, from the necessity of compression, that what remains looks "like a fragment of the winding steps of an old ruined tower." Besides, the full chapter could not amount to less than a hundred pages and he should not lay himself open to the charge of deceiving his readers by promising a biographical sketch and providing instead an abstruse tract on "ideal Realism," thus imitating Berkeley's *Siris,* "announced as an Essay on Tar-water, which beginning with Tar ends with the Trinity, the omne scibile forming the interspace." The letter ends with Coleridge's expressions of good will toward himself: "All success attend you, for if hard thinking and hard reading are merits, you have deserved it." [64]

In place of the deduction of imagination Coleridge in his own person presents three definitions as the "main result" of the unpublished part of the chapter:

The IMAGINATION then, I consider either as primary, or secondary. The primary IMAGINATION I hold to be the living Power and prime Agent of all

[62] *BL,* I, 197–198.
[63] *CL,* IV, 728. April 29, 1817.
[64] *BL,* I, 200, 201.

human Perception, and as a repetition in the finite mind of the eternal act of creation in the infinite I AM. The secondary Imagination I consider as an echo of the former, co-existing with the conscious will, yet still as identical with the primary in the *kind* of its agency, and differing only in *degree*, and in the *mode* of its operation. It dissolves, diffuses, dissipates, in order to recreate; or where this process is rendered impossible, yet still at all events it struggles to idealize and to unify. It is essentially *vital*, even as all objects (*as* objects) are essentially fixed and dead.

FANCY, on the contrary, has no other counters to play with, but fixities and definites. The Fancy is indeed no other than a mode of Memory emancipated from the order of time and space; while it is blended with, and modified by that empirical phenomenon of the will, which we express by the word CHOICE, But equally with the ordinary memory the Fancy must receive all its materials ready made from the law of association.[65]

Whatever else, Coleridge says, he thinks fit to declare concerning the powers and privileges of the imagination can be found in the essay on the supernatural in poetry which will be prefixed to *The Ancient Mariner* — another entry in the canon of Coleridge's unwritten works.

What are we to make of the fragment that Coleridge leaves for us when he makes his graceless exit — the definitions of the two imaginations and of fancy? Are they in any way intelligible as conclusions to his argument, or do they perhaps form independently a coherent aesthetic structure?

The first thing that must be said is that the distinction of primary from secondary imagination is by no means clear. Shawcross thought it the same as Schelling's distinction between our common unconscious perception of the actual world of phenomena on the one hand and on the other our free creation of an ideal world, the world of our common experience in its real significance. This latter is the province of art.[66] However, as Bate has pointed out, the concept of the artistic imagination as an "echo" of a universal agency of perception does violence to the whole trend of Coleridge's thought, and its scope necessarily includes universals, which lie beyond the restricted field of the secondary imagination.[67] Again it is tempting to view the distinction

[65] *BL*, I, 202.
[66] *BL*, I, 272.
[67] W. J. Bate, "Coleridge on the Function of Art," *Perspectives of Criticism*, ed. Harry

as parallel to that of spontaneous consciousness and philosophic consciousness in the twelfth chapter of the *Biographia*. Philosophic consciousness is artificial insofar as it is "actualized by an effort of freedom" just as the secondary imagination is co-existent with the conscious will. It is also the domain of the transcendental, of "pure" philosophy, whereas the spontaneous consciousness is the "mere reflection and *re*-presentation" natural to all men.[68] Philosophic consciousness is subsequently identified in the *Biographia* with intuition, "the ascertaining vision," the "philosophic imagination," and the "sacred power of self-intuition" — thus with the highest faculty of the finite mind. The obvious difficulty involved in identifying these two distinctions is that the spontaneous consciousness deals, in the earlier formulation, with mere reflection and re-presentation, which are normally assigned in Coleridge's lexicon to fancy (as in the last lines of Chapter XIII: Fancy deals only with fixities and definites, and must receive all its materials ready made from the law of association).[69] Further, if imagination in its highest degree is made the equivalent of philosophic intuition, is there any specifically aesthetic function — creative as distinguished from noetic — also proper to the secondary imagination? And what, then, is the relationship of secondary imagination to reason, to which the capacity of intuitive knowledge has already been assigned?

Equally untenable is the interpretation which considers the differ-

---

Levin, Harvard Studies in Comparative Literature, vol. 20 (Cambridge, Mass., 1950), p. 145.

[68] *BL*, I, 164. Philosophic consciousness is also opposed here to "lawless speculation," but this latter is not the normal spontaneous consciousness either, since it is "abandoned by *all* distinct consciousness, because transgressing the bounds and purposes of our intellectual faculties."

[69] This objection is mitigated somewhat if we go back to the very opening of the section on the notion of imagination in the *Biographia*, and recall the three kinds of inward experience with respect to reality: the passive, the spontaneous, and the voluntary. There the spontaneous acts of the mind were midway between the reception of wholly external impressions and the conscious exertion of our will on our mind. If Coleridge was speaking carelessly then in the later passage where he identified spontaneous consciousness with mere reflection (as it is not at all unlikely he was, since his concern was not with the spontaneous as such but with a description of the philosophic kind), it is possible that the fancy–primary imagination–secondary imagination distinction is correlative with the (fancy–) spontaneous consciousness–philosophic consciousness one. But Coleridge gives us no hint that this is his meaning.

ence between primary and secondary imagination as another form of the distinction between understanding and reason. For one thing, the understanding, though it can be considered a faculty of perception common to all, is certainly not "a repetition in the finite mind of the eternal act of creation in the infinite I AM." Coleridge, after all, attributed to higher animals a form of understanding.[70] And reason has a much higher aim than imagination: it is the power by which we become possessed of principles (the eternal verities of Plato and Descartes) and of ideas, which are characterized by universality and necessity.[71] Perhaps this suggests Coleridge's difficulty. The fancy-imagination distinction was originally designed to explore the differences between the creative activity of the mind and its passive arrangement of perceptions. The much wider scope of the understanding-reason distinction offered a classification of all the kinds of knowledge, at least by defining (in conjunction with the purely passive *sense* as the lowest of the three kinds of knowledge) the extremes of human knowledge. To the extent that the fancy–primary imagination–secondary imagination pattern took the place of the latter, as it did implicitly in Schelling's system where imagination reproduces and guarantees the highest intuition, confusion was bound to result because of the different starting points of the two distinctions.

Nor can Coleridge's primary imagination simply be identified with Kant's "productive" imagination. For Kant the imagination is the power which operates between the phenomena of the sense manifold and the categories of the understanding. It has two functions: as reproductive it is an active power for the synthesis of the sense manifold, which it apprehends according to laws received from the understanding, enabling the phenomena to be "reproduced" in the understanding — as such it is empirical only. As productive or transcendental it is the power of synthesis a priori, providing the necessary unity,

[70] *The Statesman's Manual, or the Bible the Best Guide to Political Skill and Foresight: A Lay Sermon, Addressed to the Higher Classes of Society*, with the author's last corrections, and notes by Henry Nelson Coleridge, in *The Complete Works of Samuel Taylor Coleridge*, with an Introductory Essay upon His Philosophical and Theological Opinions, ed. W. G. T. Shedd, 7 vols. (New York, 1854), I, 430. Hereafter cited as *SM*; the *Complete Works* hereafter cited as *C Works*.

[71] *Friend* (1809), p. 106; *CL*, II, 1198.

through the laws of the understanding, which makes possible the synthesis of the manifold of phenomena. The whole of our experience is ultimately possible because of the transcendental function of imagination, without which no concepts of objects could ever come together in one experience.[72]

Shawcross roughly identifies Coleridge's fancy with Kant's reproductive imagination, Coleridge's primary imagination with Kant's productive imagination, and the secondary imagination with what he calls Kant's aesthetic imagination.[73] The aesthetic imagination is presumably what Kant speaks of as another form of the productive imagination, contemplated in its freedom from the laws of understanding (when it is not a case of apprehending a given object of sense) and as originator of arbitrary forms of possible intuitions a priori, the conformity to which constitutes taste and results in beauty, the same disinterestedness or lack of concern for the real existence of the object being necessary here as in Coleridge's aesthetic. On the other hand, though it performs a mediating function between sense and understanding, and independently of imagination has a hypothetical creativity of its own, Kant's productive imagination possesses neither the contact with materiality nor the power of idealizing the sensible by means of the ideas of the mind that Coleridge demands for his imagination. Still, it was possibly in reading Kant that the notion of the imagination as a mediating faculty first occurred to Coleridge, if indeed it was not part of his own problem from the moment he had been able to define it. And again it may be Kant to whom the credit is due for the conception of the imagination as a universal element of the knowledge process, for this was no part of Coleridge's earlier formulations. If so, it was this very aspect of the imaginative theory that led Coleridge into philosophical bogs, for, though it was necessary if the imagination was to be developed into something more than a private gift, it constituted a temptation so to generalize the faculty that it was no longer left with a clearly defined function in the poetic process.

---

[72] *Critique of Pure Reason*, A. 120–123, Smith ed. pp. 143–146.
[73] *BL*, I, lvii–lix.

In the absence, then, of any obvious meanings that can be attached to Coleridge's definitions of the primary and secondary imagination, there are two possibilities left to us if we would make his remarks intelligible. The first is to follow the strategy of the critics who rework the distinction in terms of some larger principle of unity which they find in Coleridge's thought, and thus save the meaning of his terminology. Richards, for example, does this when he interprets the difference as lying between the "usual world of the senses" and the re-formed world of civilized values. His conception of the distinction follows from his "psychological," as distinguished from a "metaphysical," analysis of Coleridge's thought, and from his apparent interpretive hypothesis that nonempirical "value" is the subjective contribution of the mind in the knowledge process.[74] D. G. James does much the same thing in his explanation of the process by which the primary imagination constructs the world of ordinary perception. Using Kant as a starting point he elaborates a theory which explains both the imaginative apprehension of individual wholes and the abstractive and classificatory procedure of scientific knowledge, showing how both are interdependent within an inclusive epistemological structure that is in its fundamental organization imaginative.[75] However interesting and suggestive such schemes are (and that of James seems a particularly useful theory for present-day purposes), they are inevitably para-Coleridgean, constructs intended to show what Coleridge might have meant, or must have meant, had he taken the trouble to tell us so.[76]

If, for the sake of hewing to a historical mode of inquiry, we are reluctant to speculate about what Coleridge *might* have meant in the obscurer parts of his *Biographia*, there is still one way of making sense out of his distinction.[77] That is to place it in the context of

[74] I. A. Richards, *Coleridge on Imagination* (London, 1934), pp. 58–59.

[75] See the first chapter of *Scepticism and Poetry: An Essay on the Poetic Imagination* (London, 1937).

[76] Indeed this is James's explicit remark at the start of his essay, p. 18.

[77] Coleridge apparently considered removing the sentence about primary imagination — a good reason for not laboring unreasonably to discover exactly what he meant by it. Shawcross gives the reference to Sara Coleridge's remark in the 1847 edition of the *Biographia Literaria* (I, 297) that the sentence was "stroked out in a copy of the *B. L.*

his total argument, to attempt not a translation of its particular terminology but instead an inquiry into why his whole line of thought
in the *Biographia* failed, to let the celebrated distinction stand or
fall with all the theory borrowed from Schelling to support it. This
approach is more useful in our particular inquiry because it enables
us to take into account the direction which Coleridge's earliest theories
of knowledge and of poetic creativity gave to his search for the imagination, and to evaluate the results of this search in terms of its sources
and history. In simple terms this amounts to asking why the *Biographia* did not satisfy Coleridge himself. The answer seems to be
that it set at cross-purposes two fundamental principles in his thought.

The first of these basic elements was the tendency of his epistemology to require as a solution for its problems a mediation between the
knowing subject and the object known. Since the Wedgwood letters
of 1801 his speculations had been directed to the reconciliation of the
Cartesian dualism by a knowledge theory which would provide both
for a formative, creative activity of the mind and for the objective
reality of what was known. In terms of literary theory it was first
word and then poem that were identified as the intermediate elements
in our knowledge of things and in our communication of that knowledge. The theory of imagination grew out of certain experiences —
the lessons of Boyer, the reading of Bowles and especially of Wordsworth, and, obviously, Coleridge's own once-total involvement with
the creation of poems — which testified to this unity of the knowing
mind and the known object, and was an attempt, even prior to the
Biographia, to provide a rationale for the apparent connaturality of
the two. The notions of organic wholeness and of the symbolic mode
of representation were contributions to the elaboration of this theory.
The argument of the *Biographia* recapitulates this development of
Coleridge's early years. It is a search for "an intermediate faculty,
which is at once both active and passive." [78] Gradually, however, Coleridge's aesthetic imagination was drawn into the epistemological discussion and became the faculty or capacity for unifying knower and

---

containing a few marginal notes of the author, which are printed in this edition." *BL*,
I, 272.
    [78] *BL*, I, 86.

known on the highest level. The definition of the primary imagination represents perhaps the highest aspirations of this desire for a mediating power in the act of knowledge: as a universal active power in all perception it repeats the creative informing act of God. It is Coleridge's boldest attempt to escape the Cartesian dualism.

It does not succeed because the theory of Schelling on which it depends contradicts another of Coleridge's most deeply felt convictions, his antipathy to the errors of monistic pantheism. The notions of the "one life" in all created things which were so prominent a feature of Coleridge's transcendentalist years bordered closely on a kind of pantheism. He devoted a great deal of thought to the problem, especially as it involved Spinoza and Boehme. At one time it must have seemed that their theories could be saved, but he gradually came to see that this was impossible. Though in the history of his intellectual development in the *Biographia* he expresses only a cautious objection to the system of Boehme, out of loyalty and gratitude to one of the thinkers who had helped rescue him from the sterilities of mechanism, he nevertheless had to admit finally that Boehme's ideas amounted to "mere Pantheism." He was less certain about the inevitable errors of Spinoza's system, but he conceded that it was easily capable of being converted to an irreligious pantheism.[79] His admiration for both men was the principal reason why he was continuously sensitive to any implications that his own thought inclined toward pantheism.

Shawcross proposes that the imaginative interpretation of nature never could have led Coleridge into pantheism because he placed the transcendent consciousness of God above all other forms of consciousness, and thus the beauty of nature was always symbolic of a spiritual reality but not coexistent with it.[80] Perhaps it was this fundamental persuasion, or even more primarily his own innermost need for a per-

---

[79] *BL*, I, 98–99. The criticism of Boehme is from a letter of 1818, *CL*, IV, 883. The lenient judgment of Spinoza is repeated in his philosophical lectures. *The Philosophical Lectures of Samuel Taylor Coleridge: Hitherto Unpublished*, ed. Kathleen Coburn (New York, 1949), p. 385. In 1817 Coleridge writes of "the much calumniated Spinoza (whose System is to mine just what a Skeleton is to a Body, fearful because it is only the *Skeleton*)." *CL*, IV, 775. Yet he finally came to call Spinoza a pantheist. See *Table Talk*, I, 57–58, March 10, 1827.

[80] *BL*, I, xix.

sonal God, that kept Coleridge from accepting Schelling's notion of
the identity of nature and mind in an Absolute where all antitheses
disappear, and of the imagination (or intellectual intuition) as the
verification of this identity by reason of its ability to objectify the
inward intuition of the subject-object identity. It was an attractive
theory for Coleridge when he was beginning the *Biographia* because
it obviously provided the long sought-after medium between knower
and known. Yet it failed because it offered too much. It raised the
imagination to a new dignity and gave it that contact with the real
that it did not have in Kant's system, but at the same time it col-
lapsed all distinctions between the world and the self insofar as it
did not distinguish between the world and God — everything became
only a moment in the dialectical act of knowing that constituted the
existence of the Absolute.[81] "His System is extremely plausible and
alluring at a first acquaintance," Coleridge wrote in 1818. "But as a
System, it is little more than Behmenism, translated from visions into
Logic and a sort of commanding eloquence: and like Behmen's it is
reduced at last to a mere Pantheism, or 'gemina Natura quae fit et
facit, creat et creatur', of which the Deity itself is but an Out-birth." [82]
He says in the same letter that in the metaphysical chapters of his
Literary Life he was *"taken in"* by Schelling's polarities — "not aware,
that this was putting the Candle horizontally and burning it at both
ends." [83] The defects of Schelling's system did not lead Coleridge to
abandon the hope of working out a satisfactory epistemology which
would explain the mediation between object and mind and even in-
voke the divine nature as the ground of this interaction, but his later
exposition of this theory, in *The Statesman's Manual*, successfully

[81] E. D. Hirsch, Jr., has reservations about Schelling's complete pantheism. He prefers to call it a "panentheism" which overcomes the distinction between transcendence
and immanence. *Wordsworth and Schelling: A Typological Study of Romanticism* (New
Haven, 1960), p. 29. At any rate it is clear that Coleridge thought Schelling's system
pantheistic.

[82] *CL*, IV, 883, November 24, 1818. For a longer criticism, see a letter of September
30, 1818, to J. H. Green, *CL*, IV, 873–876.

[83] *CL*, IV, 874. Miss Coburn thinks that the reason Schelling and Kant are so inadequately treated in the philosophical lectures of 1818 is that Coleridge is rethinking his
commitments to their systems, and that his primary objection to Schelling is his pantheism. *Philosophical Lectures*, pp. 62–63. See also p. 390.

avoids the pantheistic implications which weaken the argument of the *Biographia*.

Another objection can be made to the theory of imagination presented in the last chapters of Volume I. The context of the discussion in the first part of the book makes it clear that Coleridge himself fully intended his theory to clarify a primarily literary or at most an aesthetic problem. In none of the uses of the term before the writing of the *Biographia* are there any hints that the faculty has a wider significance, and in the *Biographia* itself the discussion grows out of Coleridge's youthful search for the principles of poetry, the excellence which he admired in the verse of Bowles and Wordsworth, and the distinction in the merits of Shakespeare and Milton in comparison with other poets. Since what was involved was some sort of faculty that was active in the creation of poetry, it was natural to begin the philosophical examination of the power by showing the deficiencies of the prevailing philosophy of passive mechanical association as an explanation of knowledge. But there was a fatal difficulty implicit in this approach, a confusion of knowing and making. What had been a problem in poetic art was muddied by treating it exclusively as a problem in poetic insight. In one sense it is entirely a question of knowing, but of the peculiar way of knowing which is proper to the artist. The noetic grasp of reality, of the other, occurs, for the artist, only by means of images. There is no gap between idea and shape, no separation of knowing and expressing. Where a disparity may be felt, however, and painfully felt, is between the inadequate image and the unshaped but persistent persuasion — arising from the conflict of present and past experience, perhaps even from the failure of the present insight to improve on the past — that something more is wanted for complete expression. The difference between the two cases seems to be the difference between the facile aesthetic gesture or the effortless reproduction of conventional insights, and the relatively complete imaginative grasp of reality which the artist can achieve at a given time only by exploiting and extending his total capacity and experience. The craft of the artist is involved precisely in attempting to transcend the first and achieve the second; it consists in recognizing and implementing from among alternate possibilities those that best shape and clarify the governing experience. It is this aspect of making that is wanting in Coleridge's theory of imagination in the *Biographia*. It is implied in the final description ("It dissolves, diffuses, dissipates, in order to recreate; or where this process is rendered impossible, yet still at all events it struggles to idealize and to unify.") but the theory as explained previously out of Schelling has no place for a poetic art. The contradiction between the origin of his imaginative theory and the philosophy adduced to defend it may have been another reason why Coleridge abandoned his incomplete speculations at the end of the first volume.

Comparing the treatment of imagination in the *Biographia* with the descriptions given in the letters of 1802 and 1804, it is difficult to see how the formulas of 1815 represent an advance over the earlier ones. The two capacities had already been distinguished there in kind, and the function of modifying and coadunating proper to the imagination had been contrasted with the aggregating power of fancy. The imagination, besides, had been called "a dim Analogue of Creation." [84] Now, in the *Biographia*, the additions to the earlier descriptions — the distinction between the primary and secondary imaginations, the Schellingian philosophy behind the whole discussion, the fact that the imagination is now a universal element in the knowledge process, and the very faint suggestion of art involved in the association of the secondary imagination with the conscious will — add little in the way of clarification and much genuine obscurity. And the omissions from the earlier theory — notably the union of thought and feeling proper to poetry, the defect of which in Bowles was the starting point for Coleridge's first speculations on imagination — damage the *Biographia* formulations even more. It may be said, in the phrase Coleridge used of Hartley, that where he differs from his earlier theory of imagination he differs mainly to err. Possibly the failure of so ambitious a scheme as that of the *Biographia* was necessary before Coleridge could shake himself loose from the vaguely pantheistic implications of the whole unitive and integrative tendency in his earlier thought.

[84] *CL*, II, 865–866, 1034.

CHAPTER VII

Reformulations, 1815–1819

In my "literary life," the publication of which has been delay'd
two years, there are a few opinions which better information
and more reflection would now annul.

Letter of July 28, 1817

ᔐᑫ

After the collapse of the argument in the first volume of the *Bio-graphia* Coleridge never again attempted a complete description of his literary theories. Indeed, within three years his interest in speculation about the nature of poetry and art seems to have ceased entirely. Religious matters, often in conjunction with social and political problems, theories of life, and the attempts to synthesize his "Spiritual Philosophy," are the principal topics of his published writings and his correspondence between 1818 and his death sixteen years later. Before completely abandoning the theory of literature, however, Coleridge added some fragments to the philosophical structure that he had been laboring at for years. The second half of the *Biographia* (in some ways so different in concept from the first that it can hardly be thought of as substantially related to it), the first of the *Lay Sermons*, and parts of the lectures on literature of 1818 all help to complete our idea of the substance of Coleridge's literary theories, and yet they also change it from what we might have expected had we formed a judgment mainly on the familiar passages of the *Biographia*. In many ways the theory of these last years is related directly to Coleridge's ideas in the decade 1800–1810 and to the conceptual structure of the Shakespearean lectures, 1811–1814, rather than to the transcendental philosophy of his most famous work. And in the final stages of this theory it is not difficult to see the reasons why Coleridge turned eventually from literature and art to theology as a subjectively more satisfying subject for his speculations.

THE MAKING OF POEMS: THE WORDSWORTH CRITICISM
OF THE BIOGRAPHIA

The discussion of the poetic theory and practice of Wordsworth constitutes most of the original matter of the second volume of the *Biographia*. It is Coleridge's longest work of sustained literary analysis. Though it is in general less useful for our purposes than, for example, the Shakespearean lectures of 1811–1814, because it contains little that is directly speculative and has only slight specific reference to the theories of the first volume, nevertheless the discussion is carried on in a theoretical framework which restores to prominence some of the earliest Coleridgean insights into the nature of literature and integrates them in a viewpoint which implicitly corrects in many details the deficient philosophy of art in the first volume. For this reason certain parts of the criticism are of interest to us here.

The Wordsworth analysis has often, in fact, been praised at the expense of Coleridge's philosophy, as though it somehow represented the best of Coleridge as critic, and his more explicit speculations the worst. Raysor's opinion of the Shakespearean criticism — that it succeeds despite Coleridge's general ideas — has already been discussed. This is not the case with the Wordsworth analysis, Raysor says, but adds that even in this part of the *Biographia* the ideas are "inductive generalizations based upon the personal experience of poetic creation and the observation of the practice of other poets; they are not in any sense a deduction of art from a metaphysical system, like that branch of philosophy which we call aesthetics. Coleridge's unsuccessful aesthetic speculations may be fairly represented by his unfortunate theory of the imagination in the first part of the *Biographia Literaria*." [1] Elsewhere he cites in support of this position several unpublished lectures of Irving Babbitt who says, according to Raysor, that in the first

[1] *ShC*, I, xlvii–xlviii, note.

thirteen chapters of the *Biographia* "Coleridge is a follower of Schelling, while in the remainder of the book, he is an enlightened Aristotelian, criticising Wordsworth's theory and practice by reference to the universality demanded of art, and to the doctrine of decorum and probability."[2]

Two answers can be made to these observations. First, there is a rather significant difference between the critical analysis of individual poems and the speculative discussions of the metaphysical status of poetry. It is the difference between asking which poems are good and what poems are. The first question is not unrelated to the second, and a theory irrelevant to practice is as useless as a criticism unfounded in principle is dangerous, but there may be a great distance between the two which often only a thoroughly developed conceptual structure can bridge, and it does not seem the responsibility of either philosopher or critic to have to demonstrate constantly the possibility of moving from the one activity to the other.

Second, the principles by which Coleridge criticizes Wordsworth, though they have to do with a theory of imagination that functions in a quite different way from that of the first volume, are far from unrelated to the basic concepts of the first half of the book, though they are also by no means deductions from a metaphysical system. Coleridge promised to "deduce" the imagination, but he never did so. His theory in fact begins in empirical experiences which demand an explanation and, except for the Schellingian philosophy of the twelfth chapter, is wholly dependent on the experience of the "true and original realism" as a guide. It is nowhere deductive in the technical sense. He constantly praises that induction which respects the concrete details of things but which elevates them into "ideas" by means of the unifying reason. Furthermore, there is a close relation between the intent of the theory of imagination and the principles by which Wordsworth is criticized, even as Babbitt formulated them. Both the unifying of subject and object, which may stand for the principal function of imagination in the first volume, and the "Aristotelian" principle of "probability" (in conjunction with the universality and the idealizing function of art),

[2] *ShC*, II, 326, note.

which Babbitt feels is the principal criterion of the analysis in the second volume, are founded ultimately upon a conception of the work of art as imitative representation, or more exactly as mediating symbol. The qualities are correlative: imitation involves selection of details on the basis of an idea of the thing, and the mediation is achieved by the artifact by virtue of it being an analogon both of thing and of mind.

However, to talk about probability and the mediating function of art in these terms limits us to the work conceived as existing in the mind of the artist or as existing in itself. The focus of discussion is better shifted to the third element in the noetic process, the work of art as it exists in the mind of the auditor or spectator. This is the approach Coleridge takes to Wordsworth's poetry, and the clarification of this point constitutes his achievement in the second volume of the *Biographia*. By moving attention away from the problems of the artist he brings much more objectivity to the discussion and at the same time overcomes a defect in the theory of the first volume, namely the inadequate attention paid to the effect of the poem on the reader. In some ways the emphasis here seems to be a recognition that his earlier theory was unsuccessful largely because of a failure to provide for the essential ποίησις or making that is involved in the poetic process. The extensive attention to illusion (for that is what "probability" and "universality" come to) as the underlying theme of what speculation there is in the Wordsworth criticism shows Coleridge more willing to consider the art of the poet with respect to his audience. In this sense his position is, as Babbitt implies, a corrective of his earlier reliance on Schelling.

The organization of the chapters on Wordsworth is simple. In order to discuss Wordsworth's theories of poetic diction, the origin of their long-standing controversy, Coleridge proposes first to determine what a poem is and what poetry is. He gives various definitions, then illustrates them by discussing the characteristics of poetic genius. This is followed by a long criticism of Wordsworth's theory of diction, and then by an exposition of Coleridge's counterproposals involving the natural differences between the languages of poetry and prose. The last chapters devoted to Wordsworth consider the defects and merits of his actual poetry, in order to distinguish between its commonly supposed characteristics and the real elements of his genius. It is not to our purpose to follow out the Wordsworth criticism in detail, but insofar as Coleridge develops a theory of illusion to explain the effect of the work of art this second volume of the *Biographia* serves to complement the speculations of the first.

The subject of poetic illusion comes up on the very first page, where Coleridge recalls the different objects which he and Wordsworth had in mind when they wrote the poems for the *Lyrical Ballads* almost twenty years before. They had first noticed two cardinal points of poetry: "the power of exciting the sympathy of the reader by a faithful adherence to the truth of nature, and the power of giving the interest of novelty by the modifying colors of imagination." Two kinds of poems were proposed that might unite these qualities: Coleridge would use incidents and agents which were, in part at least, supernatural and would aim at interesting "the affections by the dramatic truth of such emotions, as would naturally accompany such situations, supposing them real," or in other words "to transfer from our inward nature a human interest and a semblance of truth sufficient to procure for these shadows of imagination that willing suspension of disbelief for the moment, which constitutes poetic faith." Wordsworth, on the other hand, would take subjects chosen from ordinary life, and attempt "to give the charm of novelty to things of every day, and to excite a feeling analogous to the supernatural, by awakening the mind's attention from the lethargy of custom, and directing it to the loveliness and the wonders of the world before us." [3] The aims of both were thus defined by the responses they intended to arouse in their auditors. Their disagreement turned on the methods of evoking these responses.

Wordsworth offered the *Lyrical Ballads*, Coleridge says, as an experiment to see whether subjects which were presented without "the usual ornaments and extra-colloquial style of poems in general, might not be so managed in the language of ordinary life as to produce the pleasurable interest, which it is the peculiar business of poetry to impart." To the second edition of the *Ballads* he added a preface in which, says Coleridge, "he was understood to contend for the extension of this style

[3] *BL*, II, 5–6.

to poetry of all kinds, and to reject as vicious and indefensible all phrases and forms of style that were not included in what he (unfortunately, I think, adopting an equivocal expression) called the language of *real* life." Thus the origin of a long-continued controversy. Coleridge insists that he had never been in total agreement with the original preface, and now wishes to make clear his opinions on the questions raised by Wordsworth's theories and practice.[4]

Before proceeding with his criticism of Wordsworth, he makes several remarks about poetry which in spirit recall the philosophy of the Shakespearean lectures and the speculations of his earlier years, and seem to bypass the conceptual structure of the first part of the *Biographia*. The discussion of what constitutes a poem, for example, repeats much of the material from the lectures. A poem contains the same elements as a prose composition, but differs by reason of the object proposed. If this be merely to facilitate memory by artificial arrangement, the result is nonetheless pleasurable because of the recurrence of sounds and quantities. However, of works whose immediate purpose is the communication of pleasure (the communication of truth should always be the ultimate purpose, but this distinguishes the character of the author and not of the work), the question arises: is meter enough to justify calling these poems? The answer Coleridge gives is that "nothing can permanently please, which does not contain in itself the reason why it is so, and not otherwise," and the parts must justify the attention given to them by meter.[5] The definition of a poem that he finally gives is in substance the same as that given in the fourth lecture of 1811–1812.[6]

---

[4] *BL*, II, 6–8. See *CL*, II, 830: "Altho' Wordsworth's Preface is half a child of my own Brain/ and so arose out of Conversations, so frequent, that with few exceptions we could scarcely either of us perhaps positively say, which first started any particular thought . . . yet I am far from going all lengths with Wordsworth . . . On the contrary, I rather suspect that somewhere or other there is a radical Difference in our theoretical opinions respecting Poetry."

[5] *BL*, II, 8–10.

[6] "A poem is that species of composition, which is opposed to works of science, by proposing for its *immediate* object pleasure, not truth; and from all other species (having *this* object in common with it) it is discriminated by proposing to itself such delight from the *whole*, as is compatible with a distinct gratification from each component part." *BL*, II, 10. The notion of illusion and so of making is the determining element in the

He then asks a further question: in what does poetry consist? For "a poem of any length neither can be, or ought to be, all poetry." [7] The distinction, according to Abrams, is between "those supreme achievements of the creative mind which can be sustained only for limited passages, whether in prose or verse," and the finished product or "poetry in the medium of a poem." [8] Or, again, between "a poem as a poem" and "a poem as a process of mind." [9] Coleridge does not answer his question about poetry, except by asking another: what makes a poet? To this he replies with one of his most familiar passages:

The poet, described in *ideal* perfection, brings the whole soul of man into activity, with the subordination of its faculties to each other, according to their relative worth and dignity. He diffuses a tone and spirit of unity, that blends, and (as it were) *fuses*, each into each, by that synthetic and magical power, to which we have exclusively appropriated the name of imagination. This power, first put in action by the will and understanding, and retained under their irremissive, though gentle and unnoticed, controul (*laxis effertur habenis*) reveals itself in the balance or reconciliation of opposite or discordant qualities; of sameness, with difference; of the general, with the concrete; the idea, with the image; the individual, with the representative; the sense of novelty and freshness, with old and familiar objects; a more than usual state of emotion, with more than usual order; judgement ever awake and steady self-possession, with enthusiasm and feeling profound or vehement; and while it blends and harmonizes the natural and the artificial, still subordinates art to nature; the manner to the matter; and our admiration of the poet to our sympathy with the poetry . . . Finally, GOOD SENSE is the BODY of poetic genius, FANCY its DRAPERY, MOTION its LIFE, and IMAGINATION the SOUL that is everywhere, and in each; and forms all into one graceful and intelligent whole.[10]

The description draws together several old themes and one or two new ones, in a somewhat unexpected hierarchy. Beginning in the very

<hr />

definition. As Abrams says, "By defining a poem as a means to an 'object,' 'purpose,' or 'end' (terms which he employs as synonyms), Coleridge, quite in the tradition of neoclassic criticism, establishes the making of poems to be a deliberate art, rather than the spontaneous overflow of feeling." *Mirror and the Lamp*, p. 117. For the definition in the fourth lecture of 1811–1812, see above, Chap. IV, "The definition of poetry."

[7] *BL*, II, 11.
[8] *Mirror and the Lamp*, pp. 118, 121.
[9] *Mirror and the Lamp*, p. 124.
[10] *BL*, II, 12–13.

center of the passage we find the imagination unifying a series of distinctions familiar from the Shakespearean lectures and even earlier: sameness and difference, the general and the concrete, idea and image, the individual and the representative, and so on. Note that the union of emotion and feeling with order and judgment is once again the proper activity of imagination. But all these polarities are now identified as "opposite or discordant qualities" which it is the business of imagination to balance or reconcile. This important notion of Coleridge's may seem to be an appropriation from his Schellingian philosophy, a survival of the dialectical meeting of extremes in the Absolute and of art's externalization of that process, but in fact it is a repetition of the fundamental idea of the definition of poetic genius that he had given in 1808, showing how little some of Coleridge's most typical principles really changed.[11] It is also noteworthy that the entire operation of the imagination here is placed under the "gentle and unnoticed" control of the will and the understanding, thus creating a certain ambiguity between the voluntary element in the art process and what appears to be the old Kantian subordination of the imagination to the understanding. Coleridge seems to be insisting on both: the process is clearly voluntary, and the imagination is the synthetic power. Then he stresses the objective orientation of the poetic process as well as the creative shaping: the imagination subordinates art to nature, and the manner to the matter. Finally, the description at its beginning and end frames all these elements in the conscious art, the making, involved in poetry: it is an activity of the whole soul of man, but so directed that our attention is not on the poet but on the poetry.

The following rebuttal of Wordsworth's theories centers around three of Wordsworth's propositions about poetic diction: that the proper diction for poetry in general should be taken from the language of men in real life, that the language of rustics is purer because they hourly communicate with the best of natural objects, and that there is no essential difference between the language of prose and the language

---

[11] See *ShC*, I, 166–167. The passage is quoted above, Chap. IV, "The definition of poetry." Raysor assigns it to 1808, though his reasons are not wholly clear. See Chap. IV, note 31.

of poetry. The second of these propositions is simply a question of interpreting facts. Coleridge denies that the language of rustics is any richer or more suitable for poetry, by reason of the unspoiled surroundings which are thought to form it, than any other. In fact, he says, if it were purified of provincialisms and brought into grammatical order, the rustic's language would not differ from that of any man of common sense, except in the fewer and more indiscriminate notions the countryman would have to convey. For the rustic, by reason of the lower development of his faculties, aims mostly at conveying insulated facts of his scanty experience and traditional belief; he does not perceive the connections and related bearings by which an educated man evolves the laws of things.[12] Moreover, even Wordsworth has not limited himself to the less compact manner of ordinary men when portraying rustics in his poetry.

The first and third of Wordsworth's positions are more directly connected with poetic theory. To the notion that the proper language of poetry is that of men in real life, Coleridge answers succinctly that in any sense this could apply only to certain kinds of poetry,[13] and in these kinds it is applicable only in a way that no one has ever denied, and finally that even where possible the concept is useless, even dangerous, if urged as a rule.[14] Wordsworth himself has not observed the rule. In the most interesting of his poems — "The Brothers," "Michael," "Ruth," and "The Mad Mother" — the persons are by no means taken from low or rustic life as these words are commonly understood, nor

[12] *BL*, II, 38–39.

[13] Dramatic poetry, for example, where exact imitation may be the direct object. *BL*, II, 42. Stephen Maxfield Parrish advances the idea that at the root of the disagreement about poetic diction may have been a disagreement about dramatic method. "To put it in the simplest way, the passion that Wordsworth expressed in poetry was likely to be that of his characters; the passion that Coleridge looked for was mainly that of the poet. For Wordsworth, the passion could appear only if the poet maintained strict dramatic propriety; for Coleridge, the passion was obscured unless the poet spoke in his own voice. As against Wordsworth's dramatic propriety, Coleridge cited what he might have called poetic propriety." "The Wordsworth-Coleridge Controversy," *PMLA*, 73 (1958): 371. Coleridge's criticisms of "The Thorn" bear this out. He objects to Wordsworth's putting the whole poem into the mouth of a "dull and garrulous discourser" and says that the most interesting parts of the poem are those which the poet himself might better have spoken. *BL*, II, 36–38.

[14] *BL*, II, 29–30.

is it clear that their sentiments and language are necessarily connected with their occupations and abode. In fact, these may be accounted for by causes which would produce the same results whether in country or in town, especially by the independence which raises these people from servitude but does not free them from the necessity of a simple and frugal life, and by the accompanying solid and religious education based on the Bible and hymn book.[15] Both of these causes are accidental, whereas poetry, as Aristotle shows, is essentially ideal. "Its apparent individualities of rank, character, or occupation must be *representative* of a class." [16]

The objections to the third of Wordsworth's principles, that there is no essential difference between the language of poetry and that of prose, is wholly centered on a theory of making, insofar as the criterion of the difference between prose and poem is the effectiveness of meter and of its linguistic concomitants for the purposes of the poem. Indeed so closely connected is metrical language with this purpose that the difference is said by Coleridge to be natural. The discussion must be understood in the light of the distinction between poem and poetry. Meter is necessary only for the former. Coleridge's thesis is that there are "modes of expression, a *construction*, and an *order* of sentences" which are appropriate to prose but not to poetry, likewise that there is an arrangement and a selection proper to poetry but not to prose.[17] His primary argument is that the attempt to balance spontaneous pas-

---

[15] *BL*, II, 31.

[16] *BL*, II, 33.

[17] *BL*, II, 49. Wordsworth had never denied that meter and impassioned language were naturally suited to certain kinds of poetry, but merely that there was an essential difference betwen the language of prose and that of poetry. See the 1801 preface, *Poetical Works of William Wordsworth*, II, 392, 398f, especially the latter section, in answer to the question, "Why . . . have I written in verse?" The answer involves the end sought, the pleasure of the reader, and the dramatic appropriateness of language and manner to character and subject. "Now the music of harmonious metrical language, the sense of difficulty overcome, and the blind association of pleasure which has been previously received from works of rhyme or metre of the same or similar construction, an indistinct perception perpetually renewed of language closely resembling that of real life, and yet, in the circumstance of metre, differing from it so widely — all these imperceptibly make up a complex feeling of delight, which is of the most important use in tempering the painful feeling always found intermingled with powerful descriptions of the deeper passions" (p. 401).

sion and voluntary control naturally results in artificially measured speech and in figures of speech, originally "the offspring of passion" but now "the adopted children of power." Subsidiary arguments are drawn from the organization of the feelings and attention, the curiosity gratified and re-excited, that are the proper effects of meter. Meter also makes a more elevated language appropriate, not because elevated language is essential to poetry but because it is the language of passion which, as Wordsworth himself says, is always implied in poetry. Another argument is found in man's natural instinct to subordinate all the parts of an organized whole to the more important and essential parts. Finally, the practice of the best poets of all countries and ages authorizes the opinion that there is an essential difference between the language of prose and that of metrical composition. The ultimate criterion in this process of poetic making is the effect on the audience, and only taste, the result of meditation and observation, can make this a success.[18] "Could a rule be given from *without*, poetry would cease to be poetry, and sink into a mechanical art. It would be μόρφωσις, not ποίησις. The rules of the IMAGINATION are themselves the very powers of growth and production. The *words*, to which they are reducible, present only the outlines and external appearances of the fruit. A deceptive counterfeit of the superficial form and colors may be elaborated; but the marble peach feels cold and heavy, and *children* only put it to their mouths." [19] The metaphor embodies Coleridge's general argument against Wordsworth, that the poem naturally employs certain means to achieve its end, and the consequent unity of parts in an organic whole is essential to the effect.

[18] *BL*, II, 49–57. To this long argument in defense of the natural suitability of meter to poetry some observations must be appended. Coleridge had earlier denied any difference between prose and verse except the accidental one of meter; both could be the vehicles either of truth or of pleasure. *ShC*, II, 75. See above, Chap. IV, "The definition of poetry." To the vehicles of pleasure he gave the generic name of poetry, as having a fictitious and therefore imaginative form, as opposed to a discursive form. Imaginative literature included both what is properly called poetry, and prose fiction. Coleridge now refines that earlier theory and appropriates meter to poetry proper, by reason of the emotional concentration on each part within the whole, which is not found to the same degree in other kinds of imaginative literature. The naturalness of meter for poetic expression must therefore be a question of degree.

[19] *BL*, II, 65.

The proof of the success of the poem lies in the fact of complete poetic illusion. The sources of this illusion, so central to the notion of poetry as the purposeful product of imaginative activity, are discussed at greater length in the midst of Coleridge's analysis of the characteristic defects of Wordsworth's poems. He comes to the topic by way of an objection against the rustic wisdom of some of Wordsworth's characters. How is the poet's moral purpose served, he asks, by merely attaching the name of some low profession to powers and qualities least likely to be found in it? The poet–philosopher–chimney sweep hero is unconvincing because he violates the nature of poetic illusion.[20] Coleridge then digresses somewhat from his criticism of Wordsworth to renew discussion of this fundamental element of his theory.

The concept of aesthetic illusion that Coleridge first stated in the earlier Shakespearean lectures was limited to dramatic poetry, indeed to stage representation (involving as it did the question of the unities), and it did not advance much beyond rejecting the notion of literal deception and asserting that illusion is a factor in the experiencing of all poetry. The voluntary belief in the *Biographia* is based on the truth to the ideal which the poem involves. Thus, in discussing Wordsworth's characters, Coleridge insists on the inappropriateness of the accidental in poetry, and he cites Aristotle's opinion that poetry is the "σπουδαιότατον καὶ φιλοσοφώτατον γένος," the "most intense, weighty and philosophical product of human art," by reason of its representative and idealistic nature.[21] Horace, he says, has precepts of the same import with respect to credibility in fiction, and they are "grounded on the nature both of poetry and of the human mind." The illusion of poetry, contradistinguished from delusion, is called "*negative* faith." It "simply permits the images presented to work by their own force, without either denial or affirmation of their real existence by the judgement." This is what Coleridge had a few chapters earlier

[20] *BL*, II, 105–106.

[21] BL, II, 101. What Aristotle actually said is even more suited to Coleridge's purpose: διὸ καὶ φιλοσοφώτερον καὶ σπουδαιότερον ποίησις ἱστορίας ἐστίν. "Poetry, therefore, is a more philosophical and a higher thing than history: for poetry tends to express the universal, history the particular." *Poetics*, 1451 B, *Aristotle's Theory of Poetry and Fine Art, with a Critical Text and Translation of The Poetics*, ed. and trans. S. H. Butcher, 3rd ed. (London, 1902), pp. 34–35.

called, in an off-hand phrase that has since become immortal, "that willing suspension of disbelief for the moment, which constitutes poetic faith." [22]

Elsewhere in the *Biographia*, in discussing the characters of Don Juan and of Milton's Satan, he says: "The poet asks only of the reader, what, as a poet, he is privileged to ask: namely, that sort of negative faith in the existence of such a being, which we willingly give to productions *professedly ideal* . . . The ideal consists in the happy balance of the generic with the individual. The former makes the character representative and symbolical, therefore instructive; because, *mutatis mutandis*, it is applicable to whole classes of men. The latter gives it *living* interest; for nothing *lives* or is *real*, but as definite and individual." [23] Powerful though this illusion is, it has its exact limits, and nothing destroys it quicker than too close a juxtaposition with objects of true and stronger faith. This is the case, Coleridge suggests, when an epic poet derives his fable and characters from scriptural history, as in the *Messiah* of Klopstock (Milton's story and personages, on the other hand, are merely suggested in scripture). "A faith, which transcends even historic belief, must absolutely put out this mere Analogon of faith [that is, poetic illusion], as the summer sun is said to extinguish our household fires, when it shines full upon them." The same kind of effect, Coleridge suggests, is brought about in a less degree by circumstances which violate the reader's natural credibility, and yet in which the author tries to make him believe.[24]

The relevance of the comparison of poetic illusion to dream-visions is also clearly stated shortly after the writing of the *Biographia*, and it may be noted here to complete the discussion of this topic. There are two useful texts, a fragment evidently related to the lectures of 1818 and a letter of May 13, 1816. Illusion is a middle state between the perfect delusion which French critics insisted on and the full reflective knowledge of the unreality of theatrical performances which Dr. Johnson advanced.[25] "The truth is, that Images and Thoughts possess

[22] *BL*, II, 107, 6.
[23] *BL*, II, 186–187.
[24] *BL*, II, 107.
[25] *ShC*, I, 128–129.

a power in and of themselves, independent of that act of the Judgement or Understanding by which we affirm or deny the existence of a reality correspondent to them." This is what happens in dreaming. We neither believe nor disbelieve that our dreams are actual, but "the comparing power is suspended, and without the comparing power any act of Judgement, whether affirmation or denial, is impossible." In dreams bodily sensations are the causes of images, not, as when we are awake, their effects. "Add to this a voluntary Lending of the Will to this suspension of one of it's own operations (i.e. that of comparison and consequent decision concerning the reality of any sensuous Impression) and you have the true Theory of Stage Illuison." [26]

Whatever tends to prevent the mind from placing itself in this state "in which the images have a negative reality" must be a defect; the improbable therefore is such a defect, "not because it *is* improbable (for that the whole play is foreknown to be) but because it cannot but *appear* as such." Coleridge adds, however, with critical perceptiveness, that probability depends on the degree of excitement, so that things are accepted at the height of the action which would be intolerable in the opening scenes; on the other hand, it is true that "improbabilities will be endured as belonging to the groundwork of the story rather than to the drama, in the first scenes, which would disturb or disentrance us from all illusion in the acme of our excitement, as, for instance, Lear's division of his realm and banishment of Cordelia." The great rule is that all the elements of the drama be means to the chief end, "that of producing and supporting this willing illusion." [27]

The teleological conception of poetic art that is central to this theory of illusion restores to Coleridge's larger philosophy of literature a balance that it had lost in the limited discussion of imagination in the first part of the *Biographia*. The broader and more inclusive operation of poetic creativity that is outlined in the descriptions of the poem and of the poet at the beginning of the Wordsworth criticism looks back for its support to the theories of the Shakespearean lectures and to Coleridge's epistemological speculations in the period 1800–1808.

[26] *CL*, IV, 641–642.
[27] *ShC*, I, 129–130.

It thus justifies the claim that this is the more authentic Coleridgean tradition, rather than the ideas represented by the much-quoted passages of the earlier part of the *Biographia*. However, it is only in details and by implications that the Wordsworth criticism offers any corrective of the former theories. It is, though not necessarily to the extent that Babbitt would assert, restricted by the implications of the imitative hypothesis. For a partially successful attempt to escape these limitations, and for a more thorough revaluation of the fundamental argument of the first volume, that the imagination as Schelling conceived it was the essential mediator in the aesthetic process between mind and object, we have to look elsewhere, specifically to *The Statesman's Manual* and the lectures on literature of 1818.

THE DIVINE GROUND: THE STATESMAN'S MANUAL, 1816

In 1816 Coleridge arranged with the firm of Gale and Fenner for the publication of a second edition of *The Friend* and for that of the unfinished *Sibylline Leaves* and *Biographia Literaria*. As a mark of respect for his new publishers he also undertook to write a tract on the distresses of the day, to be called a *Lay Sermon*. While working on this essay, Coleridge expanded his plans to include two more sermons, the three to be addressed in turn to the higher classes, the higher and middle classes, and the working classes. The first appeared in the fall of 1816 and was called *The Statesman's Manual; or The Bible the Best Guide to Political Skill and Foresight: A Lay Sermon, Addressed to the Higher Classes of Society*. The second of these tracts appeared in the spring of the following year, under the title *A Lay Sermon, Addressed to the Higher and Middle Classes, on the Existing Distresses and Discontents*. The third essay in the series was never written.[28]

The two finished works are not in substance related to our study. The first is directly concerned with the Bible as a guide for the conduct of public affairs, and the second with the contemplation of prin-

---

[28] The first of these tracts is usually published under the title *The Statesman's Manual*, and the second is sometimes identified by the text which is its epigraph, "Blessed are ye that sow beside all waters." We shall avoid confusion by referring to them, after Miss Coburn's practice, as *The Statesman's Manual* and the *Lay Sermon*.

ciples as the best means of alleviating contemporary social distresses.
The second, in particular, because of the detailed discussion of topical
issues, is not of interest to us. However, the first of the essays has the
curious appearance of being in many respects a commentary on the
Biographia and an extension of some of its principles. Where the
earlier work had been largely concerned with the imagination as a
solution to the problem of the inward self and the outward thing, in
The Statesman's Manual this theme is recast in terms of a metaphysic
of history in which religion is seen as the ground of a resolution of the
tension between reason and understanding and thus as the guarantee
of the possibility of a mediation between subject and object. The
whole argument is scattered throughout the text and in several elaborate appendices, but it is not difficult to reconstruct. To read *The
Statesman's Manual* from this point of view gives it a much greater
importance as a documentation of Coleridge's literary philosophy than
its superficial characteristics as a religious tract would otherwise lead
us to believe, and it makes the somewhat various beauties of Coleridge's digressive prose fall into place as parts of a comprehensible
argument.

Coleridge's object in the first of the two sermons is to show that the
Bible is the best source of the true principles of political science. The
argument is the familiar Coleridgean one, the superiority of principles
and relations to isolated facts. "In the infancy of the world signs and
wonders were requisite in order to startle and break down that superstition which . . . tempts the natural man to seek the true cause and
origin of public calamities in outward circumstances, persons, and incidents . . . But with each miracle worked there was a truth revealed,
which thenceforward was to act as its substitute." [29] To neglect these
truths and instead to expect wonders for our instruction is to tempt
God. The true origin of human events is so concealed from us by the
shifting phenomena in the cycle of change, and by the belief of every
age that its situation is different, that there will never be lacking spe-
cious explanations why the history of the past does not apply to us.
"And no wonder, if we read history for the facts instead of reading it

[29] *C Works*, I, 425.

for the sake of the general principles, which are to the facts as the root and sap of a tree to its leaves." [30] It is a common tendency to attribute national events to particular persons, measures, intrigues, occasions, rather than to speculative principles and to current modes of thinking. "Yet it would not be difficult, by an unbroken chain of historic facts, to demonstrate that the most important changes in the commercial relations of the world had their origin in the closets or lonely walks of uninterested theorists." For most men speculative philosophy has always been a *terra incognita.* "Yet it is not the less true, that all the epoch-forming revolutions of the Christian world, the revolutions of religion and with them the civil, social, and the domestic habits of the nations concerned, have coincided with the rise and fall of metaphysical systems. So few are the minds that really govern the machine of society, and so incomparably more numerous and more important are the indirect consequences of things, than their foreseen and direct effects." [31] Coleridge goes on to demonstrate that scripture is the source of knowledge of principles, a guide and warning to us in the study of history. We shall follow a parallel but slightly different path into the theme that supports the biblical discussion — the importance of understanding ideas.

This position is arrived at by an analysis of the inadequacy of the understanding. In contrast with reason, which distinguishes men made in the image of God, the understanding is present in some degree even in many inferior animals. In comparison with the principles contained in the Bible, the understanding snatches at truth, but is frustrated and disheartened by the fluctuating nature of its objects.[32] Its products are notions, "the depthless abstractions of fleeting *phaeno-mena,* the shadows of sailing vapors, the colorless repetitions of rainbows," which "have effected their utmost when they have added to the distinctness of our knowledge," and being adverse to lofty emotion require "the influence of a light and warmth, not their own, to make them crystallize into a semblance of growth." This lifelessness is con-

[30] *C Works,* I, 426.
[31] *C Works,* I, 428.
[32] *C Works,* I, 430–431.

trasted with the qualities of a principle, which is actualized by an idea, "and every idea is living, productive, partaketh of infinity, and (as Bacon had sublimely observed) containeth an endless power of semination." Thus, "notions, linked arguments, reference to particular facts and calculations of prudence, influence only the comparatively few," those who have been trained up for them. Far otherwise with ideas. "At the annunciation of principles, of ideas, the soul of man awakes and starts up, as an exile in a far distant land at the unexpected sounds of his native language, when after long years of absence, and almost of oblivion, he is suddenly addressed in his own mother-tongue." "On what other ground," asks Coleridge, "but the cognateness of ideas and principles to man as man does the nameless soldier rush to the combat in defence of the liberties or the honor of his country?" [33]

The hollow abstractions of the histories written in Coleridge's time are the result of the contagion of mechanical philosophy, the product "of an unenlivened generalized understanding." Scriptural history, however, is the living educt of the imagination, "that reconciling and mediatory power, which incorporating the reason in images of the sense, and organizing (as it were) the flux of the senses by the permanence and self-circling energies of the reason, gives birth to a system of symbols, harmonious in themselves, and consubstantial with the truths of which they are the conductors." The context of the description here recalls the earliest statement of the specific distinction of imagination from fancy, where the modifying and coadunating faculty was attributed to Hebrew poetry in contrast to the dead natural objects of Greek religious verse.[34] Thus in a derivative but more than metaphorical sense, "the Sacred Book is worthily entitled *the Word of God*. Hence too, its contents present to us the stream of time continuous as life and a symbol of eternity, inasmuch as the past and the future are virtually contained in the present." In the scriptures both facts and persons have a twofold significance; they are at once portraits and ideals.[35]

[33] *C Works*, I, 433–434.
[34] *CL*, II, 864–866.
[35] *C Works*, I, 437.

The word symbol had been discussed separately by Coleridge and once or twice associated with discussions of the imagination or its effects. Now he goes into a detailed explanation of the term which amplifies earlier treatments. "It is among the miseries of the present age," he says, "that it recognizes no *medium* between literal and metaphorical. Faith is either to be buried in the dead letter, or its name and honors usurped by a counterfeit product of the mechanical understanding, which in the blindness of self-complacency confounds symbols with allegories." Coleridge rectifies the confusion and gives a distinction which reaches to a very profound truth:

Now allegory is but a translation of abstract notions into a picture-language, which is itself nothing but an abstraction from objects of the senses; the principal being more worthless even than its phantom proxy, both alike unsubstantial, and the former shapeless to boot. On the other hand a symbol (ὁ ἔστιν ἀεὶ ταυτηγόρικον) is characterized by a translucence of the special in the individual, or of the general in the special, or of the universal in the general, above all by the translucence of the eternal through and in the temporal. It always partakes of the reality which it renders intelligible; and while it enunciates the whole, abides itself as a living part in that unity of which it is the representative. The other are but empty echoes which the fancy arbitrarily associates with apparitions of matter, less beautiful but not less shadowy than the sloping orchard or hill-side pasture-field seen in the transparent lake below. Alas, for the flocks that are to be led forth to such pastures! [36]

The doctrine of symbol here is based upon an expanded conception of the imagination, or, perhaps better, a theory of imagination purified of its too close relationship with the Schellingian Absolute, and more simply stated as holding the middle ground between the literal, which supposes identity of subject and object, and the metaphorical, which supposes essential diversity fancifully linked. Here the symbol is the product of that mediation; the fundamental principle which makes this function possible is that the symbol is an analogon of the real and of the ideal — more exactly it is an analogon of the ideal-real union, since it is not constructed discursively by adding a concept to a sensible image (or an abstract notion to a picture, as an allegory is formed) but

[36] *C Works*, I, 437–438.

by the interpenetration of its formal and material principles in a manner not the same or different from real existents but partly the same, partly different, that is, analogously. Coleridge insists that a symbol partakes of the reality which it represents, that it involves sameness with difference, and this is only possible if it has an existence analogous to that of the reality it renders intelligible. Much of this he had said before in 1804, but nowhere so explicitly and confidently.

The symbol, however, is only the expression, the incarnation of the subject-object, or reason-understanding fusion. The ground of it remains to be discovered. Coleridge proposes religion as the solution, of which scripture is the text. "The Bible alone contains a science of realities," he says, and he offers a contrast between the discursive processes of the mind and the intuition which captures the total reality. "That hidden mystery in every the minutest form of existence, which contemplated under the relations of time presents itself to the understanding retrospectively, as an infinite ascent of causes, and prospectively as an interminable progression of effects; — that which contemplated in space is beholden intuitively [that is, by sense intuition] as a law of action and re-action, continuous and extending beyond all bound; — this same mystery freed from the *phaenomena* of time and space, and seen in the depth of real being, reveals itself to the pure reason as the actual immanence or in-being of all in each." The ground of this insightful grasp of the being of a thing can only be found in God: "Are we struck with admiration at beholding the cope of heaven imaged in a dew-drop? The least of the *animalculae* to which that drop would be an ocean, contains in itself an infinite problem of which God omnipresent is the only solution." [37]

For a fuller explanation of how precisely Coleridge viewed the relationship of reason and religion, we must go to the longest of the appendices (Appendix B) which Coleridge attached to the first *Lay Sermon*. The argument, though protracted, is not complicated in its outline: religious faith is the perfecting complement and base of all knowledge, just as God is the ground of all existence. Coleridge begins with a form of the Kantian distinction between reason and under-

[37] *C Works*, I, 450.

standing. Reason is "the knowledge of the laws of the whole considered as one," while the understanding is "the science of *phenomena*, and of their subsumption under distinct kinds and sorts (*genera* and *species*). Its functions supply the rules and constitute the possibility of experience; but remain mere logical forms except as far as materials are given by the sense or sensations." The language used here is to be carefully interpreted. Reason has the ideas of oneness (unity) and allness (omneity, or infinity) as its two elements; the union is called totality. "We can neither rest in an infinite that is not at the same time a whole, nor in a whole that is not infinite." The understanding constantly represents totality with some kind of limit, so that the natural man is prone either to atheism (the infinite without the one) or anthropomorphic monotheism (unity without the infinite). The unbalanced and abstract rational intellect was the source of the original temptation by which Adam fell, and in all ages has offered the same snare, to which the atheists of the French Revolution succumbed in their worship of reason. The saving complement to this tendency is provided by religion which considers the particular and individual, and thus is identified with the understanding, but the individual as it exists and has its being in the universal, and so is one with pure reason.[38]

Coleridge then proposes a tri-unity in man of reason, religion, and the will. "For each of the three, though a distinct agency, implies and demands the other two, and loses its own nature at the moment that from distinction it passes into division or separation." The reason taken singly and exclusively becomes "mere visionariness in intellect, and indolence or hard-heartedness in morals," in short Jacobinism — "that philosophy of the French Revolution, which would sacrifice each to the shadowy idol of all." As the science of all as a whole, reason must be interpenetrated by a power that represents the concentration of all in each — "a power that acts by a contraction of universal truths into individual duties, such contraction being the only form in which those truths can attain life and reality." Thus religion is the executive of our nature; it is, as he has said before, "philosophy evolved from idea into act and fact by the superinduction of the extrinsic conditions

[38] *C Works*, I, 456–457.

of reality." Yet even religion itself, by too exclusive devotion to the specific and individual without the contemplation of the universal, changes into superstition, becomes more earthly and servile, and "goes wandering at length with its pack of amulets, bead-rolls, peri-apts, fetishes, and the like pedlary, on pilgrimages to Loretto, Mecca, or the temple of Juggernaut." [39] Both reason and religion, if they will coexist, must be actuated by the will, which is "the sustaining, coercive and ministerial power." As immanent in reason and religion the will appears indifferently as wisdom or love. In its abstraction it becomes Satanic pride and rebellious self-idolatry, such as Milton has so phil-osophically embodied in *Paradise Lost*.[40]

By way of completeness, Coleridge once again states the distinction between understanding and reason, this time in relation to imagina-tion. The understanding or experiential faculty is what Shakespeare called "discourse of reason," that is, an instrumental faculty belonging to reason. Its characteristic is clearness without depth:

> It contemplates the unity of things in their limits only, and is consequently a knowledge of superficies without substance . . . The completing power which unites clearness with depth, the plenitude of the sense with the com-prehensibility of the understanding, is the imagination, impregnated with which the understanding itself becomes intuitive, and a living power. The reason (not the abstract reason, not the reason as the mere organ of science, or as the faculty of scientific principles and schemes *à priori*; but reason), as the integral spirit of the regenerated man, reason substantial and vital . . . this reason without being either the sense, the understanding, or the imagination, contains all three within itself, even as the mind contains its thoughts, and is present in and through them all; or as the expression per-vades the different features of an intelligent countenance.[41]

Like the description of the ideal poet in the beginning of the second part of the *Biographia*, this passage presents the imagination in a context far different from that of Schelling's philosophy. No longer the supreme faculty of intuitive knowledge, it is here restored to its Kant-ian position as the mediator between reason and the plenitude of

[39] *C Works*, I, 457–458.
[40] *C Works*, I, 458.
[41] *C Works*, I, 460–461.

sense. Yet the pattern of the mind's powers that Coleridge describes here is not genuinely Kantian, however much the reason–understanding-with-imagination–sense division suggests a similarity. Coleridge carefully distinguishes his integral reason from "the faculty of scientific principles and schemes *a priori*," and his own imagination here seems to be a higher faculty than understanding (it is the "completing power" which impregnates the understanding and makes it "intuitive"). This does not fully clarify the ambiguity noticed in the description of the poet, where the imagination was under the control of both the will and the understanding. Undoubtedly Coleridge was hesitating about the precise position of his synthetic faculty; to make it inferior to understanding which is an animal faculty capable only of imperfect knowledge seems contrary to all that he claims for it elsewhere, while to elevate it to the dignity of reason brings back all the Schellingian problems. A more exact statement of his solution appears in the 1818 lectures.

There is no doubt, however, that reason is now the highest and most complete function of the mind for Coleridge, the possession of which constitutes man's relationship both to the divine nature (reason as being, contemplated objectively) and to the natural world analogously patterned after this highest mode of being. Thus he finds it easy to turn from the Bible to that other revelation of God, "the great book of his servant nature," coming back, one might say, full circle to one of the very earliest ideas of his Christian Philosophy. As he writes he is gazing on a flowery meadow, and thinking about the undivided reason, "neither merely speculative nor merely practical, but both in one"; he seems to see in the meadow more than an arbitrary illustration of this power, not a simile (the work of fancy), but rather "the same power as that of the reason — the same power in a lower dignity, and therefore a symbol established in the truth of things. I feel it alike, whether I contemplate a single tree or flower, or meditate on vegetation throughout the world, as one of the great organs of the life of nature." The description continues, exhibiting the communion of all the elements in the one plant, the mutuality of their growth, "the ceaseless plastic motion of the parts in the profoundest rest of the whole," so that "it becomes the visible *organismus* of the entire silent or elementary life of nature and, therefore, in incorporating the one extreme becomes the symbol of the other; the natural symbol of that higher life of reason, in which the whole series (known to us in our present state of being) is perfected." [42] The symbolizing and mediating function is here proper to the "undivided" reason, which can integrate organically all modes of being by virtue of its analogous relation to all existents. True knowledge does not consist in word juggling and system building. "If to mint and to remember names delight thee, still arrange and classify and pore and pull to pieces, and peep into death to look for life, as monkeys put their hands behind a looking glass!" Rather, the analogical relationship of all existing things requires "that like can only be known by like: that as truth is the correlative of being, so is the act of being the great organ of truth: that in natural no less than in moral science, *quantum sumus, scimus.*" [43]

The ground of this analogy can only be God. "The fact, therefore, that the mind of man in its own primary and constituent forms represents the laws of nature, is a mystery which of itself should suffice to make us religious: for it is a problem of which God is the only solution, God, the one before all, and of all, and through all!" [44] If reason and understanding merely unite in a composition of their capacities, the result will be acquiescence in the general doctrines of natural religion — belief in a God, in immortality, and probably in the history and ethics of the Gospel. This would be a speculative faith, in the nature of a theory. But what the mind intuitively beholds it tends to become. "In all things and in each thing — for the Almighty Goodness doth not create generalities or abide in abstractions — in each the meanest object it bears witness to a mystery of infinite solution." [45] Falling back on one of his basic similes, Coleridge compares with the operation of the eye the analogous nature of the mind or reason, its primary object (the divine nature), and the way in which it thus must impose upon nature, while detecting in nature the pattern that

[42] *C Works*, I, 462–463.
[43] *C Works*, I, 465.
[44] *C Works*, I, 465.
[45] *C Works*, I, 471.

both receive from their creator. "As it [the mind] is the image or symbol of its great object, by the organ of this similitude, as by an eye, it seeth that same image throughout the creation; and from the same cause sympathizeth with all creation in its groans to be redeemed." [46]

He appeals to the same ground of being as the final guarantee of knowledge in the last of the chapters on method in *The Friend* of 1818. "The finite form can neither be laid hold of, nor is it anything of itself real, but merely an apprehension, a frame-work which the human imagination forms by its own limits, as the foot measures itself on the snow; and the soul truth of which we must again refer to the divine imagination, in virtue of its omniformity." [47] Coleridge's language is typically careless in the negative part of his statement — he certainly does not intend to deny the real existence of objects, nor to assert a wholly subjective knowledge of externals. Rather his point is that what we know of things we know by virtue of the structure of the human imagination, and that the ultimate source of both this mind and its object is the omniform divine imagination which has shaped both us and what we know after its own contours, thus bonding object and subject in the divine ground. [48]

He finds support for this position in both Bacon and Plato. Bacon's philosophy, he says, in his philosophical lectures of 1818, asserts "the necessity of that one great Being whose eternal reason is the ground

[46] *C Works*, I, 470–471.

[47] *Friend*, III, 261.

[48] "For Coleridge, the coalescence of subject and object *must* imply the reality of both, for they are inseparable; there is no knowledge of an object except in its meeting with a subject — no rock is known until *I* know rock; and conversely, *I* do not know anything (am not conscious) until I know *some-thing*." "So the 'infinite I AM' is the formula this system yields for God: He created objects, which *do* exist; our 'perception' (a repetition in the finite mind) also, specifically, 'creates' them, *as they are*, but known as vital because the act of knowledge is itself vital. The essential paradox is that objects do exist; but that *we* have to create them. There is, for Coleridge, no other form of knowledge than the creative." "Dead" objects do not exist at all, in spite of Coleridge's words in *BL*, II, 259. They cannot be dead because they are only known as alive. They are better thought of as "objects, '*as* objects-as-opposed-to subjects'." This is what Coleridge meant in saying, "The Artist must imitate what is active *through* form and figure," neither separately nor both together, but the thing within, which is active through them. Nicholas Brooke, "Coleridge's 'True and Original Realism,'" *Durham University Journal*, n.s., 22 (1961):59–61.

and absolute condition of the ideas in the mind, and no less the ground and the absolute cause of all the corresponding realities in nature — the reality for ever consisting in the law by which each thing is that which it is." [49] The central problem of philosophy according to Plato, he says in *The Friend* of 1818, is to find a ground for all that exists conditionally, and so reduce the aggregate of human knowledge to a system. The objects of sense are in flux, while laws or scientific principles are not principles unless they are permanent and always the same, either the products or the connate forms of pure reason (in a note he refuses to decide which position Plato held). But the material world is found to obey the same laws as had been deduced independently from the reason. "The only answer which Plato deemed the question capable of receiving, compels the reason to pass out of itself and seek the ground of this agreement in a supersensual essence, which being at once the *ideal* of the reason and the cause of the material world, is the pre-establisher of the harmony in and between both." [50] Thus the correlation between idea and law is ultimately founded on the conformity of reality to the mind by reason of their common source in the creative act of God.

Above all principles by which man attempts to be reconciled with himself, with others, and with the world around him, Coleridge now places religion as "the substantiating principle of all true wisdom, the satisfactory solution of all the contradictions of human nature, and of the whole riddle of the world." It is not a sort of knowledge, but a form of being, or rather the truest knowledge of which all science is symbolic. "The material universe," he says in the last lines of the long discussion of philosophic method in *The Friend*, "is but one vast complex MYTHOS (i.e. symbolical representation); and mythology the apex and complement of all genuine physiology." But this is a principle which cannot be learned by logic or excited by rhetoric. "For it is an immutable truth, that WHAT COMES FROM THE HEART, THAT ALONE GOES TO THE HEART; WHAT PROCEEDS FROM A DIVINE IMPULSE, THAT THE GODLIKE ALONE CAN AWAKEN." [51]

[49] *Philosophical Lectures*, p. 334.
[50] *Friend*, III, 162.
[51] *Friend*, III, 265.

By postulating the analogy of the divine mode of being with all the created modes of being as the source of the unity of subject and object in the knowledge process, Coleridge redefined his earlier theory of mediation on an altogether different level. In doing so he avoids the unfortunate pantheistic implications of Schelling's mediating imagination, and is able to give a much richer account of the value and operation of symbolic knowledge, but of course he also makes this theory dependent upon a kind of fideism doubtless unacceptable to many of his readers. This involves no difficulty for Coleridge, and, in fact, the appeal to the verification by individual religious experience does not differ, except in scope, from the earlier appeal to the "true and original realism" as a support for the epistemological theories of the *Biographia's* first volume. The significant aspect of this religious resolution of a lifelong problem is that it indicates the direction Coleridge's thought now begins to take. The literary problem, long ago metamorphosed into a philosophical problem, now leads finally to a religious problem. But before we leave Coleridge at the threshold of a new Christian Philosophy one final document must be examined.

ART AS MEDIATION: THE LECTURES OF 1818

After 1814 Coleridge gave two more series of lectures on literary subjects, one on a mixed collection of topics in the winter and spring of 1818, and another on Shakespeare's plays in the winter of 1818–1819. Of the latter series there is almost no record except the prospectus and brief newspaper accounts of two of the talks.[52] The lectures on literature of 1818 are by no means complete, but manuscripts exist for a half-dozen of the talks and there are reports of some of the others. The course covered an enormous number of works; Coleridge called them "*various*, rather than *miscellaneous*" and said that the common bond was that they were all in kind, though not in the same degree, productions of genius. He began with a portrait of "Manners, Morals, Literature, Philosophy, Religion, and the State of Society in general"

[52] *ShC*, II, 318–323. There was also a course on the history of philosophy in the winter of 1818–1819, which Miss Coburn has edited.

in the (so-called) Dark Ages of Europe, then proceeded through the medieval romance and ballad literature of England, France, and Italy, Chaucer, Spenser, Shakespeare, Beaumont and Fletcher and the dramatic poetry of their contemporaries, Cervantes, Rabelais, Swift, Sterne (a lecture on wit and humor), Donne, Dante, even the Arabian Nights (on the romantic use of the supernatural in poetry and prose fiction), and tales of witches and magic, a lecture on poetry, philosophy and religion, and finally the English language and style.[53]

The matter of all these lectures is not of uniform interest to us, especially in their fragmentary state. Many of them consist of detailed analysis of the works in question, or generalizations about literary history. However, there are some passages where Coleridge again takes up themes from his earlier speculations about the nature of literature and amplifies and clarifies them. Two in particular are of importance here: the theory of allegory and symbol that forms the background for his discussion of Spenser and Cervantes, and the correlative conception of art as mediating between nature and mind which is the substance of the thirteenth lecture.

In *The Statesman's Manual* Coleridge had distinguished the allegorical from the symbolical. The difference had turned on the relation between the sign and the referent: an allegory was only a translation of abstract notions into a picture language, but a symbol, by being a part of that which it represented, both signified and partook of the union of universal and particular in the referent. The analysis here adds little to the earlier notion of allegory. Coleridge defines allegory as "the employment of one set of agents and images to convey in disguise a moral meaning, with a likeness to the imagination, but with a difference to the understanding, — those agents and images being so combined as to form a homogeneous whole." [54] This distinguishes it from metaphor, which is rather a part of allegory. Because of the obvious and intended separation of the sense from the symbol in allegory, its characters are on a kind of middle step between actual

[53] *Coleridge's Miscellaneous Criticism*, ed. T. M. Raysor (Cambridge, Mass., 1936), pp. 3–5, for the syllabus. Hereafter cited as *MC*.

[54] *MC*, pp. 32–33. Metaphor had already been mentioned: "Substitute a simile for the thing it resembles, instead of annexing it, and it becomes a metaphor" (p. 28).

persons and mere personifications. "But for this very cause it is incapable of exciting any lively interest for any length of time, for if the allegoric personage be strongly individualized so as to interest us, we cease to think of it as allegory; and if it does not interest us, it had better be away." The dullest parts of Spenser are those where we have to think of his agents as allegories, but Bunyan's characters on the other hand are so entertaining that we fail to attend to his lessons; "the Bunyan of Parnassus had the better of the Bunyan of the conventicle." [55]

When he comes to speak of symbol, in discussing Cervantes, Coleridge adds an element not mentioned in any of his previous treatments of this topic. The earlier definition is briefly indicated — the symbolical, as distinguished from the allegorical, "is always itself a part of that, of the whole of which it is the representative" [56] — but then Coleridge goes on to suggest a new dimension of symbol theory. "Of most importance to our present subject is this point, that the latter (the allegory) cannot be other than spoken consciously; — whereas in the former (the symbol) it is very possible that the general truth represented may be working unconsciously in the writer's mind during the construction of the symbol." [57] The allegory, in other words, is the product of deliberate choice of image for meaning, of the discursive faculty, while the symbol responds to a law of inner congruity based on the most fundamental community of thing, thought, and expression. Here is the suggestion of a possible way out of the representational prison: conscious art, with its ever present implications of a dualism of form and content, seems to be about to yield to a thoroughly organic and analogical theory of symbol. Unfortunately it is a way that Coleridge does not explicitly take. Yet, though he never repudiates the imitative hypothesis as such, what he has said already about the ground of the analogy between mind, image, and object, and what he

[55] MC, p. 31.

[56] He gives an unfortunate example: " 'Here comes a sail,' — (that is, a ship) is a symbolical expression. 'Behold our lion!' when we speak of some gallant soldier, is allegorical." The exclusive literalness with which this instance illustrates that a symbol must be a part of the whole which it represents is inconsistent with what Coleridge says elsewhere, and even in the context here, about symbol. MC, p. 99.

[57] MC, p. 99.

subsequently says about poetry as mediation, indicate a markedly different way of approaching the unity and the noetic value of the work of art.

It will help to make this clear if we turn back to Coleridge's remarks about Beaumont and Fletcher in an earlier lecture. He characterized them as possessing the common species of wit, later associated with the understanding, and the distinctive note of which is apparently its incapacity to achieve an organic unity of thought and expression based on the idea of the thing. "What had a grammatical and logical consistency for the ear, what could be put together and represented to the eye, these poets took from the ear and eye, unchecked by any intuition of an inward impossibility, just as a man might fit together a quarter of an orange, a quarter of an apple, and the like of a lemon and of a pomegranate, and make it look like one round diverse colored fruit." This is not the method of nature, however, which "works from within by evolution and assimilation according to a law." [58]

Nor is it the method of Shakespeare, and here Coleridge gives his clearest statement of the revised relation of reason and imagination in the creative act, "for he too worked in the spirit of nature, *by evolving the germ within by the imaginative power according to an idea* — for as the power of seeing is to light, so is an idea in mind to a law in nature. They are correlatives that suppose each other." [59] The germ within is what the marble peach lacked, its own life, and therefore its analogous relation to the being of the artist, whose inward eye conceives an idea of the thing and whose imaginative power fuses image with idea in the production of the symbolically real. This "idea of the thing" is not purely subjective. "[There is] no greater or more common vice in dramatic writers than to draw out of themselves." [60] For the individual person, even that of the author, is only *natura naturata*, "an effect, a product, not a *power*." "It was Shakespeare's prerogative to have the *universal* which is potentially in each *particular*, opened out to him in the *homo generalis*, not as an abstraction of observation

[58] *MC*, pp. 42–43.
[59] *MC*, p. 43. Italics added.
[60] *MC*, p. 44. The interpolation apparently is Raysor's.

from a variety of men, but as the substance capable of endless modifications, of which his own personal existence was but one, and to use *this one* as the eye that beheld the other, and as the tongue that could convey the discovery." [61] This is the same process of "observation and meditation, and the former in view of an earlier meditation," of which Coleridge already had found Shakespeare so obvious an example.[62]

The basis for these notions is the theory of the mediating function of art, of which Coleridge gives his fullest explanation in the thirteenth lecture of the series, called "On Poesy or Art." [63] Among the many instances of Coleridge's "borrowings," this essay is outstanding because so much of it, sometimes the very words, comes from a single source, Schelling's lecture "On the Relation of the Formative Arts to Nature." [64] Raysor observes that the essay must be judged leniently since it was never intended for publication by Coleridge, and he cannot be blamed for failing to indicate his sources in incomplete notes made for an oral lecture.[65] Like any other case of indebtedness, this example raises yet again the question of Coleridge's originality. It can only be answered that, however much some sections of the work depend on Schelling, the conceptual structure of the whole essay is one that Coleridge himself had been developing for years. Anyone who has studied the progress of Coleridge's ideas since his first intimations of a theory of imagination before the turn of the century must of necessity agree with Sara Coleridge's remark: "If it be Schelling's — and that the leading

[61] *MC*, p. 44.

[62] See above, Chap. IV, "The poet as knower."

[63] An expanded version of the text, which exists now only in Notebook 22, was later published by H. N. Coleridge in *Literary Remains*, and is included in the Shawcross edition of *BL*. This is the version that will be followed here, though the question of exactly how much of the text Coleridge himself intended as part of the essay and how much is due to H. N. Coleridge's ingenuity cannot be settled satisfactorily in the absence of a finished manuscript. Raysor, who gives the original notebook manuscript, finds the interpolations in the *Literary Remains* text characteristic of Coleridge. *MC*, p. 204.

[64] Sara Coleridge has indicated the similarities and echoes in an appendix to her *Notes and Lectures upon Shakespeare and Some of the Old Poets and Dramatists with Other Literary Remains of S. T. Coleridge*, ed. Mrs. H. N. Coleridge, 2 vols. (London, 1849).

[65] *MC*, pp. 205. One other consequence of the unfinished state of the text is the great number of obscurities of expression and, for Coleridge, an unusually large number of vague and confusing transitions between the sentences and paragraphs of the lecture.

thought of the whole is his, I freely own — it is Coleridge's also." [66]

The central idea of the essay is stated in the opening paragraph: Art, used collectively for painting, sculpture, architecture, and music, is the mediatress between, and reconciler of, nature and man. It is therefore the power of humanizing nature, of infusing the thoughts and passions of man into every thing that is the object of his contemplation; color, form, motion, and sound are the elements which it combines, and it stamps them into unity in the mold of a moral idea.[67] Coleridge explains this mediation in a compressed but carefully phrased analysis. Among primitive people there is no art properly speaking but only reproduction or literal copying of things which give pleasure. His example is savage music. In its lowest state it is "a mere expression of passion by sounds which the passion itself necessitates; — the highest amounts to no more than a voluntary reproduction of these sounds in the absence of the occasioning causes, so as to give the pleasure of contrast, — for example, by the various outcries of battle in the song of security and triumph." This condition is not true of poetry, which is rather "the apotheosis of the former state." Here "by excitement of the associative power passion itself imitates order, and the order resulting produces a pleasurable passion, and thus it elevates the mind by making its feelings the object of its reflection." This it accomplishes by allowing passion to color the sights and sounds that accompanied the original feelings, and yet controlling passion by the "calming power which all distinct images exert on the human soul." [68] The union of thought and feeling described here recalls the balance of the reciprocal impulses of passion and orderly arrangement that was the origin of metrical verse in the *Biographia*.[69]

The beginning of art is the presentation of an "outward image" to the mind. Only the specifically human, however, can be the realm of art, so Coleridge excludes whatever is common to all animals, and limits his discussion "to the effect produced by the congruity of the animal impression with the reflective powers of the mind; so that not

[66] *Notes and Lectures*, II, 363.
[67] *BL*, II, 253.
[68] *BL*, II, 253–254.
[69] *BL*, II, 49–50.

the thing presented, but that which is re-presented by the thing, shall
be the source of the pleasure." This leads to a more explicit statement
of the key idea of the essay: "Art itself might be defined as of a middle
quality between a thought and a thing, or, as I said before, the union
and reconciliation of that which is nature with that which is exclusively human." [70] Its mediation consists in its existence as "the figured language of thought." Things are characterized by diversity and
variety; thought by unity. Nature appears to us as diverse, and art
mediates between it and mind by forming that diversity into unity.
Thus art is distinguished from nature by "the unity of all the parts in
one thought or idea." In fact, nature itself is unified but does not seem
so to us; it would give us the impression of a work of art, "if we could
see the thought which is present at once in the whole and in every
part." Nature is, therefore, to a religious observer "the art of God." In
general, "a work of art will be *just* in proportion as it adequately con-
veys the *thought*, and *rich* in proportion to the *variety of parts* which
it holds in unity." [71]

Coleridge now turns to the way in which this mediation is accomplished.[72] This involves a more exact definition of imitation. He
begins with an example. "The impression on the wax is not an imitation, but a copy, of the seal; the seal itself is an imitation." A philo-

---

[70] Coleridge is not very clear when he says that it is "not the thing presented, but
that which is re-presented by the thing," that is the source of pleasure. Insofar as he is
trying to indicate the mediating function of art, then this formula is useful to show that
it is the object to which the medium refers that governs the relationship. Elsewhere,
however, he makes clear that he regards the mediating artifact as the source of the
pleasure. It must be contemplated with "disinterestedness," that is, without reference
to the real existence, *as an object of desire*, of the thing referred to. See *BL*, II, 254.

[71] *BL*, II, 254–255. Italics added.

[72] He first makes the point that all the fine arts can be called by the old definition of
painting, *muta poesis*. He wishes to distinguish therefore between poetry and poesy.
"Poesy" is the generic and common term, and indicates that all the fine arts have as
their purpose "to express intellectual purposes, thoughts, conceptions, and sentiments
which have their origin in the human mind, — not, however, as poetry does, by means
of articulate speech, but as nature or the divine art does, by form, color, magnitude,
proportion, or by sound, that is, silently or musically." *BL*, II, 255. Coleridge is con-
sistently careless in the subsidiary parts of his distinctions and definitions, and this text
furnishes another example of this negligence: The idea that all art "expresses" conceptions, and so forth, which are essentially "intellectual" occurs nowhere in Coleridge as a
serious proposition.

sophical discrimination must define the kind; Coleridge therefore says that "in all imitation two elements must coexist, and not only coexist, but must be perceived as coexisting." These are likeness and unlikeness, or sameness and difference. They are constituents in all art. "The artist may take his point of view where he pleases, provided that the desired effect be perceptibly produced, — that there be likeness in the difference, difference in the likeness, and a reconcilement of both in one." Likeness to nature without check of difference arouses disgust, because we are deluded. The supposed reality is revealed to be a deception. In a work of genuine imitation, "you begin with an acknowledged total difference, and then every touch of nature gives you the pleasure of an approximation to truth." [73]

But the combination of likeness and difference still does not specify very clearly the nature of art. It is further an imitation of the beautiful in nature. What is beauty? "It is, in the abstract, the unity of the manifold, the coalescence of the diverse; in the concrete, it is the union of the shapely (*formosum*) with the vital." Shawcross points out that this differs from the definition of beauty given in the essays "On the Principles of Genial Criticism." There it was "the shapely joined with the agreeable," and open to the charge that the pleasurable was insufficiently united to the formal.[74] Here it is the organic unity of the elements that is stressed. In the "dead organic" a kind of beauty may be perceived in regularity of form; in the "living organic" mere regularity is not enough to provide the formal.[75] What then does? Coleridge distinguishes between two senses of nature. "If the artist copies the mere nature, the *natura naturata*, what idle rivalry!" Form cannot come from outside. If he employs a given form, supposed to be beautiful, only emptiness and unreality result. The artist must "master the essence, the *natura naturans*, which presupposes a bond between nature in the higher sense and the soul of man." [76]

He continues to explore the meaning of this bond which enables art to perform its mediation. One element of it explains both the onto-

[73] *BL*, II, 255–256.
[74] *BL*, II, 257, 318, 234.
[75] *BL*, II, 256–257.
[76] *BL*, II, 257.

logical perfection of nature and its subordination to man: this might be called the identity of formal and final causes, or the constitutive power of final causes in nature. "The wisdom in nature is distinguished from that in man by the co-instantaneity of the plan and the execution; the thought and the product are one, or are given at once; but there is no reflex act, and hence there is no moral responsibility." Man, however, has the power of reflection and of choice. The objects of nature present, as in a mirror, "all the possible elements, steps, and processes of intellect antecedent to consciousness, and therefore to the full development of the intelligential act." Further, "man's mind is the very focus of the rays of intellect which are scattered throughout the images of nature." The genius of the fine arts lies in their ability to superinduce upon the forms of these images, which are fitted to the limits of the mind, the moral reflections to which they approximate, to make nature thought, and thought nature. Art, therefore, reveals to mind its own shape in nature.[77]

But this reconcilement of the external and the internal in the work of art must be partly unconscious. The artist cannot begin by "mere painful copying," for this way he will produce only masks, not forms breathing life. This is why Coleridge says that the artist must "eloign himself from nature in order to return to her with full effect." What he seems to mean is that the artist must contemplate in his own mind the ideas which correspond to the laws in nature and which, with them, have a common source elsewhere. "He merely absents himself for a season from her, that his own spirit, which has the same ground with nature, may learn her unspoken language in its main radicals, before he approaches to her endless compositions of them." [78]

There is no true alternative, says Coleridge, between the idealistic theory of knowledge ("that every thing around us is but a phantom, or that the life which is in us is in them likewise") and the copy theory ("that to know is to resemble, when we speak of objects out of ourselves, even as within ourselves to learn is, according to Plato, only to recollect").[79] By virtue of the unity between knower and

[77] BL, II, 257–258.
[78] BL, II, 258.
[79] BL, II, 259. Coleridge condemned the same position in the closing paragraphs of

known, art discovers what its object is. "The artist must imitate that which is within the thing, that which is active through form and figure, and discourses to us by symbols — the *Natur-geist,* or spirit of nature, as we unconsciously imitate those whom we love; for so only can we hope to produce any work truly natural in the object and truly human in the effect." The ground of all is the idea which creates the form, but it cannot itself be the form. "It is above form, and is its essence, the universal in the individual, or the individuality itself, — the glance and the exponent of the indwelling power." [80]

After some remarks on the other fine arts, sculpture, painting, architecture, and music, Coleridge summarizes his conception of mediation. It is essentially organic and vital, as the difference between "form as proceeding, and shape as superinduced." The latter is mechanical, "either the death or the imprisonment of the thing; — the former is its self-witnessing and self-effected sphere of agency, Art would or should be the abridgement of nature." Its final object is "to give the whole *ad hominem.*" [81]

The discussion is incomplete, especially so at the end of the lecture notes, where Coleridge's own manuscript has a series of disconnected comments and a postscript, and H. N. Coleridge's text is filled out with interpolated observations on the various media of art. Nor is the elaborate theological grounding for the possibility of mediation and of symbol that was given in *The Statesman's Manual* mentioned anywhere in the lectures. Perhaps the omission is due to the fragmentary state of the text. But no explanation seems really necessary. Coleridge's subject in the lecture was the nature of the aesthetic mediation between man and nature; his starting point was the assumed fact of the mediation, and his purpose to clarify the specific circumstances in which the process takes place, its limitations but also its potency as a noetically formative experience. Within the scope of his argument there was

---

the essays on method in *The Friend.* There it was the fault of the understanding, by which we think of ourselves as separated beings, nature in antithesis to mind, subject to object. By reason, in contrast, we know ourselves one with the whole. *Friend,* III, 261–262.

[80] *BL,* II, 259.
[81] *BL,* II, 262.

no need for an explanation of the theory previously worked out, of the divine nature as the substrate for the modes of existence which make mediatory contact between subject and object possible. He is content with merely pointing out that the spirit of the artist "has the same ground" as the nature he transforms, and that in the contemplation of this ground is to be found the higher criterion of the art process.[82]

Coleridge's achievement here is to restate much of his older theory in a context which makes clear that we can differentiate only abstractly between the functions of the mind, and indeed this may be one of the explanations why the imagination seems to decline in importance, or to be assimilated to the reason, in his writings after the *Biographia*: the aesthetic process is seen as one complete act. The whole mind creates the work of art by an operation that is integral and essentially synthetic: as imagination it shapes what it perceives in the fragments of its sense perception according to the ideas which it has contemplated as universal and necessary — or alternatively it embodies these ideas in sensible shapes. Coleridge struggles in this lecture to avoid the language of that destructive dichotomy between idea and expression, but discursive language does not allow him or us to characterize perfectly the unique embodiment of the concrete-universal that the art object is. The closest he can come is to compare the art process with the working of nature, which is distinguished "by the co-instantaneity of the plan and the execution; the thought and the

---

[82] *BL*, II, 258. A final text to illustrate this relationship of the poem to the creative ground of being in God can be found in a letter of 1815 (Coleridge is criticizing Cottle's *Messiah*): "The common end of all *narrative*, nay, of *all*, Poems is to convert a *series* into a *Whole*: to make those events, which in real or imagined History move on in a *strait* Line, assume to our Understandings a *circular* motion — the snake with it's Tail in it's Mouth. Hence indeed the almost flattering and yet appropriate Term, Poesy — i.e. poiēsis = *making*. Doubtless, to *his* eye, which alone comprehends all Past and all Future in one eternal Present, what to our short sight appears strait is but a part of the great Cycle — just as the calm Sea to us *appears* level, tho' it be indeed only a part of a *globe*. Now what the Globe is in Geography, *miniaturing* in order to *manifest* the Truth, such is a Poem to that Image of God, which we were created into, and which still seeks that Unity, or Revelation of the *One* in and by the *Many*, which reminds it, that tho' in order to be an individual Being it must go forth *from* God, yet as the *re*ceding from *him* is to *pro*ceed towards Nothingness and Privation, it must still at every step turn back toward him in order to *be* at all — Now a straight Line, continuously retracted forms of necessity a circular orbit." *CL*, IV, 545.

product are one." The whole purpose of art is to attach meaning and value to the shapes of nature by a fusion which has no parts, "to make nature thought, and thought nature." The end result is "the figured language of thought," the image — evolved by the imaginative power according to an idea — with which the artist confronts us, the analogon he has made of his own experience, which he invites us to experience again for ourselves.

These reconsiderations of earlier theory confirm the conclusion that the central principle of Coleridge's literary philosophy is the mediating function of art, and that the most characteristic of his ideas on aesthetics — the conception of imagination as the synthetic faculty, of the organic metaphor to express the mode of existence of artifacts, of the reconciliation of opposites or of multeity in unity as the paradigm of artistic making, and of the symbol as the shape of the mind's nondiscursive experience of the external — are all finally intelligible only in the context of the imaginative abridgement of reality by the mind that constitutes the essential activity of art. Indeed not only are these conceptions best understood in terms of the purpose of art, but in these last documents all the elements tend to merge into a single imaginative act and become accordingly motive, mode and product of one aesthetic function. It would be too bold to say that Coleridge's philosophy of literature is complete by the time he finishes the lectures of 1818; the very necessity here of constructing this last phase out of several different manuscripts would make that claim unwise. Nonetheless, from this point on the problems of literary theory ceased to interest Coleridge to any great extent, and one reason may have been that the speculations which began two decades earlier with Wordsworth's poetry and Locke's epistemology had now come to a perfection of sorts in the conception of art as "the mediatress between, and reconciler of, nature and man."

CHAPTER VIII

Another Coleridge, After 1819

> Christian faith is the perfection of human intelligence.
> *Aids to Reflection*, preface.

Our study comes to an abrupt end in 1819. After the lectures of that year literature and literary theory never again seem to have held Coleridge's interest as they did from 1811 through the writing of the *Biographia*. He turned his attention instead almost entirely to religious questions, to Christian apologetic, the social and political implications of theological principles, and, in his letters and notebooks, to scientific theories about the principle of life and to plans for a new synthesis of his philosophy. There are hints of literary ventures — an epic on the destruction of Jerusalem, a series of critical letters, works on Shakespeare and on romantic poetry, the completion of *Christabel* [1] — but, except for some new poems, a few reviews and miscellaneous articles for journals, and an essay for the Royal Society of Literature *On the Prometheus of Aeschylus* (1825), the published works of Coleridge's last years are wholly religious or politico-religious in theme: the *Aids to Reflection* (1825), a study of "the principles of moral Architecture on the several grounds of prudence, morality, and religion," [2] and *On the Constitution of Church and State* (1830), a tract on the nature of both these institutions in connection with the Catholic Emancipation Bill of 1829. Most of his speculative energy is devoted once again to the construction of a philosophical system. The Dynamic Philosophy

---

[1] Chambers, *Coleridge*, pp. 283, 287.

[2] S. T. Coleridge, *Aids to Reflection in the formation of a manly character on the several grounds of prudence, morality and religion, illustrated by select passages from our elder divines, especially from Archbishop Leighton* (London, 1825), p. vi.

in the *Logosophia* of his earlier years now becomes a "Spiritual Philosophy" and the work is renamed the *Opus Maximum*. Here, too, Coleridge's ultimate interest is in a religious conclusion to his thought. The plan consists now of only two treatises in place of the original six: a preliminary one on logic and, as the main essay, an "Assertion of Religion." [3] Of the principal posthumous works, including *Table Talk* (1835) and *Confessions of an Inquiring Spirit* (1840), only the *Literary Remains* (1836–1839) is at all concerned with our subject, and that is mainly a collection of loose ends from earlier projects, gathered together and revised a good deal by H. N. Coleridge: manuscript notes from the lectures of 1818, marginalia on literary subjects, and much later material on theological writers. Unless the unedited notebooks and manuscript fragments of Coleridge's last years yield much new material, the evidence on which a study of his philosophy of literature can be based ends with the lectures of 1818 and 1819.[4]

Yet merely to point out the obvious fact that Coleridge's sentiments and enthusiasms changed direction between his fortieth and fiftieth years is no satisfactory conclusion to our investigation. It is true that the problem of why Coleridge ultimately lost interest in speculation about the imaginative apprehension of reality in literature and art is separable from the problem of the concrete development and interpretation of the theory that he had evolved. The latter is a coherent enough question and can be adequately discussed within the temporal limits 1790–1819. On the other hand, the change of Coleridge's interests after the *Biographia* and the subsequent subordination of literary theory to theological and metaphysical matters of an entirely different sort are questions that involve a much wider view of Coleridge's thought (and not only his thought but also pertinent biographical data — his declining health, money problems, the continual struggle with drug addiction, even the security of his refuge with the Gillmans) and would require, necessarily, detailed study in the published and especially the

---

[3] Chambers, *Coleridge*, pp. 312–313.

[4] An examination of the notebook manuscripts in the British Museum which include material from the years after 1818 tends to confirm this conclusion. But the extremely difficult matter of dating the entries — most of the notebooks were used simultaneously for several years and the notations are by no means consecutive — makes any conjectures based on their contents necessarily dubious, at least until we have the completed results of Miss Coburn's painstaking scholarship.

unpublished writings of his later years before they could be adequately answered.

Still, it seems entirely too cautious to end this investigation without some indication of where a solution may lie, however tentative such a suggestion must necessarily be. Coleridge, after all, had spent nearly ten years of his life lecturing and writing about literature and critical theory, and, for a good many years before that, these had been among the principal subjects of his philosophical investigations, and before he had begun to philosophize he had been writing poetry for some years. If the virtual abandonment of these interests after 1819 is to appear intelligible in any way, and the unity of Coleridge's philosophical outlook to be preserved in spite of this *volte-face*, then some attempt must be made to formulate an explanation, even though inevitably from a standpoint within the problem itself, within the limits of the evidence already offered and not from the vantage point of the knowledge that a wider study of the religious and philosophical speculations in the writings and notebooks of Coleridge's last years could provide. That study remains to be done.

Without wishing to do anything more here than propose a tentative solution to what must be, even without these reservations, a complex and elusive problem — the search for the primary motivations and determinations of an individual's thinking — I suggest that one of the decisive conditions of Coleridge's intellectual life was the epistemological problematic that prevailed in the early years of his adulthood — more precisely, the way in which he conceived of and defined the problems of knowledge as he first became aware of the need for a more satisfactory epistemology in the decade before 1800. The pattern of the origin, development, and eventual abandonment of a philosophy of literature was determined largely by the way in which Coleridge posed for himself the most primary noetic questions at the very beginning of his philosophical speculations.

There seem to have been, for him at least, two aspects to the problem of finding a guarantee and an explanation of knowledge.[5] The first

[5] This analysis of the two formulations of the epistemological problem will be recognized as an elaboration of the two tensions in Coleridge's thought already noticed in discussing the *Biographia* — namely, the requirements of his imagination theory and the somewhat contradictory implications of his distrust of anything smacking of pantheism.

was philosophical, indeed essentially literary: how to justify his own persuasion of the mind's ability to penetrate to the meaning of the "one mighty alphabet," the "lovely shapes and sounds intelligible" of the world around him. As he described it in the *Biographia*, the problem was to furnish a theory that would explain the sense of empathy between the poet's mind and the external world that was so powerful a characteristic of Wordsworth's poetry. He did not have to wait until 1797 to discover this phenomenon, however; the concept of the "one life" in all things can be found in his own earlier verse, in "Religious Musings" for example, and can probably be traced back to his youthful reading of Plato and the Plotinians, if not to the romances and magical stories of his childhood. Yet when he began to study the subject seriously in 1800 he found this fundamental persuasion challenged by the whole weight of the orthodox philosophy of the day, the school of Locke and especially of his associationist successors. In the face of a wholly passive, mechanistic, and, in Coleridge's view, finally materialistic theory of the operation of the mind, he had to discover a justification for the partly subjective activity by which the mind formed out of the merely measurable and quantitative aspects of experience a knowledge of the world of spirit. Neither the extreme subjective idealism of Berkeley, the critical distinctions of Kant, nor, ultimately, the pantheism of Spinoza and Boehme could adequately account for this knowledge. The only solution was to postulate the reality of this community of self and thing, and then search for a function of mind which would be able to construct it. Thus the epistemological problem as Coleridge conceived it — an inherited associationism unable to account for a felt transcendence — required the kind of answer that he finally proposed in his theory of an intermediary and synthetic imagination.

The other aspect of the knowledge problem was, perhaps, more typical of Coleridge than of the age, but, given his character and life history, no less important for the direction of his thought. It grew out of the immense importance he attached, in youth as well as in old age, to questions about the existence of God and the nature and extent of religious obligations — under which social, political, and even philosophical questions may also be subsumed since they are primarily for Coleridge moral questions involving the nature of personal obligation as derived from an analysis of man's nature. "I retired to a cottage in Somersetshire at the foot of Quantock," he writes about the spiritual crisis of 1797, "and devoted my thoughts and studies to the foundations of religion and morals. Here I found myself all afloat. Doubts rushed in; broke upon me." [6] The exact problem that faced Coleridge, it seems, was the inadequacy of "the rationalism of the understanding," to use Boulger's phrase, for giving any insight into the most important religious questions. Unitarianism, Anglicanism, and especially the so-called philosophical defense of traditional religion by Locke and the physico-theologians and "evidence-writers" were as much infected as the criticisms of Hume by the deadly reliance on scientific and rationalistic criteria which the empiricists had introduced into philosophical and theological discussion. Against this excessive rationalism only some kind of appeal to a knowledge higher than the discursive and schematic could be successful. The accomplishment of this purpose was, as Boulger points out, the main reason for Coleridge's attraction to Kant's distinction between reason and understanding: used negatively it shows that God and his existence are not subjects for scientific inquiry.[7] This is essentially the position of Coleridge in the description of his early religious difficulties in the *Biographia*. The "sciential" reason by itself can show only the falsity of demonstrations about God, but the will under the influence of the lessons of nature and the promptings of conscience can move us to faith.[8] Thus Coleridge proposes an imperfect version of what he later comes to call the "practical" reason, the highest function of the mind under the influence of will. By distinguishing reason from understanding he gave at an early age an answer, however undeveloped it was to remain for some time, to the religious problem as he conceived it. He relegated the demonstrations of extreme rationalism to the understanding, and proposed for his own purposes a "higher" reason, ultimately a kind of fideism, to provide the profound and certain knowledge on which religion is grounded.

It seems possible now to say that these versions of the two problems — both philosophical, but the one basically aesthetic in origin and the

[6] *BL*, I, 132.
[7] James D. Boulger, *Coleridge as Religious Thinker* (New Haven, 1961), p. 75.
[8] *BL*, I, 135.

other fundamentally religious — determined the outlines of Coleridge's intellectual development after 1800. Further, the complications of the *Biographia* were due, partly at least, to the failure to keep distinct the two sets of questions involved. And finally, the clarification of problems that followed the confusion of theory in the first half of the *Biographia* led to some improvement in the literary philosophy of the last years but eventually resulted in Coleridge's total silence on literary questions as they were superseded in his interest by the more attractive and more critical problems of religion, moral philosophy, and the construction of a synthesis which would relate the two to a complete theory of life and thought.

The tension between the two problems was inevitable, granted their existence and importance for Coleridge, because they differed substantially in the kind of solution they required. The epistemological problem demanded for its resolution a theory of the unity of knower and known that was active and creative, while the religious problem required a higher and more certain kind of knowledge than the merely schematic and discursive operations of the mind could provide. The tension involved what may be called the horizontal and the vertical aspects of knowledge. Up to the writing of the *Biographia* it was the first problem that absorbed most of Coleridge's attention. In the middle of that work he seems to have reached the conclusion that the solution of the epistemological or poetic problem would also serve as the solution to the religious problem, that the imagination was not only the synthesizing and mediating faculty in the act of aesthetic creation but also the fundamental operation involved in all knowing and, at its most intense and controlled level, the faculty of insight into ultimate philosophical and religious truths.

The failure of this ambitious design led finally to a separation of the two problems in Coleridge's mind. Thereafter, in the Wordsworth criticism, the digressions and appendices of *The Statesman's Manual*, and in the lectures of 1818, he repaired the theory of imagination wholly within the limits of the original epistemological-aesthetic problem, and did not attempt any further extensions to a general knowledge theory or to the terrain of the truths of theology and theosophical philosophy. The result of these corrections was his most significant contribution to a philosophy of literature: the concept of the work of art as a symbol mediating between multiform reality and the knowing person, and of the aesthetic act of both poet and auditor as symbolic experience achieved through the shaping power of imagination. In the context of traditional British realism he offered a theory which defended the creativity of the mind and, while insisting on a fairly classical concept of imitation, developed an organic vitalism that kept this theory from abstract formalism. If his vision did not entirely escape the limitations of the mimetic premise, it was nonetheless the first modern statement of the autonomy of poetic knowing, strengthened by an explanation of the ontological relationship of the poem to other kinds of existents.

The most interesting element in Coleridge's post-*Biographia* theory — and little noticed by critics, it seems, though quite consistent with all his earlier metaphysical and literary assumptions — is the reconciliation of the demands of these opposite traditions by an appeal to the analogous existence of both subject and object, grounded in divine creativity. Without some kind of basis for the ultimate possibility of interaction between knower and known, Coleridge's theory of the mediating function of art and of the imagination as the faculty of this process would have been simply an assertion that carried him safely over the crux of the argument, like Hartley's "infinitesimal elementary body" acting between the soul and the gross body.[9] Of course, even the explanation that Coleridge gives is open to the criticism that it only removes the difficulty one step further, that it too is but an assertion which requires an act of religious faith to justify it. But Coleridge would not have thought this an objection, because he insists that his explanation centers exactly on the division between philosophy and religion, the point where argument ends and the confidence of faith begins.

The frontier which divides philosophy and religion in Coleridge's thought also separates the two problems we have been discussing, and it seems noteworthy that the very theory of analogy that enabled Coleridge to explain the imaginative mediation between subject and object in the creation of art also defines quite clearly the limitations

[9] Hartley, *Observations*, I, 34.

of that activity and the impossibility of it ever providing that certain knowledge of religious and moral principles which Coleridge wanted. The imagination could give images, symbols, "the figured language of thought," insight into the particular existences of things, but not the universal and necessary truths of theology or the highest "spiritual" philosophy. Thus, though the discussion of imagination led to God it could, within its own terms, say nothing about him, and the original version of the problem of religious knowledge came back into prominence.

For the rest of his life the investigation and defense of religion, and the synthesis of it with his metaphysics, were Coleridge's principal concerns, and the distinction of reason from understanding was both tool and weapon. Whether he ever succeeded in overcoming the divergence between the solutions demanded by these two problems and thus in resolving the claims of imagination and reason is a question that cannot be answered here. It involves the sixteen years that he was yet to live after the last lectures on literature in 1819, and it deals with a different Coleridge than the one we have been talking about — not wholly different, for the analysis attempted here has indicated the fundamental dispositions around which his thought patterned itself and it is clear that the sources of his interest in literary theory were not entirely unrelated to the tendencies that also made him a religious philosopher. But if pre-eminence must be given to one or the other, it should be to Coleridge the religious man, for however much we think of him as poet, literary critic, or metaphysician, it seems likely that the questions he finally asked were, and all the while had been, religious questions. But that is a thesis which requires another study to substantiate it, and not the least of the difficulties in the way of doing so is the mass of unpublished material which lies in the manuscripts and notebooks of Coleridge's final years. That will tell us a great deal about his thought and may require the revision of things that have been said in this study, some confidently but many with the realization that the matter is far from closed. In the true Coleridgean tradition, the present work is only a fragment.

WORKS CITED

INDEX

Works Cited

Abrams, Meyer. *The Mirror and the Lamp: Romantic Theory and the Critical Tradition*. New York: Oxford University Press, 1953.

Aristotle. *Aristotle's Theory of Poetry and Fine Art, with a Critical Text and Translation of The Poetics*. Edited and translated by S. H. Butcher. 3rd edition. London: Macmillan and Co., 1902.

Badawi, M. M. "Coleridge's Formal Criticism of Shakespeare's Plays," *Essays in Criticism*, 10 (1960): 148–162.

Baker, Herschel. *William Hazlitt*. Cambridge, Mass.: Harvard University Press, 1962.

Bate, Walter Jackson. "Coleridge on the Function of Art," in *Perspectives of Criticism*. Edited by Harry Levin. (Harvard Studies in Comparative Literature, vol. 20) Cambridge, Mass.: Harvard University Press, 1950.

—— *From Classic to Romantic: Premises of Taste in Eighteenth Century England*. Cambridge, Mass.: Harvard University Press, 1946.

Benziger, James. "Organic Unity: Leibniz to Coleridge," *PMLA*, 66 (1951): 24–48.

Berkeley, George. *The Works of George Berkeley, Bishop of Cloyne*. Edited by A. A. Luce and T. E. Jessop. 9 vols. London: Thomas Nelson and Sons, 1948–1957.

Boulger, James D. *Coleridge As Religious Thinker*. New Haven: Yale University Press, 1961.

Brooke, Nicholas. "Coleridge's 'True and Original Realism,'" *Durham University Journal*, n.s., 22 (1961): 58–69.

Chambers, E. K. *Samuel Taylor Coleridge: A Biographical Study*. Oxford: Clarendon Press, 1938.

Cohen, Ralph. "Association of Ideas and Poetic Unity," *Philological Quarterly*, 36 (1957): 464–475.

Coleridge, Samuel Taylor. *Aids to Reflection in the formation of a manly character on the several grounds of prudence, morality and religion, illustrated by select passages from our elder divines, especially from Archbishop Leighton*. London, 1825.

—— *Anima Poetae: From the Unpublished Note-books of Samuel Taylor Coleridge*. Edited by E. H. Coleridge. London, 1895.

—— *Biographia Literaria*. Edited with his aesthetical essays by J. Shawcross. 2 vols. Oxford: Oxford University Press, 1907; repr., 1958.

—— *Coleridge on Logic and Learning: With Selections from the Unpublished Manuscripts*. Edited by Alice D. Snyder. New Haven: Yale University Press, 1929.

—— *Coleridge's Miscellaneous Criticism*. Edited by T. M. Raysor. Cambridge, Mass.: Harvard University Press, 1936.

—— *Coleridge's Shakespearean Criticism*. Edited by T. M. Raysor. 2 vols. London: Constable and Co., 1930.

—— *Collected Letters of Samuel Taylor Coleridge*. Edited by Earl Leslie Griggs. 4 vols. Oxford: Clarendon Press, 1956–1959.

—— *The Complete Poetical Works of Samuel Taylor Coleridge*. Edited by Ernest Hartley Coleridge. 2 vols. Oxford: Clarendon Press, 1912.

—— *The Complete Works of Samuel Taylor Coleridge, with an Introductory Essay upon His Philosophical and Theological Opinions*. Edited by W. G. T. Shedd. 7 vols. New York, 1854.

—— *Essays On His Own Times: Forming a Second Series of The Friend*. Edited by Sara Coleridge. 3 vols. London, 1850.

—— *The Friend*. Penrith, 1809–1810.

—— *The Friend: A Series of Essays in Three Volumes, To Aid in the Formation of Fixed Principles in Politics, Morals, and Religion, with Literary Amusements Interspersed*. 3 vols. London, 1818.

—— *Inquiring Spirit: A New Presentation of Coleridge from His Published and Unprinted Prose Writings*. Edited by Kathleen Coburn. London: Routledge and Kegan Paul, 1951.

—— *The Notebooks of Samuel Taylor Coleridge*. Edited by Kathleen Coburn. 2 vols. (Bollingen Series L) New York: Pantheon Books, 1957–1961.

—— *Notes and Lectures upon Shapespeare and Some of the Old Poets and Dramatists with Other Literary Remains of S. T. Coleridge*. Edited by Mrs H. N. Coleridge. 2 vols. London, 1849.

—— *The Philosophical Lectures of Samuel Taylor Coleridge: Hitherto Unpublished*. Edited by Kathleen Coburn. New York: Philosophical Library, 1949.

—— *Specimens of the Table Talk of the Late Samuel Taylor Coleridge*. Edited by H. N. Coleridge. 2 vols. London, 1835.

—— *The Statesman's Manual, or the Bible the Best Guide to Political Skill and Foresight: A Lay Sermon, Addressed to the Higher Classes of Society, With the Author's Last Corrections, and Notes* by H. N. Coleridge. In *The Complete Works*. Edited by W. G. T. Shedd. New York, 1854. Vol. I.

Colmer, John. *Coleridge: Critic of Society*. Oxford: Clarendon Press, 1959.

Cottle, Joseph. *Reminiscences of Samuel Taylor Coleridge and Robert Southey*. London, 1847.

Fairchild, Hoxie N. "Hartley, Pistorius, and Coleridge," *PMLA*, 62 (1947): 1010–1021.

Gillman, James. *The Life of Samuel Taylor Coleridge*. Vol. I (the only part published). London, 1838.

Gilson, Etienne. *History of Christian Philosophy in the Middle Ages*. New York: Random House, 1955.

Gray, Arthur. *Jesus College*. London, 1902.

Hanson, Lawrence. *The Life of S. T. Coleridge: The Early Years*. London: George Allen and Unwin, 1938.

Hardy, Barbara. "Keats, Coleridge and Negative Capability," *Notes and Queries*, July 5, 1952, pp. 299–301.

Hartley, David. *Observations on Man, His Frame, His Duty, and His Expectations*. 2 vols. London, 1749. 3 vols., octavo, 1791.

Haven, Richard. "Coleridge, Hartley, and the Mystics," *Journal of the History of Ideas*, 20 (1959): 477–494.

Hazlitt, William. *The Complete Works of William Hazlitt*. Edited by P. P. Howe. 21 vols. London and Toronto: J. M. Dent and Sons, 1930–1934.

Helmholtz-Phelan, Anna von. *The Indebtedness of Samuel Taylor Coleridge to August Wilhelm von Schlegel*. (Bulletin of the University of Wisconsin, no. 163; Philology and Literature Series, vol. 3, no. 4, pp. 273–370) Madison, Wisconsin: University of Wisconsin Press, 1907.

Hirsch, E. D., Jr. *Wordsworth and Schelling: A Typological Study of Romanticism*. (Yale Studies in English, vol. 145) New Haven: Yale University Press, 1960.

House, Humphrey. *Coleridge: The Clark Lectures 1951–1952*. London: Rupert Hart-Davis, 1953.

James, D. G. *The Romantic Comedy*. London: Oxford University Press, 1948.

———— *Skepticism and Poetry: An Essay on the Poetic Imagination*. London: George Allen and Unwin, 1937.

Jones, David. *Epoch and Artist: Selected Writings*. Edited by Harman Grisewood. London: Faber and Faber, 1959.

Kallich, Martin. "The Association of Ideas and Akenside's *Pleasures of Imagination*," *Modern Language Notes*, 62 (1947): 166–173.

———— "The Association of Ideas and Critical Theory: Hobbes, Locke, and Addison," *English Literary History*, 12 (1945): 290–315.

———— "The Associationist Criticism of Francis Hutcheson and David Hume," *Studies in Philology*, 43 (1946): 644–667.

Kant, Immanuel. *Critique of Practical Reason and Other Writings in Moral Philosophy*. Translated and edited with an introduction by Lewis White Beck. Chicago: University of Chicago Press, 1949.

———— *Immanuel Kant's Critique of Pure Reason*. Translated by Norman Kemp Smith. London: Macmillan and Co., 1933.

———— *Kant's Critique of Aesthetic Judgment.* Translated, with seven introductory essays, notes, and analytical index, by J. C. Meredith. Oxford: Clarendon Press, 1911.

Locke, John. *An Essay Concerning Human Understanding.* Edited by A. C. Fraser. 2 vols. Oxford, 1894.

Lovejoy, A. O. *Essays in the History of Ideas.* Baltimore: The Johns Hopkins Press, 1948.

Lowes, John Livingston. *The Road to Xanadu: A Study in the Ways of the Imagination.* Boston and New York: Houghton Mifflin and Co., 1927.

Marsh, Robert. "The Second Part of Hartley's System," *Journal of the History of Ideas,* 20 (1959): 264–273.

McKenzie, Gordon. *Organic Unity in Coleridge.* (University of California Publications in English, vol. VII, no. 1) Berkeley: University of California Press, 1939.

Muirhead, J. H. *Coleridge as Philosopher.* London: George Allen and Unwin, 1930, repr. 1954.

Parrish, Stephen Maxfield. "The Wordsworth-Coleridge Controversy," *PMLA,* 73 (1958): 367–374.

Piper, Herbert. "The Pantheistic Sources of Coleridge's Early Poetry," *Journal of the History of Ideas,* 20 (1959): 47–59.

Priestley, Joseph. *Hartley's Theory of the Human Mind, on the Principle of the Association of Ideas; with Essays Relating to the Subject of It.* London, 1775.

Richards, I. A. *Coleridge on Imagination.* London: Kegan Paul, Trench, Trubner, and Co., 1934.

Schneider, Elisabeth. *Coleridge, Opium and Kubla Khan.* Chicago: University of Chicago Press, 1953.

Stallknecht, Newton P. *Strange Seas of Thought.* Durham, North Carolina: Duke University Press, 1945.

Tucker, Abraham. *The Light of Nature Pursued.* 2nd edition, revised and corrected. 7 vols. London, 1805.

Waples, Dorothy. "David Hartley in *The Ancient Mariner,*" *Journal of English and Germanic Philology,* 35 (1936): 337–351.

Werkmeister, Lucyle. "Coleridge, Bowles, and 'Feelings of the Heart,'" *Anglia,* 78 (1960): 55–73.

Whalley, George. "The Bristol Library Borrowings of Southey and Coleridge, 1793–8," *The Library, Transactions of the Bibliographic Society,* fifth series, 4 (September 1949): 114–132.

Wilde, Norman. "The Development of Coleridge's Thought," *Philosophical Review,* 28 (1919): 147–163.

Willey, Basil. *The Eighteenth Century Background: Studies on the Idea of*

Nature in the Thought of the Period. London: Chatto and Windus, 1940.

Woodring, Carl R. *Politics in the Poetry of Coleridge*. Madison, Wisconsin: University of Wisconsin Press, 1961.

Wordsworth, William. *The Poetical Works of William Wordsworth*. Edited by E. de Selincourt and Helen Darbishire. Second ed. 5 vols. Oxford: Clarendon Press, vols. I–III, 1952–1954; vols. IV–V from the first edition, 1947 and 1949.

Index